100 Recipes from
New York's Premier Indoor Food Hall

CHELSEA

MARKET

COOKBOOK

Michael Phillips with Rick Rodgers
Photography by Jennifer May

Stewart, Tabori & Chang | New York

CONTENTS

INTRODUCTION

························

I t's late on a spring Wednesday morning at Chelsea Market. Behind the big plate glass window at Sarabeth's Bakery, four bakers are deftly stretching and dividing huge mounds of dough into loaves, mesmerizing passing tourists. The butchers at Dickson's Farmstand Meats set out specialty cuts of beef and trays of fat homemade sausages. Behind her small worktable outside Bowery Kitchen Supply, the knife lady is at work, skillfully honing knives on her whetstone for the Market's vendors as well as for local cooks. Food Network crew members, identifiable by their headsets, pass through the brick concourse on the way to their studios. A neat line forms inside Amy's Bread, as walkers fresh from a constitutional on the High Line try to decide what to purchase. The greengrocers at Manhattan Fruit Exchange are arranging the delicacies of the season, including tight scrolls of fiddlehead ferns and tied-up bunches of pale green garlic. At The Lobster Place, customers are carefully choosing freshly steamed lobsters, soon to be devoured at one of the Market's dining tables. And gathering his group (one of four in the Market at this moment) in front of a brass-framed glass case full of memorabilia from the building's past, a tour guide begins to tell the story of Chelsea Market.

A block long and a block wide and just a short walk from the Hudson River in the section of Manhattan known as the Meatpacking District, Chelsea Market has become—in just fifteen years—one of the greatest indoor food halls of the world, with more than thirty-five vendors purveying everything from soup to nuts, wine to coffee, cheese to cheesecake. Attracting six million national and international visitors annually, it is one of the most trafficked, and written-about, destinations of any kind in New York City, and countless New Yorkers use it as their everyday market. Chelsea Market is a neighborhood market with a global perspective.

The area has always been the locus of food in the city, beginning with the Algonquin Indians, who traded their game and crops on the banks of the Hudson River at this same spot. The trains of the High Line once served the wholesale butchers who lined the streets beneath the tracks and cooled their provisions with blocks of Hudson River ice, and the National Biscuit Company established its factory—now reclaimed as Chelsea Market—here to take advantage of the butchers' lard in the nineteenth century. This long history—and the stripped-down brick architecture of the building—gives the Market a unique character. For foodies and even casual tourists, it is possible to enter the Market at one end in the morning and not exit the other until lunchtime, without ever growing bored—and certainly without ever going hungry.

Now, to celebrate its first fifteen years, here is *The Chelsea Market Cookbook*. We've gathered over ninety recipes from the array of shops, as well as friends and family of Chelsea Market and Jamestown, the firm that manages and operates the Market. This book is a veritable market basket of goodies, with a little of this and some of that, all adding up to a very tasty repast.

Many of the recipes are authentic international classics, such as the Carne Asada Tacos (page 81) from Los Tacos No. 1 and Pad Gra Prow (Thai Chicken with Holy Basil; page 109) from Chelsea Thai. You'll find recipes for some of the vendors' most popular offerings, including Amy's Bread's indulgent Pecan Sticky Buns (page 179) and Sarabeth's Pain de Mie (page 181), and frozen treats from L'Arte del Gelato, Ronnybrook Farm Dairy and People's Pops. Eateries that sit at the top of many New Yorkers' Top 10 lists—Morimoto, Buddakan, and The Green Table—have shared their best dishes. Celebrity chefs Giada De Laurentiis, Alexandra Guarnaschelli, and others (some of whom are associated with our tenant, the Food Network), who have learned to love the Market for its huge selection of the very best ingredients, have also contributed. The Market's annual sold-out dining events "Sunday Supper" and "Chilifest" are both represented so you can feel like you attended. You'll discover recipes for every occasion, from a casual breakfast to a special dinner party with friends.

In addition to the recipes themselves, along the way we've collected "Market Voices," where the vendors talk about their business in personal terms and our expert purveyors expound on their specialties, with information on everything from how to set a table to making the perfect pot of coffee. There are also "Tips from the Pros," with concise advice on how to make your home cooking better.

As linchpins in the Chelsea neighborhood, Jamestown and the Market have a long history of giving back to the community. In this philanthropic spirit, proceeds of the author's share from this book will benefit both Charity: Water, an organization bringing clean, safe water to people in developing nations, and Wellness in the Schools, which inspires healthy eating, environmental awareness, and fitness as a way of life for kids in public schools across the country.

With *The Chelsea Market Cookbook*, you can re-create the delicious and varied food from the Market in your home kitchen.

Michael Phillips

January 2013

A BRIEF HISTORY OF CHELSEA MARKET,
THE MEATPACKING DISTRICT,
AND THE NEW YORK CITY FOOD SHED

Chelsea Market's motto is "Building Community through Food," a concept that New Yorkers, with their famously diverse appetites for good food, completely understand, and live every day. Cultural historians call the various ways that a community feeds itself a "food shed"—a virtual structure of producers, purveyors, sellers, and more. The area around Chelsea Market—centered on Fourteenth Street near the Hudson River—has long been a vital part of New York City's shed.

Before refrigeration and jet planes made it possible for us to buy foodstuffs from around the world, all of the food for a community was locally produced. Crops were planted, grown, and harvested locally, within an easy transport distance to market, and many of the grains were processed into flour at the town mill for baking. Fish were caught from nearby bodies of water. Livestock, from chickens to cattle, were sometimes raised within the city limits.

The natural waterfront of the Hudson once ran right up to the Tenth Avenue entrance of today's Market. The Algonquin Indians nestled in a cove on the river's edge and reaped bountiful harvests from the rich soil, naming their village Sapokanican, which means tobacco field. With the arrival of the Dutch West India Company and the establishment of the territories of New Netherland in 1609, the Indians peacefully continued to live along the shores, and traded food with the settlers. (A journal entry from a Dutch visitor, mentions "a roasted haunch of venison. . . bought of the Indians. . . The meat was exceedingly tender and good, and also quite fat. We were also served with wild turkey, which was also fat and of a good flavor; and a wild goose, but that was rather dry. Everything we had was the natural production of the country.") However, in the early 1630s, Wouter Van Twiller, the Dutch director-general of the capital city New Amsterdam, displaced the Native Americans to build a farm in the region.

After a complicated series of European wars, the British acquired New Netherland in 1664, and later rechristened it New York. Meanwhile, the farmland north of the settlement was evolving into a suburb that eventually became known as Greenwich Village. Around 1808, a fort was built in the upper border of the Village to protect the Hudson River, and in 1812 it was named Fort Gansevoort after a recently departed Revolutionary War hero. The fort dominated the northern half of Greenwich Village for over forty years, until it was leveled to make room for a landfill that altered the shape of the river shore.

In the late 1780s, a produce and poultry market was established on the street where the fort would be built, close to the busy piers. Eventually known as the Farmers' Market, this enterprise became the core of the burgeoning food industry, spurred by advances in food production and technology. Another local food business was the National Biscuit Company (subsequently known as Nabisco), which was located where Chelsea Market now stands. The bakery's many innovations illustrate how putting food on the table was changing at the end of the nineteenth century. Crackers and cookies used to be delivered to the stores in recycled flour barrels, and sold directly out of the barrels. It took vision and, consequently, a lot of space, to take cookies out of a barrel and into a box.

In 1890, eight large eastern bakeries amalgamated to form the National Biscuit Company (*biscuit*, the British word for cookie, was still in use), and soon absorbed a dozen more firms. It immediately began building a Romanesque-style complex of six-story bakeries, near the refineries in the Chelsea neighborhood that would supply lard for baked goods and close enough to the Domino Sugar refinery on the East River, the center of the nation's sugar industry at the time. (The district is named for Chelsea, an estate where the General Theological Seminary, an Episcopalian school, now stands.) National Biscuit Company's various locations throughout the country soon provided half of the nation's cookies, including many that are still beloved: Premium Saltines, Vanilla Wafers, Fig Newtons, Nabisco Sugar Wafers, Barnum's Animal Crackers, and, in 1913, both the Oreo and the Mallomar. The company was painstaking about consistency and shelf life, and their neat, sealed, and hygienic packaging replaced the cracker barrel. Over time, the bakery had acquired the entire tract between 16th and 17th streets, from Ninth to Tenth Avenues, including some outlying properties. In fact, the bakery on 16th Street was connected to the accounting department on 15th Street by a pedestrian bridge a couple of stories above street level, which still stands near Tenth Avenue.

During this period, the meatpacking industry grew alongside the brick buildings of the National Biscuit Company. For many years, livestock lived among humans in the city. What is now Hell's Kitchen was called

Hog City because of its profusion of pigpens. Many cattle were raised along Tenth Avenue, fed by the slops from adjoining distilleries. By the early twentieth century, livestock was raised and slaughtered outside of the city, but the carcasses were transported to the wholesale butchers that had clustered near the Gansevoort Piers.

To transport goods to and from this vital food production center, railroads were built along the west edge of Manhattan. Understandably, railroads operating at street level were dangerous, and Tenth Avenue got the unsavory nickname, "Death Avenue." A special kind of worker, the West Side Cowboy, came into being. Riding a horse, blowing a trumpet, and waving a red flag or lantern (depending on the hour), the cowboy would warn other vehicles that a train was on its way. By the mid-1930s, the railroad tracks had been elevated. A spur went to the National Biscuit Company to drop off ingredients and take away cases of sweets. (The former railcar shed that runs along Tenth Avenue now protects a variety of food carts, serving up ice cream, ice pops, and more during the warm weather months.)

But new technologies continued to affect the area and its growing industries. In the late 1950s, after almost sixty years in New York, the vertical ovens at the bakery were outmoded, and Nabisco moved its plant to New Jersey to acquire the space needed for assembly-line production. While the meatpacking industry of the district held on for a bit longer, it was slipping into a decline, and the area became known mainly as the home to the raunchiest nightlife in Manhattan. A late-night trip to the meatpacking district could show some of New York City's seediest, most violent, or most disreputable scenes, from men in blood-splattered jackets carting meat carcasses, to sex workers plying their trade, often playing out right next to each other. New Yorkers, ever curious, were sensationalized enough by these barely legal or lawless activities that some could be seen "slumming" in the neighborhood just for fun—the most exciting place in New York to be at 3 a.m. on a weeknight was surely sitting at a table at Florent, a twenty-four-hour eatery in the thick of the district. Then more and more wholesale butchers moved to the city's new central market, Hunts Point, in the Bronx. Food transportation had evolved from railroads and small delivery trucks to large refrigerated trucks and jets that traveled across the country and the world. The last food delivery by rail to the neighborhood was a load of frozen turkeys in 1980. As the meatpackers relocated, they were replaced by a few cutting-edge art galleries, restaurants, hotels, and clothing stores, a sign of what was to come. From there, the area slowly worked its way to becoming fashionable.

In the 1990s, the investor Irwin B. Cohen organized a syndicate to buy the principal National Biscuit buildings, from Ninth to Eleventh avenues and 15th to 16th Streets. Over the next several years, Mr. Cohen reinvented the older complex, between Ninth and Tenth Avenues, re-renting the upper floors to an emerging group of technology companies.

On the ground floor, he created the long interior concourse of food stores (formerly the bakery's open-air loading dock) that the world knows as Chelsea Market. It was filled with a group of innovative, individually owned food purveyors who wanted to sell their wares from a well-appointed modern building with a strong link to New York's culinary past. (A common thread among these trailblazers: Many of them left the corporate arena to follow their bliss in the food world.) The Market quickly became a resource for both the home cook and the professional, as local residents and chefs shopped at retailers/wholesalers like original tenants Manhattan Fruit Exchange, Bowery Kitchen Supply, Amy's Bread, and Sarabeth's Bakery.

At the same time, the neighborhood was undergoing a transformation, led by like-minded investors such as Keith Barket at Angelo Gordon, Charlie Bendit and Paul Pariser at Taconic, and Glen Siegel and Adam Miller of Belvedere. Jamestown, another member of this real estate community, started investing in 1998, which began the transformation of the area into what would be called Silicon Alley, an urban main street of technology companies. In 2003, Jamestown took over the controlling interest of the Market.

The meatpacking district began its rise as a fashion industry magnet when Milk Studios drew top designers to shoot their creations at the 15th Street photography loft. Art galleries followed, and the area developed as a fine arts center to such a degree that soon the Whitney Museum will become one of our neighbors. Upscale restaurants, both inside and outside of the Market, affirmed the area as a destination for food lovers. The High Line, an urban park built on the reclaimed railroad tracks, opened in 2011. As singular as Chelsea Market, the High Line attracts another kind of visitor to the Market, who takes advantage of the culinary treasures of the concourse and the food stalls in the former railroad shed after a leisurely promenade three stories above this one-of-a-kind food hall.

The old cookie bakery is now filled not only with some of the best food stores and restaurants in New York, but also with such leaders in technology as Google and the Food Network. This makes the Market—and indeed the entire Chelsea District—unique in the world for its stew of art, fashion, media, technology, and, of course, food.

A NOTE ON MEASURING

When gathering the recipes for this book, we wanted to make them accessible to the many visitors who come to the Market every day. Virtually every country in the world except the United States measures cooking ingredients by weight. The only other exceptions are Liberia and Myanmar (also known as Burma). Therefore, in addition to the standard American volume measurements in cups, we also supply metric measurements by weight for all of the appropriate ingredients.

Weighing certain ingredients (such as flour) has become common practice even with dedicated American home cooks, and many kitchens now have a digital scale for this purpose and other measuring jobs. Inexpensive but accurate models are available at kitchenware stores and online. Without a scale, the most common method for measuring flour has long been to dip the measuring cup into flour and sweep off the excess. The problem is that each person packs the flour in the cup differently, and the amount can easily differ by 1 ounce (about 28 grams) per cup. (We have rounded metric measurements slightly to the nearest increment of five, so 28 grams becomes 30, and 116 grams is rounded to 115.)

If you want to measure the flour by volume with measuring cups, note that in this book we used the spoon-and-sweep method: Gently spoon the flour into a dry-ingredients measuring cup (not a glass liquid measuring cup) to fill the cup to overflowing. Sweep off the excess flour with a knife so it is level with the lip of the cup.

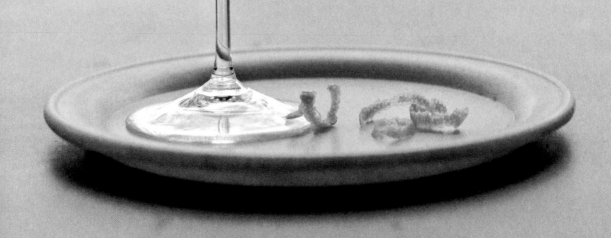

CHAPTER 1

LIFT A GLASS

COCKTAILS & OTHER BEVERAGES

CHAMPAGNE-ORANGE COCKTAIL

SERVES 1

1 sugar cube, preferably Demerara

3 dashes orange bitters, preferably The Bitter Truth

About 3 fluid ounces (90 ml) Champagne, chilled, as needed

Orange twist, removed from an orange with a channel knife (see Note), for garnish

CHELSEA WINE VAULT

NOTE: *A channel knife, which can be purchased at kitchenware shops, is a bartender's tool to remove citrus zest in a long, thin strip. You can also use a vegetable peeler to remove a 2-inch (5-cm) strip for the same amount of citrusy flavor, though a thin strip will look more elegant.*

There are many variations on the Champagne cocktail, a convivial mix of sparkling wine, a sugar cube, and aromatic bitters. This one, developed by Sarah Marley, has an orange undertone that is bright and citrusy without being too bitter, making it perfect as an aperitif or with brunch. The Chelsea Wine Vault recommends a light, dry Champagne, such as Delamotte Blanc de Blancs Brut NV. Their preferred brand of orange bitters is The Bitter Truth. (See photo on previous page.)

1. Place the sugar cube in a Champagne flute. Shake the bitters over the sugar to moisten it. Let stand for 1 minute.

2. Add enough Champagne to fill the glass. Garnish with the orange twist and serve immediately.

WHITE SANGRIA
WITH STRAWBERRIES AND LIME

SERVES 4 TO 6

1 (750-ml) bottle dry white wine, such as Forstreiter Grooner Grüner Veltliner or Château Lamonthe de Haux Bordeaux Blanc

1½ tablespoons superfine sugar

1 cup (160 g) sliced fresh strawberries

1 lime, half thinly sliced and half juiced

12 fluid ounces (1½ cups/360 ml) sparkling water, chilled

Ice cubes for serving

CHELSEA WINE VAULT

Few beverages are more refreshing on a hot summer day as tart, fruity sangria. White wine is lighter than red, allowing the strawberry flavor to come through. The creator of this sangria, Krista Lee, says that the base can be refrigerated for up to a day, with the ice and sparkling water added just before serving. For the very best results, search out Chelsea Wine Vault's recommendations, as their motto is "We only buy wine we love." (See photo on opposite page.)

1. At least 2 hours before serving, stir the wine and sugar together in a large pitcher to dissolve the sugar. Add the strawberries, lime slices, and lime juice. Cover and refrigerate for at least 2 hours or up to 1 day.

2. Just before serving, add the sparkling water and ice and stir to combine.

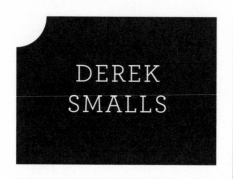

DEREK SMALLS

THE TIPPLER

SERVES 1

½ medium cucumber

2 fluid ounces (¼ cup/60 ml) Zubrowka Bison Grass Vodka

1 fluid ounce (2 tablespoons/30 ml) fresh grapefruit juice

2 teaspoons honey

Splash of sambuca (optional)

3 drops The Bitter Truth Jamaican Bitters #1, or 3 dashes Angostura bitters

4 fresh mint leaves

Ice cubes, for serving

Fresh mint sprig, for garnish

Fans of the movie *This is Spinal Tap!* will recognize the name Derek Smalls: He's the character who has an interesting encounter involving a cucumber and an airport metal detector. Cucumber juice plays a part in this cocktail. Bison grass vodka is infused with grass stalks that tint and flavor the spirit.

1. Cut off a thin slice of the cucumber and reserve it for garnish. Peel the remaining cucumber and shred it on the large holes of a box grater over a wire sieve placed in a small bowl. Press hard on the cucumber to extract the juice. Measure 4½ teaspoons of the juice.

2. Combine the cucumber juice, vodka, grapefruit juice, honey, 1 teaspoon of water, the sambuca, if using, bitters, and mint leaves in a cocktail shaker. Half-fill the shaker with ice. Cover the shaker and shake 10 times. Strain the mixture into an ice-filled glass. (To remove any mint residue from the drink, The Tippler's bartenders strain the mixture through a fine-mesh sieve into the glass, but at home, you may want to skip the sieve.) Garnish with the reserved cucumber slice and a mint sprig, and serve immediately.

TIPS FROM THE PROS

BITTERS
The Tippler

There are two ingredients in cocktail making that can be called bitters, but they are entirely different.

Aromatic bitters are used as cocktail flavorings. These were once very popular and have made a huge comeback. For years, Angostura and Peychaud's were the only brands in continuous production, but with the renaissance of cocktail making, that has all changed. (At one time, a cocktail was a specific drink of spirits and sugar doused with bitters but, over the years, came to mean any kind of mixed alcoholic beverage.) Aromatic bitters are distilled from herbs, spices, and other ingredients to make a large range of flavors from fruity (orange, lemon, and rhubarb) to exotic (such as Caribbean, Jamaican, Creole, mole, and whiskey barrel). They are very intense, so use them a drop or a dash at a time.

And then there is the category of bitter Italian liqueur called amaro (which means "bitter"). It is basically sweet, but it has distinct aromatic flavors from herbs, spices, and botanicals. Examples include Ramazzotti, Cynar, and Averna. They are traditionally sipped after dinner (especially if you have Italian relatives reliving the flavors of the old country), but they are now breaking out of the box, as more bartenders are using them in mixed cocktails.

TOP CAT

THE TIPPLER

SERVES 1

1 fresh strawberry, halved

2 fluid ounces (¼ cup/60 ml) Averna amaro

½ fluid ounce (1 tablespoon) fresh lemon juice

Crushed ice, for serving

4 fluid ounces (½ cup/120 ml) orange-flavored soda, as needed

Orange slice, for garnish

Tad Carducci of the Tippler tells how this cocktail was invented: "I created the Top Cat to pay homage to my grandfather, who used to sneak the kids Averna mixed with orange juice after gluttonous Sunday family dinners. We thought he was the coolest person alive. Little did we suspect that he was actually ensuring that we'd be asleep in a matter of minutes, so that the adults could commence in drinking grappa and playing cards."

1. Muddle the strawberry in a cocktail shaker. Add the Averna and lemon juice, and half-fill the shaker with ice. Cover and shake for about 5 seconds.

2. Fill a tall glass with ice. Using a cocktail strainer, strain the Averna mixture into the glass. Fill the glass with the soda. Stir the drink with a long spoon until the glass is frosty. Garnish with the orange slice and serve immediately.

BERRY BLUE SHAKE

ONE LUCKY DUCK

SERVES 2

1 (12-ounce/340-g) bag frozen mixed berries

1 small banana, preferably frozen, sliced

1 (11.2-ounce/330-ml) can coconut water

2 tablespoons agave nectar, or more to taste

1 tablespoon spirulina powder

½ teaspoon vanilla extract

This purple-blue smoothie is a great way to start the day. In addition to coconut water, bananas, and mixed berries, it includes spirulina, a blue-green algae that is a good source of protein, vitamins, and antioxidants, and also deepens the shake's color. If you wish, substitute 1⅓ cups (315 ml) almond milk for the coconut water.

1. Process the berries, banana, coconut water, agave nectar, spirulina, and vanilla in a blender until smooth. Pour into two tall glasses and serve immediately.

As befits a restaurant with Asian influences, this cocktail includes Eastern flavors like oolong tea and lemongrass. While the instructions are for a single drink, you will have enough tea and lemongrass syrup for a pitcher, so consider serving it as the "house cocktail" at your next dinner party, especially if Asian food is on the menu.

1. Make the syrup: Bring the sugar and 4 fluid ounces (½ cup/120 ml) water to a boil in a small saucepan over high heat, stirring often to dissolve the sugar. Add the lemongrass and remove the pan from the heat. Let it stand for 30 minutes. Strain the syrup through a sieve into a covered container, pressing hard on the lemongrass to extract any liquid. Discard the lemongrass. (The syrup can be covered and refrigerated for up to 1 month.)

2. Make the tea: Put the tea bag in a mug and add the boiling water. Let it stand for 3 minutes. Remove the tea bag, pressing to extract any liquid. Let the tea cool.

3. Stir the vodka, 1 fluid ounce (2 tablespoons/30 ml) of the tea, 1½ teaspoons of the lemongrass syrup, and the lemon juice together in a cocktail shaker. Half-fill the shaker with ice cubes. Cover the shaker and shake 8 to 10 times.

4. Fill an iced-tea glass with ice. Using a cocktail strainer, strain the vodka mixture into the glass. Garnish with the lemon wedge and serve immediately.

TRANQUILITY

BUDDAKAN

SERVES 1

FOR THE LEMONGRASS SYRUP:

½ cup (100 g) sugar

1 stalk lemongrass, bottom part only, trimmed and chopped

FOR THE TEA:

1 oolong tea bag

8 fluid ounces (1 cup/240 ml) boiling water

1½ fluid ounces (3 tablespoons/45 ml) citrus-flavored vodka, such as Smirnoff

¼ fluid ounce (1½ teaspoons) fresh lemon juice

Ice cubes, for serving

Lemon wedge, for garnish

SNOWGRONI

THE TIPPLER

SERVES 1

$^2/_3$ cup (100 g) coarsely cracked ice (see Note)

1½ fluid ounces (3 tablespoons/45 ml) sweet vermouth

1 fluid ounce (2 tablespoons/30 ml) London-style dry gin

1 fluid ounce (2 tablespoons/30 ml) Campari

Orange twist, removed from an orange with a channel knife (see Note, page 14), for garnish

NOTE: *To crack ice, wrap ice cubes in a heavy kitchen towel. Using a flat meat mallet or a rolling pin, smash the ice in the towel until it is coarsely crushed. (If you really get into having crushed ice, get a Lewis bag—a heavy canvas bag designed to hold the ice while you smash it.)*

This is a slushy take on the ultimate Italian cocktail, the Negroni, which is made using gin, Campari, and sweet vermouth. There is such a thing as a vodka Negroni, but it lacks the gin's herbaceous flavor, and is pretty wimpy. Make this as written, and you just may switch from vodka to gin in other cocktails. Tad of The Tippler confesses: "The Snowgroni got us in hot water with some cocktail purists who thought we were corrupting the classic. We thought it was high time to stir up the pot a bit. But, we couldn't find a pot, so we used a blender instead."

1. Process the ice, vermouth, gin, and Campari in a blender until smooth and slushy. Pour the mixture into an old-fashioned glass. Garnish with the orange twist and serve immediately.

The thirst-quenching combination of citrus-scented Earl Grey tea, refreshing mint, and fresh oranges makes an enticing iced tea that you will serve all summer long (if not all year!). Take it a step further with a shot of Campari or Aperol to make a refreshing cocktail. The tea is quite sweet, and while you can reduce the sugar by half, remember that the tea will eventually be slightly diluted by the ice cubes, so don't cut back too much.

1. Using a vegetable peeler, remove the zest of 1 orange in wide strips. Squeeze the juice from 3 or 4 oranges until you have 1½ cups (360 ml) of juice. Cut the remaining orange(s) into ¼-inch- (6-mm-) thick rounds, and then in half crosswise to make half-moon shapes.

2. Bring the sugar and 1 cup (240 ml) of water to a boil in a small saucepan over high heat, stirring often to dissolve the sugar. Remove it from the heat. Add the zest and dried mint. Let them steep for 10 minutes. Strain through a sieve into a large heatproof bowl, pressing hard on the solids in the sieve to extract any liquid; discard the solids.

3. Bring 7 cups (1.7 L) of water to a boil in a medium saucepan over high heat. Remove it from the heat and add the tea. Let it steep for 4 minutes. Strain the tea through a sieve into the bowl with the syrup; press hard to extract any liquid. Discard the tea. Let the mixture cool.

4. When you are ready to serve, stir the orange juice into the tea mixture. Pour the tea into an ice-filled pitcher and add the sliced oranges, reserving 6 to 8 orange slices for the garnish. Pour the tea into ice-filled tall glasses. Garnish each serving with a reserved orange slice and a mint sprig.

VARIATION: Orange Mint Tea Cocktail: Add 1½ fluid ounces (3 tablespoons/45 ml) bitter Italian aperitif, such as Campari or Aperol to each serving and stir gently.

MOROCCAN MINT ICED TEA

SPICES AND TEASE

SERVES 6 TO 8

5 large seedless oranges

1 cup (200 g) sugar

1 cup (15 g) dried spearmint leaves

7 Earl Grey tea bags or 7 teaspoons loose Earl Grey tea

Ice cubes, for serving

Fresh mint sprigs, for garnish

LOTS OF HOT CHOCOLATES

JACQUES TORRES CHOCOLATES

SERVES 1

FOR THE HOT CHOCOLATE:

1 cup (240 ml) whole milk

2 ounces (55 g) bittersweet chocolate, finely chopped, plus more, shaved, for garnish (optional)

Whipped cream, for garnish (optional)

FOR VANILLA HOT CHOCOLATE:

½ vanilla bean, split lengthwise, or ½ teaspoon pure vanilla extract

FOR PEPPERMINT HOT CHOCOLATE:

1 peppermint candy cane

FOR MOCHA HOT CHOCOLATE:

1 teaspoon freeze-dried coffee granules, dissolved in 1 tablespoon hot water

FOR RASPBERRY HOT CHOCOLATE:

5 fresh raspberries

FOR SPICED HOT CHOCOLATE:

Pinch each of ground allspice, ground cinnamon, ancho chile powder, and chipotle chile powder

Is there anything more delicious on a cold winter day than a cup of steaming hot chocolate? Rather than just a plain cup, here are a few variations to warm your heart and soul. You can vary the intensity of the chocolate by adding more or less chopped chocolate in the hot milk. As a variation on the traditional marshmallow garnish, Jacques recommends topping hot chocolate with a big scoop of whipped cream and shavings of bittersweet chocolate.

1. Make the hot chocolate: Heat the milk in a small, heavy-bottomed saucepan over medium heat until slightly warm. Whisking constantly, gradually add the chocolate. Cook, still whisking constantly, just until the milk begins to form bubbles around the edge of the pan. Do not allow the milk to boil.

2. Pour the mixture into a mug. Garnish with whipped cream and/or shaved chocolate, if desired.

FOR VANILLA HOT CHOCOLATE: Using the edge of a small, sharp knife, scrape the seeds from the split vanilla bean into the milk, then add the pod to the saucepan. Whisk in the chocolate as directed above. Remove the vanilla pod before serving. Or, if using the extract, simply add it to the hot chocolate just before serving.

FOR PEPPERMINT HOT CHOCOLATE: Stir the milk in the saucepan with the candy cane, allowing it to melt partially into the mixture as it heats. Proceed as directed above.

FOR MOCHA HOT CHOCOLATE: Add the dissolved coffee with the chocolate and proceed as directed above.

FOR RASPBERRY HOT CHOCOLATE: Proceed as directed above until the chocolate has melted, then using a wooden spoon, crush the raspberries into the milk.

FOR SPICED HOT CHOCOLATE: Add the allspice and cinnamon to the hot milk. Add the chile powders to taste, keeping in mind that freshly ground chile can be very hot. Proceed as directed above.

VARIATION: Hot White Chocolate: Use ½ cup (120 ml) each whole milk and heavy cream in place of the milk; 3½ ounces (100 g) white chocolate, chopped, in place of the bittersweet chocolate; and ½ teaspoon pure vanilla extract for the flavoring. Prepare as directed above.

SHAKING UP GREAT COCKTAILS

THE TIPPLER

We, friends, are in the midst of an exciting era. It is one that the Tippling Bros. are wont to call the Platinum Age of drinking. Never before in our nation's history have we, as a people, been so acutely aware of things libational. From biodynamic wines to craft beers and artisanal spirits, we are becoming ever-more savvy of what we imbibe. It makes perfect sense, as we are experiencing the same thing with food. Thanks to celebrity chefs, the Food Network, farm-to-table restaurants, and the like, we are incredibly passionate about what we eat. Food—great food, real food—has become mainstream. The Tipplers are tickled to be plying our trade at this particular time (see what we did there with the alliteration?), especially when it comes to cocktails.

The following are a handful of mixological techniques and tips to guide you on the journey to becoming a bona fide craft cocktail maker. However, keep in mind the mixologist's most important asset—the palate. Trust it, but challenge it! Use what you know about flavor, texture, and temperature in foods you love to eat and apply it to your alcoholic creations.

THE TIPPLER TOOLBOX

You don't have to buy out your local kitchenware shop (although they might not mind if you do), but you should have a few basic cocktail-making implements.

A COCKTAIL SHAKER: Get the real thing, known as a Boston shaker, which has a glass vessel acting as the bottom half and a metal container to provide the top. Combine your ingredients in the bottom part with ice, add the metal top, and shake it, baby. (Actually, not all drinks are shaken—some recipes may ask you to simply stir to keep the liquid clear instead of frothy.) The three-part cobbler shaker—with a bottom container, a spouted lid, and a top—works almost as well as the Boston style, but it is meant to be more decorative than efficient. A professional bartender uses a Boston shaker, so why shouldn't you? But if you have a nice antique cobbler, don't kick it out of bed . . . as it were.

A JIGGER: This is both the name of a unit of measure (1½ fluid ounces/3 tablespoons/45 ml) and a measuring tool. The 2-ounce (60-ml) size jigger is good because it can measure large and small amounts. The big rule is—use your jigger! (We know this sounds slightly dirty, but too bad.) Don't eyeball the liquids in your drinks, and always measure them so the cocktail tastes terrific every time you make it.

COCKTAIL STRAINERS: There are two kinds, and as they are cheap, just get both. A julep strainer is designed to fit over a glass mixer bottom (like the Boston shaker). A Hawthorne strainer is ringed with a wire spring so it sits snugly over the metal mixer top. After a drink is mixed, the strainer serves to remove chunks of flavorings and ice as the beverage makes its journey from mixer to glass.

MUDDLER: This long mashing tool has become increasingly important to the bartender's tool bag since the rise of the Mojito and Caipirinha, both of which use crushed (muddled) limes. Yes, you can use a wooden spoon, but a muddler does a much better job.

BAR SPOON: It looks like a slightly fancier iced-tea spoon with a twisted handle. The twists allow the bartender to dribble liqueurs down the stem into a glass so they stack up into layers to make the classic Pousse-Café cocktail and others. If you ever make a Pousse-Café, then you obviously have too much time on your hands. However, some newer drinks, like the B-52, have a float of liqueur as well. If you are only using the bar spoon to stir drinks in the shaker, a regular iced-tea spoon will work just fine.

THE FLAVOR FACTOR

What makes a cocktail great? As in wine, as in food, and as in life itself, balance is key. The best wines (the ones that stimulate every part of our palate and leave us wanting more) are perfectly balanced. In wine, we look for harmony between acid and tannins, fruit and alcohol, because when this happens, we experience a bigger-picture, integrated experience. Balance in cocktails hinges on basically the same components. The best cocktails can play with acids (usually in the form of citrus juice), fruits (there's that citrus again, but also other fruits), sugars (syrups and liqueurs), tannins (think of the wood flavors in bourbon, or the smoke in scotch), and alcohols (duh)—when you consider all of these possible flavors, you can make a cocktail worth drinking. A well-made Whiskey Sour, with the proportions just right, can go from OK to Omigod.

GET THE JUICES FLOWING

Many cocktails use alcohol in conjunction with fresh fruit juice. Don't even think of using bottled citrus juices. Period. Don't do it. Stop. Use fresh. Need we say more?

When juicing fresh citrus, there are a couple of tricks you can employ to squeeze the most out of your fruit. First, invest in a high-quality juicer. Whether it's a manual hand-held version or a high-tech electric gadget, do your research and get the best. There is a lot of variation between brands and styles and you want one that will work efficiently and will last.

Do not try to juice cold citrus! It will be a fruitless venture (see what we did there?). Room temperature lemons, limes, oranges, and grapefruits will yield about 30 percent more juice than those that came directly from the fridge. At The Tippler, we keep the night's supply of citrus at room temperature, ready to juice. Otherwise, drop clean citrus into a bowl of hot water for 10 minutes prior to juicing. Or microwave them on high in 10-second increments until they feel softer. When cutting citrus to make juice, think of the fruit as a globe, and cut the fruit in half through the equator.

THE BUILD-OUT

Follow this model for mixing cocktails: Start with a clean mixing glass. If using lemon or lime juice, add that first. Follow with your sweetener, whether it is syrup or liqueur. Then, continue with the spirit(s), adding the ice last. This sequence, which usually goes from the lightest ingredient to the heaviest (and often this corresponds from the least expensive to the priciest, except for the ice), helps them combine without a lot of stirring or shaking.

VARIATIONS ON A THEME

Most modern drinks are just riffs on a theme. The "Sour" family of cocktails is a great launching pad for creative mixing because the formula is so straightforward. Start with this basic formula: 1½ ounces (45 ml) spirits, 1 ounce (30 ml) sour (in the form of citrus juice), and ¾ ounce (about 20 ml) sweet. The sweet is usually provided by simple syrup, made by boiling one part (by weight) of sugar to one part water. (For example, 7 ounces each sugar and water, or 1 cup sugar and a scant cup of water in American volume measurements.) This syrup dissolves better than sugar alone in some recipes, and while you can buy it, it is so simple (punning again) to make.

With that formula in mind, you can make a Whiskey Sour with whiskey, lemon juice, and simple syrup. From here, it gets very interesting:

For a **DAIQUIRI**, switch to white rum, lime juice, and simple syrup.

For a **GIMLET**, use gin, lemon juice, and simple syrup.

For a **MARGARITA**, use 100 percent blue agave tequila, lime juice, and orange liqueur for the simple syrup.

For a **SIDECAR**, keep the Margarita formula, but use Cognac instead of tequila.

So, keep going. You never know what you will find. Although curiosity killed the cat, it has only occasionally thwarted the mixologist. "What if I added this to that?" is the bartender's code. Release your inner mad scientist. Mistakes are as valuable as successes. Remember the Tippling Bros. mantra: "Stay true to the roots, but don't be afraid to color outside the lines."

CHAPTER 2

OPENING GAMBITS

APPETIZERS & SNACKS

SPICE-&-HERB MARINATED OLIVES

THE TIPPLER

MAKES 1 QUART (1 L)

2 tablespoons extra-virgin olive oil

2 garlic cloves, coarsely chopped

1 teaspoon pickling spice

1 teaspoon fennel seeds

½ teaspoon hot red pepper flakes

1 (3-inch/8-cm) sprig fresh rosemary

Finely grated zest of 1 orange

Finely grated zest of ½ lemon

Finely grated zest of ½ lime

1 bay leaf

1 quart (1 L) assorted olives, drained

Pickling spice is the surprise ingredient in these impossible-to-stop-eating marinated olives. They keep for a long time, so make a batch to have on hand to serve when friends come over for drinks. (See photo on previous page.)

1. Combine the oil, garlic, pickling spice, fennel, red pepper flakes, rosemary, orange zest, lemon zest, lime zest, and bay leaf in a large skillet. Add the olives. Cook over medium heat, stirring occasionally, until the large olives begin to soften, about 5 minutes. Remove the mixture from the heat and let cool completely. Serve it at room temperature. (The olives can be stored in an airtight container in the refrigerator for up to 1 month.)

SPICY MIXED NUTS

THE TIPPLER

MAKES ABOUT 3½ CUPS (490 G)

1 (10.3-ounce/288-g) can salted mixed nuts

1 cup (5 ounces/140 g) whole raw almonds

1 tablespoon extra-virgin olive oil

2½ teaspoons cayenne pepper

1 teaspoon sweet Spanish or Hungarian paprika

Kosher salt

The next time you need a snack to serve with cocktails, consider these devilishly spicy nuts. You can use whatever mixture you like, but The Tippler's recipe is almond heavy. These are impossible to stop eating, even as you attempt to quench the fire in your mouth with your libation.

1. Position a rack in the center of the oven and preheat to 350°F (175°C).

2. Toss the mixed nuts, almonds, oil, cayenne, and paprika together in a medium bowl. Spread them on a large rimmed baking sheet. Bake, stirring occasionally, until they're fragrant, about 10 minutes. Season with salt. Transfer the nuts to a bowl and let them cool. (They can be stored in an airtight container at room temperature for up to 1 week.)

Mention bruschetta and most people think of the classic version with raw tomatoes. While you may have had kale and beans combined before in minestrone, here they are a bruschetta topping. Grilling is a very unique way to prepare the kale. Flageolets are pale green, pebble-size beans of French heritage, but you can substitute domestic small navy beans. If you wish, adapt the recipe for indoor cooking by using the Roasted Tomatoes on page 150, toasting the bread slices in a broiler, and cooking the kale, in batches, in a grill pan.

1. Make the beans: Place the beans in a medium saucepan and add enough cold water to cover by 2 inches (5 cm). Bring them to a boil over high heat. Cook for 2 minutes. Remove the pan from the heat and cover. Let it stand for 1 hour. Or, soak the beans in cold water to cover by 2 inches (5 cm) for at least 4 and up to 12 hours.

2. Drain the beans and rinse under cold water. Return the beans to the saucepan. Add the stock, wine, carrot, celery, onion, smashed garlic, herbes de Provence, and bouquet garni (the tied herbs). Pour in enough water to barely cover the beans. Bring them to a boil over high heat. Reduce the heat to low and cover. Simmer until the beans are tender, adding hot water as needed to keep them covered, about 1 hour. During the last 10 minutes of cooking, add the salt and pepper. Discard the bouquet garni. Remove the pot from the heat and cover to keep warm. (The beans can be cooled, covered, and refrigerated for up to 2 days. Reheat in the cooking liquid before serving.)

3. Meanwhile, prepare an outdoor grill for cooking over medium heat. For a gas grill, preheat it to 450°F (230°C.) For a charcoal grill, let the coals burn until you can hold your hand just over the cooking grate for about 3 seconds.

4. Toss the kale with 2 tablespoons of oil in a large bowl. Brush the tomato halves all over with 2 more tablespoons of oil. Brush the bread slices with about 3 tablespoons of oil. Put the tomato halves, cut-sides up, on the grill grate. Grill with the lid closed, turning occasionally, until the tomatoes are tender and lightly browned, about 8 minutes. Transfer them to a platter and tent with aluminum foil to keep warm. Mound the kale on the cooking grate. Grill with the lid closed, using long tongs to occasionally turn the mass of kale over, until the kale is lightly browned and wilted, about 3 minutes. (If you move the kale as a mass, very few, if any, leaves will fall through the grate.) Transfer them to the platter. Season the tomatoes and kale with salt and pepper and tent with foil to keep warm.

5. Add the sliced bread to the cooking grate. Cover and cook, turning once, until the bread is toasted, about 2 minutes per side. Transfer it to another platter.

6. To serve, cut the tomatoes in half lengthwise into quarters. Drain the beans and transfer them to a bowl. Rub the toasts with the garlic. Top each toast with a tomato quarter, a few kale leaves, and a spoonful of beans. Serve immediately.

GRILLED KALE, TOMATO & FLAGEOLET BRUSCHETTA

SPICES AND TEASE

SERVES 6 TO 8

FOR THE BEANS:

1 cup (110 g) dried flageolet or navy beans, rinsed and picked through for stones

1 cup (240 ml) Chicken Stock (page 56) or reduced-sodium chicken broth

½ cup (120 ml) dry white wine

1 small carrot, cut into ¼-inch (6-mm) dice

1 small celery rib, cut into ¼-inch (6-mm) dice

1 small yellow onion, finely chopped

2 garlic cloves, smashed and peeled

2 teaspoons herbes de Provence

1 sprig each of fresh thyme, rosemary, and flat-leaf parsley, tied with kitchen twine

1 teaspoon kosher salt

½ teaspoon freshly ground black pepper

1½ pounds (680 g) dark curly or black Tuscan (*cavalo nero*) kale, tough stems removed, well rinsed

Extra-virgin olive oil

6 plum (Roma) tomatoes, stem ends trimmed, cut in half lengthwise

1 crusty baguette, cut on the diagonal into 24 slices about ½ inch (12 mm) thick

Kosher salt and freshly ground black pepper

4 large garlic cloves, peeled

Oysters on the half shell have a long history in New York's dining culture, and the likes of Belle Époque financier Diamond Jim Brady and his cohorts consumed mountains of them every day. The briny bivalves are well represented at Chelsea Market. Some folks buy them shucked at The Lobster Place and devour them at one of the concourse dining tables. Others order a plate of oysters downstairs at The Tippler to enjoy with a drink. Here's The Tippler's recipe for a tart, crisp condiment to complement the saline oyster flavor.

1. Make the mignonette: Mix all of the mignonette ingredients together in a small bowl. Cover and refrigerate until chilled, about 2 hours. The cucumber will give off some juices.

2. Divide the oysters among six chilled plates. (If you have oyster plates, so much the better. Or, spread a layer of crushed ice on deep plates, and nestle the oysters in the ice.) Divide the mignonette among six small serving bowls. Serve the oysters immediately, allowing the guests to add the mignonette sauce as desired to each oyster.

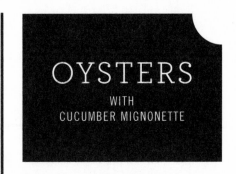

OYSTERS
WITH
CUCUMBER MIGNONETTE

THE TIPPLER

SERVES 6; MAKES 24 OYSTERS

FOR THE MIGNONETTE:

1 cup (145 g) diced (¼ inch/6 mm) seedless (English) cucumber

2 tablespoons fresh lemon juice

1 tablespoon soy sauce

1 tablespoon rice vinegar

1 teaspoon red wine vinegar

Freshly ground black pepper

24 oysters of your choice, on the half shell

TIPS FROM THE PROS

OYSTERS
The Lobster Place

At The Lobster Place, the ultimate New York fish store with an amazing array of seafood at equally amazing freshness, oysters are shucked right before your eyes by a battery of skilled fishmongers. There is always a large selection, concentrating on oysters from the East Coast's frigid waters, with an occasional guest appearance from a West Coast cousin.

The majority of oysters sold at The Lobster Place are farmed. The bivalves are grown in floating bags or on the ocean floor, and are typically harvested by hand. These methods are environmentally sound, and the oysters help improve the surrounding water quality by cleaning out tiny particles and debris. Some of our favorite oysters include:

BEAU SOLEIL (New Brunswick, Canada): *Soft, tender meat and a full briny flavor.*

INDIAN CREEK (Prince Edward Island, Canada): *Full and firm, with a great balance of sweet and salty.*

KUMAMOTO (California): *A West Coast oyster, small and creamy with a noticeable cucumber flavor.*

MARTHA'S VINEYARD (Massachusetts): *Brightly flavored saltiness and a sweet finish.*

MYSTIC (Connecticut): *Medium salinity with clean finish.*

WASHBURN ISLAND (Massachusetts): *Briny flavor and crisp finish.*

WELLFLEET (Massachusetts): *Light body and bracing saltiness.*

WIDOW'S HOLE (New York): *Crisp, clean brine and juicy meat.*

WILEY POINT (Maine): *Perfectly plump meat in brightly flavored brine.*

DEVILED EGGS

WITH BACON & PICKLE RELISH

THE GREEN TABLE

SERVES 6

2 slices bacon

6 large eggs, hard-boiled, cooled, and peeled (see Tips)

2 tablespoons mayonnaise

1 tablespoon plus 1½ teaspoons sweet pickle relish

1½ teaspoons Dijon mustard

¼ teaspoon sweet paprika, or more to taste

¼ teaspoon cayenne pepper, or more to taste

Kosher salt and freshly ground black pepper

Aleppo pepper or additional sweet paprika, for sprinkling

Like potato salad (see Ruthy's iconic version on page 72), deviled eggs bring back memories of family celebrations and Independence Day picnics. The Green Table offers a devilishly spicy recipe dressed up with bacon and just enough relish to add a touch of sweet tang. A pastry bag does an attractive and efficient job of filling the whites, but you can simply use a small spoon, if you prefer.

1. Cook the bacon in a large skillet over medium heat, turning occasionally, until it is crisp and brown, about 8 minutes. Transfer it to paper towels to drain and cool. Finely dice the bacon.

2. Cut each egg in half lengthwise and remove the yolks. Place the egg white halves, cut-side up, on a platter. Rub the yolks through a coarse-mesh wire sieve into a medium bowl. Add the mayonnaise, relish, mustard, paprika, and cayenne and mix well. Season with salt and pepper. Fit a pastry bag with a ½-inch (12-mm) large open star tip. Fill the bag with the yolk mixture, then pipe the mixture into each of the whites. (The deviled eggs can be made to this point, covered with plastic wrap, and refrigerated for up to 1 day.)

3. To serve, sprinkle the eggs with the bacon, followed by the Aleppo pepper. Serve chilled.

TIPS FROM THE PROS

HARD-BOILED EGGS
The Green Table

Cooking hard-boiled eggs seems like a very easy job. So why are there so many eggs with green yolks (caused by overcooking) and marred whites (indicating a bad peeling experience)? Here is the best technique for perfect hard-boiled eggs.

First, start with eggs that are at least a week old. The liquid in the eggs will have evaporated slightly to create a larger air pocket at the wider end of the eggs, making it easier to peel the cooked eggs.

Carefully place the eggs in a single layer in a large heavy saucepan. Add enough cold water to cover the eggs by ¼ inch (6 mm). Bring to a boil over medium heat. Reduce the heat so the water is simmering briskly, but the eggs aren't being jostled by the bubbling. Cook for 2 minutes. (Use a kitchen timer!) Remove the pan from the heat and cover. Let stand for 12 minutes. Carefully drain the eggs and rinse with cold running water. Submerge the eggs in a bowl of well-iced water for 10 minutes or so to cool completely. (Cold eggs are much easier to peel than ones that are just out of the pot.)

One at a time, rap an egg on the work surface to crack the shell all over. Starting at the larger end of the egg and working under a stream of cold running water, peel the egg.

Tapenade is something that every cook should have stashed in the refrigerator. Covered with a film of olive oil, it keeps well, ready to be put into service. This Provençal blend of olives, capers, garlic, and herbs is most often thought of as an appetizer to spread on baguette slices or crackers, but it can also be tossed with pasta for a quick supper, or used as a condiment on sandwiches. Here is The Tippler's version, heavy on the capers (as it should be, since *tapeno* means "caper" in Provençal dialect), and you will find that there are few snacks that go better with a glass of chilled white or rosé wine.

1. In a food processor, with the machine running, drop the garlic through the feed tube to mince it. Stop the machine and add the olives, basil, capers, anchovies, and pepperoncini. Pulse about 10 times, or until coarsely chopped. With the machine running, gradually add the oil to make a thick paste.

2. Transfer the tapenade to a covered container and spread it evenly. Pour a thin layer of oil on the top of the tapenade to cover. (It can be refrigerated for up to 6 weeks. Bring it to room temperature and pour off the surface oil before serving; add additional oil to cover any remaining tapenade.)

TAPENADE

THE TIPPLER

MAKES ABOUT 3 CUPS (600 G)

5 garlic cloves, smashed and peeled

2 cups (310 g) pitted and rinsed kalamata olives

½ cup (20 g) packed fresh basil leaves

⅓ cup (45 g) drained nonpareil capers

7 oil-packed anchovy fillets, drained

2 pepperoncini (Italian pickled peppers), drained, stemmed, and coarsely chopped

1 cup (240 ml) extra-virgin olive oil, plus more for storing

TUNA PIZZA
WITH ANCHOVY AIOLI

MORIMOTO

SERVES 4

FOR THE ANCHOVY AIOLI:

2 large egg yolks

1 tablespoon white wine vinegar

1 tablespoon fresh lemon juice

2 teaspoons anchovy paste

¼ teaspoon soy sauce

½ cup (120 ml) vegetable oil

¼ cup (60 ml) extra-virgin olive oil

Kosher salt and freshly ground black pepper

4 (7-inch/17-cm) flour tortillas

2 tablespoons extra-virgin olive oil

½ cup (120 ml) sauce for barbecued eel
   (*kabayaki*, available at Asian grocers) or
   teriyaki sauce

10 ounces (275 g) sushi-grade tuna, thinly
   sliced across the grain

2 jalapeño peppers, seeded and thinly
   sliced

½ cup (115 g) thinly sliced red onion

½ cup (115 g) halved cherry tomatoes

⅓ cup (50 g) pitted kalamata olives

Baby cilantro or sprouts, for garnish

Typical of Chef Morimoto's combining of culinary traditions, this Tuna Pizza is one of his most popular recipes. An instant pizza base is created from a grilled flour tortilla, then topped with tuna sashimi and a sprinkling of colorful vegetables and olives. A tangy anchovy aioli is drizzled over the top as a garnish and for extra visual appeal.

1. Make the aioli: Combine the yolks, vinegar, lemon juice, anchovy paste, and soy sauce in a food processor. Process well. Combine the vegetable and olive oils. With the machine running, very slowly add the combined oils in a slow, thin stream, processing until the mayonnaise is emulsified and thick. Season with salt and pepper to taste. If desired, transfer the aioli to a plastic squeeze bottle.

2. Prepare an outdoor grill for cooking over direct medium heat. For a gas grill, preheat it to 400°F (205°C). For a charcoal grill, let the coals burn until they are covered with white ash and you can hold your hand just over the cooking grate for 3 seconds. (Or set a cast-iron grill pan on the stovetop over medium heat.)

3. Brush each tortilla lightly on both sides with the oil. Grill the tortillas on one side for 1 to 2 minutes. Rotate them 90 degrees and grill for another 1 to 2 minutes, until crosshatch marks appear and the tortillas are fairly crisp. Turn the tortillas over and brush them each with 2 tablespoons of the eel sauce. Grill until the bottom sides are crisp and the sauce dries, 1 to 2 minutes. Transfer the tortillas to a wire rack to cool.

4. Arrange the tuna slices over the sauce side of the cooled tortillas. Scatter the jalapeños, onion, tomatoes, and olives over the tortillas. Drizzle the aioli decoratively over the pizzas. Garnish with the cilantro and serve.

TIPS FROM THE PROS

ANCHOVY AIOLI
Masaharu Morimoto

While the intensely flavored mayonnaise in the tuna pizza is used as a decorative sauce, it's also an excellent accompaniment to steamed or grilled fish and makes a fabulous potato salad. Stored in a tightly covered container, the sauce will keep well in the refrigerator for up to 5 days. Note that true French aioli always contains garlic. The word aioli *is used as a conceit in this context, as there is no garlic in the recipe.*

Pork belly has become the new filet mignon: You will now find this once-humble cut (the same as bacon, only unsmoked) on countless restaurant menus. Simmered into submission, glazed, and tucked into homemade steamed buns, this is one of the best recipes you will ever come across for this exalted meat. Start early in the day (or even the day before) so the braised pork has time to chill before slicing. You can buy frozen bao (*buns*) at Asian markets, but making them is half the fun. You will need a three-tiered bamboo steamer to make these.

1. Make the braised pork belly: Position a rack in the center of the oven and preheat the oven to 350°F (175°C).

2. Place the pork belly on its side in a baking dish just large enough to hold it. Whisk 2 cups (480 ml) water with the sugar, soy sauce, oyster sauce, and sesame oil in a medium bowl. Pour the mixture over the pork belly. Cover the dish tightly with aluminum foil. Bake for 1 hour.

3. Remove the dish from the oven, uncover it, and flip the pork belly over. Cover again and continue baking until the pork is very tender when pierced with the tip of a small sharp knife, about 1¼ hours more.

4. Remove the dish from the oven. Transfer the pork to a plate. Pour the braising liquid into a heatproof bowl. Let the pork and braising liquid cool for 1 hour. Wrap the pork in plastic wrap and place it on a baking sheet. Top with another baking sheet and weigh it down with a baking dish filled with a few heavy cans. Refrigerate the whole thing to compress and chill the pork belly, at least 4 hours or up to 1 day. Cover the braising liquid and refrigerate it until ready to serve, up to 1 day.

5. Make the shallots and cabbage: Stir the vinegar, sesame oil, sugar, and salt together in a small saucepan over low heat to dissolve the sugar and salt. Remove from the heat and let the mixture cool. Cut the ginger into thin strips. Add the shallots, ginger, and chile and stir well. Let the mixture stand for at least 30 minutes or up to 2 hours. Mix the pickled shallots and their liquid with the cabbage in a small serving bowl. Let stand at room temperature until ready to serve, up to 2 hours.

6. Make the pork belly sauce: Skim off and discard the solidified fat on the top of the chilled braising liquid. Combine the liquid, hoisin, and honey in a medium saucepan and bring to a simmer over high heat. Sprinkle the cornstarch over 1 teaspoon of water in a small bowl and stir to dissolve. Stir into the simmering liquid and cook until the liquid is thickened, about 30 seconds. Let it cool. (The sauce can be covered and stored at room temperature for up to 2 hours.)

7. Make the buns: Sprinkle the yeast over the warm water in a small bowl. Let it stand for 5 minutes, then stir until it is dissolved. Pour the water and yeast into the bowl of a heavy-duty standing mixer and add the half-and-half. Add the flour, sugar, and baking powder. Place the bowl on the mixer and fit it with the beater attachment. Add ½ cup (120 ml) cold water. Mix on low speed just until the mixture forms a soft dough.

(continued)

CHAR SIU PORK BELLY BUNS

BUDDAKAN

SERVES 6 TO 8; MAKES 16 SMALL BUNS

FOR THE BRAISED PORK BELLY:

2 pounds (910 g) pork belly with skin, in one piece

½ cup (100 g) sugar

½ cup (120 ml) soy sauce

½ cup (120 ml) oyster sauce

1 teaspoon toasted sesame oil

FOR THE SHALLOTS AND CABBAGE:

1 tablespoon unseasoned rice vinegar

1 tablespoon hot sesame-chile oil

1 teaspoon sugar

1 teaspoon kosher salt

2 shallots, thinly sliced

1 (1-inch/2.5-cm) piece fresh ginger

1 small hot red chile, cut into thin strips

1 cup (45 g) thinly shredded napa cabbage

FOR THE PORK BELLY SAUCE:

2 tablespoons hoisin sauce

1 tablespoon honey

1 teaspoon cornstarch

FOR THE BUNS:

1 teaspoon active dry yeast

1 tablespoon warm (105° to 115°F/ 40° to 45°C) water

2 tablespoons half-and-half

2 cups (230 g) cake flour

2 tablespoons sugar

1 teaspoon baking powder

Vegetable oil, for brushing

(If the dough seems too sticky or dry, add more flour or water, a tablespoon at a time, to reach the right consistency.) Turn the dough out onto a lightly floured work surface.

8. Divide the dough into 16 equal pieces. Form each into a ball. Working with one ball at a time, on a lightly floured work surface, roll the dough into a ¼-inch- (6-mm-) thick oval about 4 inches (10 cm) long. Brush it lightly with the vegetable oil. Fold it in half crosswise, making folded buns about 2 inches (5 cm) long. Transfer the buns to a lightly floured large rimmed baking sheet. Cover with a damp kitchen towel. Let the buns stand in a warm, draft-free place until doubled in size, about 1 hour.

9. Choose a large saucepan that will snugly accommodate the bamboo steamer on top. Half-fill the saucepan with water and bring it to a boil over high heat. Line the bottom of each bamboo steamer tray with a round of parchment paper.

10. Arrange the buns at least 1 inch (2.5 cm) apart in the steamer trays. Stack the trays over the saucepan of boiling water. Cover and cook until the buns are puffed and cooked through, about 5 minutes.

11. Transfer the buns from the steamer racks to a platter. (The buns can be cooled, covered with plastic wrap, and stored at room temperature for up to 8 hours. When ready to serve, reheat them in the steamer racks over boiling water for about 3 minutes.)

12. When ready to serve, position the broiler rack about 6 inches (15 cm) from the heat source and preheat the broiler.

13. Unwrap the pork and cut it across the grain into ½-inch (12-mm) slices, removing any bones. Arrange the sliced pork on a broiler pan. Brush it with some of the cooled sauce. Broil until the sauce is bubbling, about 2 minutes. Turn the pork over, brush it with more sauce, and cook until the other side is glazed, about 2 minutes more. Transfer the pork to a small serving platter.

14. Transfer the remaining sauce to a small serving bowl. Serve the pork with the buns, vegetables, and sauce, letting each guest unfold and fill a bun with the ingredients to taste.

CHOOSING CHEESE

LUCY'S WHEY

Oh, how daunting the cheese case appears, with its great diversity of contents! There are cheeses standing stately and tall, ones slouching and oozing, those with lush and sticky coral rinds, cheeses with porous blue and gray ravines. Some cheeses have smooth, golden yellow pastes, while others have white and crumbly centers. Some large wedges of cheeses clearly come from gargantuan wheels, while others are smaller, peach-size morsels.

And that's only looks! What about texture? And, of course, what of taste? Where to begin? As cheesemongers, it's our job to make sure that the process of selecting cheese is enjoyable and informative, and that it leads the customer to that delicious moment when the cheese is eaten.

There are questions that we ask each person who visits Lucy's Whey in order to glean what kind of cheese they might be looking for. Often the first question we ask is one of texture: "Do you want a hard or a soft cheese?" Anyone can answer this question regardless of cheese knowledge, and the response gives us insight into the customer's preferences. From there maybe we'll ask, "Do you like subtle and mild, or strong and pungent?" Once we've gathered a few likes and dislikes, we can begin to offer tastes of cheese that we think will fit the customer's needs—the end goal being to choose the perfect cheese for each customer.

That's only one scenario. Of course, people visit Lucy's Whey with all varieties of cheese needs. Sometimes they want only a single cheese, other times a selection of cheeses. Maybe it's for before dinner, maybe it's for after dinner. Maybe they want cheeses hailing from New York State, or maybe Vermont. Maybe they're making a quiche with dinosaur kale from the greenmarket and want the perfect cheese to melt between the greens and eggs. Maybe they dare to attempt our famous Cheddar and fig grilled cheese sandwich (see page 140) at home!

We develop relationships with customers who return again and again, and each time they stop by we can talk further about the cheeses in the case, the different styles available, and the variations in production that yield these diverse cheeses. We describe the farms on which the cheeses were made, the animal breeds that gave the milk, and the cheesemakers who impart a bit of themselves into each wheel of cheese.

With both first-time visitors to Lucy's Whey and cheese counter regulars, we share our favorite ways to enjoy cheese at home. Here are a few ideas beyond the standard cheese plate that we think are fun ways to bring cheese into your own kitchen.

GRILLED CHEESE SANDWICH NIGHT: Sometimes just one flavor combination isn't enough! If you're serving a crowd, this is the perfect way to experiment with different melting cheeses and accompaniments. Make several different sandwiches and cut them into bite-size pieces so everyone can try the variety. The acidity of pickled food—including vegetable and fruit condiments, such as chutneys—contrasts the creaminess of the cheese, and we love them on our grilled cheese sandwiches.

Some of our favorite combinations include:

- Cheddar, sea salt, unsalted butter, and pickles
- A pungent washed-rind cheese, such as Grayson, with fig compote
- An Alpine-style semisoft cheese, such as Ascutney Mountain, with a savory tomato jam
- Creamy smoked Gouda with spicy fruit chutney and ham

Use whatever condiments you have on hand to experiment (good mustards, pickles, and sweet chutneys work especially well) with a selection of cheeses, and vary the kinds of bread you use for even more variety. Melt them on a panini press, or if you don't have one, follow the instructions on page 140, using a couple of skillets to keep things moving. Or you can always toast the sandwiches on a griddle or broil them open-faced.

VERTICAL TASTING NIGHT: This is the ultimate way to really discover cheese nuances and get to the bottom of the differences between cheeses. "Vertical" refers to tastings within the same family, or cheeses that have undergone a similar cheese-making process. Here are some suggestions:

- Collect a few blue cheeses of different milk types and note the differences in smell, taste, and texture, and how the bluing affects different milks. Serve with various fruits (apples, pears, and grapes) as well as crusty bread to discover interesting pairings. For a delicious dessert, pair them with a dessert wine or a rich stout.

- Choose several washed-rind cheeses (that is, those with firm, pungent rinds) with textures ranging from puddinglike to semi-firm and see how they vary from salty and vegetal to umami-rich and beefy. Serve with a few beers (lager, wheat, and ale) and see what matches up well.

- Select five soft goat's-milk cheeses made in different regions. Choose some from various corners of the United States, and others from different European countries. Compare and contrast the cheeses, keeping in mind the landscape and climate of the locale from which each cheese hails. You might want to offer wines from the regions, too. Try a grassy, herbaceous California Sauvignon Blanc for a cheese from that state, or a Sancerre to go with a French chèvre from the Loire Valley.

BEER & CHEESE PAIRING: Invite a group of friends and request that they each bring beer and cheese. Experiment to discover the most delicious pairing! A couple of suggestions are feta or goat cheese with wheat beer, or Cheddar with brown ale. Offer artisan breads and top-notch pretzels to round out the meal.

FROMAGE FORT: This is the best solution for all of your leftover cheese bits—and it's the original cheese dip! Throw all of your leftover cheese nubbins in a blender with a clove or two of garlic and a splash of dry white wine or vegetable broth, and blend until you have a smoothish paste. Serve it with bread or crackers, or spread it on some crusty bread and melt for an oozy and garlicky sandwich.

These are just a few of our favorite suggestions for bringing cheese into your kitchen. Of course, the options are endless, and hopefully these ideas will inspire you to return to your own cheese counter for further experimentation.

CHAPTER 3

THE SOUP POT

SOUPS, STOCKS & CHILIS

THE VELVETY CREAM OF TOMATO SOUP

SARABETH'S BAKERY

SERVES 8

6 tablespoons (¾ stick/85 g) unsalted butter

1 small yellow onion, chopped

½ cup (80 g) chopped shallots

2 scallions, top green parts only, thinly sliced

1 garlic clove, minced

1 (28-ounce/800-g) can whole tomatoes in thick tomato purée

2 cups (480 ml) milk

2 cups (480 ml) heavy cream

⅓ cup (40 g) all-purpose flour

About ⅓ cup (15 g) fresh dill fronds, torn into tiny sprigs

½ teaspoon kosher salt

¼ teaspoon freshly ground black pepper

¾ cup (90 g) shredded sharp Cheddar cheese

Sarabeth's signature soup has been on her menu for many years, and many a market visitor has come to Chelsea with the sole purpose of tucking into a bowl. One important tip: Don't salt the soup until it has finished simmering, or it will curdle. Also, Sarabeth feels that it is important to tear, not chop, the dill, as it gives the soup extra flavor and texture. (See photo on previous page.)

1. Melt 2 tablespoons of the butter in a large nonreactive saucepan over medium heat. Add the onion, shallots, scallion tops, and garlic. Cook, stirring occasionally, until the onion is softened and translucent, about 4 minutes.

2. Coarsely chop the tomatoes. (This is easiest to do by pulsing them with their purée in a food processor fitted with the metal blade.) Add the tomatoes, milk, and cream to the saucepan and bring them to a simmer, stirring often.

3. Meanwhile, in a small saucepan, melt the remaining 4 tablespoons (60 g) butter over low heat. Whisk in the flour to make a roux. Cook, whisking almost constantly, for about 3 minutes, making sure the roux doesn't brown. Whisk about 1½ cups (360 ml) of the hot tomato mixture into the roux. Pour the roux mixture back into the tomato mixture.

4. Reduce the heat to very low. Cook without simmering for approximately 30 minutes to blend the flavors. Increase the heat to medium and cook, stirring constantly, just until the soup begins to simmer and thicken. Remove the saucepan from the heat. Add the dill and season the soup with the salt and pepper.

5. Ladle the soup into bowls. Top each serving with about 1½ tablespoons of cheese and serve hot. (The soup can be prepared up to 2 days ahead without the cheese, cooled completely, covered, and refrigerated. It can also be frozen for up to 2 months. The soup will thicken when chilled; when reheating, thin the soup with milk to the desired thickness.)

During the hot New York summers, many people are on the lookout for a cooling soup to help take away the sizzle. Ronnybrook Farm Dairy says that this soup was created to use up three overabundant things from their upstate farm: cucumber, mint, and of course, yogurt. If you are in a hurry to chill the soup, transfer it to a large bowl and set it in a larger bowl of ice and water. The soup does double duty as a great sauce for grilled shrimp or lamb.

1. In batches, purée the cucumbers, yogurt, water, mint, oil, lemon juice, garlic, and 1 teaspoon salt in a blender. Transfer the mixture to a large bowl. Cover and refrigerate until chilled, at least 3 hours.

2. To serve, taste and re-season the chilled soup with salt. Ladle it into bowls and sprinkle it with the lemon zest and mint. Serve chilled.

COLD CUCUMBER SOUP

WITH YOGURT AND MINT

RONNYBROOK FARM DAIRY

SERVES 6

3 cucumbers (2½ pounds/1 kg), peeled, seeded, and coarsely chopped

3 (6-ounce/170-g) containers plain nonfat or low-fat yogurt, preferably Ronnybrook Creamline

1 cup (240 ml) iced water

¼ cup (10 g) packed fresh mint leaves

2 tablespoons extra-virgin olive oil

2 tablespoons fresh lemon juice

1 garlic clove, coarsely chopped

Kosher salt

Freshly grated zest of 1 lemon, for garnish

Chopped fresh mint leaves, for garnish

VEGETABLE SOUP
WITH CHICKEN MATZO BALLS

CHELSEA MARKET FAMILY RECIPE

SERVES 6

FOR THE CHICKEN MATZO BALLS:

1 pound (455 g) ground chicken

⅓ cup (40 g) matzo meal or dried plain bread crumbs

1 small yellow onion, grated on the large holes of a box grater

1 large egg, beaten

2 tablespoons finely chopped fresh flat-leaf parsley

1 teaspoon kosher salt

½ teaspoon finely chopped fresh thyme, or ¼ teaspoon dried thyme

¼ teaspoon freshly ground black pepper

FOR THE SOUP:

2 tablespoons vegetable oil

1 yellow onion, chopped

2 celery ribs with leaves, ribs cut into ½-inch (12-mm) dice, leaves chopped

1 carrot, cut into ½-inch (12-mm) dice

6 cups (1.5 L) reduced-sodium chicken broth

½ teaspoon finely chopped fresh thyme, or ¼ teaspoon dried thyme

1 bay leaf

Kosher salt and freshly ground black pepper

Chopped fresh flat-leaf parsley, for garnish

There are many people who would say that chicken soup with matzo balls is the ultimate New York City dish. The twist with this version is that the balls are made with ground chicken as well as matzo, to make a more substantial bowl of soup. Canned chicken broth, bolstered with the flavors from fresh ground chicken and vegetables, is quickly transformed into a satisfying meal that will have Bubbie *kvelling*.

1. Make the chicken matzo balls: Using your hands, mix the chicken, matzo meal, onion, egg, parsley, salt, thyme, and pepper together in a large bowl. Cover and refrigerate for at least 15 minutes or up to 4 hours.

2. Make the soup: Heat the oil in a large pot over medium heat. Add the onion, celery, celery leaves, and carrot and cover. Cook, stirring occasionally, until the vegetables soften, about 5 minutes. Add the broth, thyme, and bay leaf and bring to a boil over high heat. Reduce the heat to medium-low, and simmer, with the lid ajar, for 15 minutes.

3. Using wet hands, shape the chicken mixture into 24 equal balls. One at a time, drop the balls into the simmering soup. Simmer, with the lid ajar, until the meatballs are cooked through, about 20 minutes. Season with salt and pepper.

4. Ladle the soup into bowls, sprinkle it with parsley, and serve hot.

This creamy soup is found in every Thai restaurant (including, of course, Chelsea Thai), but the advantage to making it at home is that you can season it to your taste. Adjust the salty fish sauce and fresh lime juice to get the balance that you like. Be careful not to add the lime juice while the soup is cooking, as it will make the citrus flavor bitter instead of smooth. You will find galangal, kaffir lime leaves, and lemongrass at Asian markets.

1. Bring the stock, lemongrass, galangal, and lime leaves to a boil in a large saucepan over high heat. Reduce the heat to low and simmer until the stock is well flavored, about 20 minutes. Using a wire sieve, scoop out the solids, hold them over the pan, and press hard on them to extract their flavor. Discard the solids.

2. Add the chicken and mushrooms and increase the heat to medium. Simmer until the chicken is opaque, about 7 minutes. Stir in the coconut milk and return the soup to a simmer. Remove it from the heat.

3. Stir in the lime juice and fish sauce, taste, and add more if desired. Stir in the cilantro and chile.

4. Ladle the soup into bowls and serve it hot with the lime wedges.

CHICKEN, MUSHROOM & COCONUT MILK SOUP
(TOM KA GAI)

CHELSEA THAI

SERVES 6

1 quart (1 L) Chicken Stock (page 56) or reduced-sodium chicken broth

2 (3-inch/8-cm) pieces peeled lemongrass (white part only), smashed under the flat side of a large knife

1 (2-inch/5-cm) piece fresh galangal or ginger, thinly sliced

8 to 10 kaffir lime leaves, fresh or frozen

1½ pounds (680 g) boneless skinless chicken breasts, sliced across the grain about ¼ inch (6 mm) thick

8 ounces (225 g) thinly sliced fresh white button mushrooms

1 (15-ounce/445-ml) can unsweetened coconut milk

⅓ cup (75 ml) fresh lime juice, as needed

⅓ cup (75 ml) Thai or Vietnamese fish sauce (*nam pla* or *nuoc cham*), as needed

¼ cup (25 g) coarsely chopped fresh cilantro

1 small hot fresh red chile, finely minced, or ½ teaspoon hot red chile flakes

Lime wedges, for serving

SEAFOOD & ANDOUILLE GUMBO

THE GREEN TABLE

SERVES 6

½ cup (120 ml) canola oil or rendered duck fat

½ cup (60 g) unbleached all-purpose flour

2 yellow onions, cut into ½-inch (12-mm) dice

2 green bell peppers, cut into ½-inch (12-mm) dice

2 celery ribs, cut into ½-inch (12-mm) dice

1 garlic clove, minced

1 teaspoon Old Bay seasoning

½ teaspoon garam masala

½ teaspoon dried thyme

¼ teaspoon cayenne pepper

Kosher salt

1 (8-ounce/225-g) container shucked oysters, or 6 large oysters, such as Wellfleet, shucked, liquor reserved

1 quart (1 L) Seafood Stock or Quick Seafood Stock (page 57) or reduced-sodium seafood stock

4 ounces (115 g) andouille sausage, cut into ½-inch (12-mm) dice

8 ounces (225 g) medium (26 to 31 count) shrimp, preferably wild-caught or eco-farmed, peeled and deveined

¼ cup (25 g) finely chopped fresh flat-leaf parsley

1 scallion, white and green parts, finely chopped

Hot cooked rice, for serving

Gumbo is a soup that thinks it's a stew, and this one is chock-full of vegetables, seafood, and sausage. Intriguingly spiced with both Old Bay Seasoning and garam masala, it is especially good if made a day ahead, to allow the flavors to develop. Don't be afraid to cook the roux until it is really browned, as that is another key to this fine gumbo's rich profile.

1. Heat the oil in a large nonreactive Dutch oven, preferably enameled cast iron, over medium heat. Whisk in the flour. Cook, whisking almost constantly, until the mixture has turned a deep chestnut color and smells toasty, adjusting the heat as necessary to avoid burning, 15 to 20 minutes.

2. Add the onions, green peppers, and celery and cover. Reduce the heat to low. Cook, stirring occasionally, until the onions are translucent and tender, about 10 minutes. Stir in the garlic, Old Bay, garam masala, thyme, cayenne, and a sprinkle of salt. Cover and continue cooking to bring out the spices' flavors, about 1 minute.

3. Drain the oysters, reserving the liquor. Cover and refrigerate the oysters until ready to serve. Add the stock and oyster liquor to the Dutch oven and whisk until smooth. Add the sausage and bring the mixture to a simmer over medium heat. Reduce the heat to medium-low and simmer until the flavors are combined, about 20 minutes. (The gumbo can be made to this point, cooled, covered, and refrigerated for up to 1 day. Return it to a simmer before proceeding.)

4. Add the shrimp, parsley, and scallion and cook until the shrimp turn opaque, about 1 minute. Season with salt.

5. For each serving, ladle the soup into a large bowl. Add a raw oyster (the heat will cook the oyster) and top with a large spoonful of hot rice. Serve hot.

CHICKEN, BEEF, OR VEAL STOCK

CHELSEA MARKET FAMILY RECIPE

MAKES ABOUT 1½ QUARTS (1.4 L)

3 pounds (1.4 kg) chicken wings

1 tablespoon vegetable oil

1 small yellow onion, chopped

1 small carrot, chopped

1 small celery rib, with leaves, chopped

4 sprigs fresh flat-leaf parsley

¼ teaspoon dried thyme

¼ teaspoon black peppercorns

1 bay leaf

There are many good broths for sale at the Market, but there are few kitchen jobs as satisfying as simmering up a big pot of stock. The difference between stock and broth is negligible, although some would say that broth is seasoned and can be consumed as soup, but stock is unseasoned and used strictly as a recipe ingredient in foods that will be seasoned anyway. Reduced-sodium broth is often called for in recipes to help reduce the chance of oversalting the final recipe. So make a batch of stock (be sure to freeze some), and see what a difference it can make in your cooking.

1. Using a cleaver or heavy knife, cut the chicken wings between the joints. Heat the oil in a large pot over medium heat. Add all of the wings and cook, stirring occasionally, until the wings are very lightly browned and a light brown film begins to form in the pot, about 10 minutes. Transfer the wings to a plate. Add the onion, carrot, and celery to the pot and cook, stirring often, until the vegetables soften, about 5 minutes.

2. Add 2 cups (480 ml) water to the pot and stir to loosen the browned bits in the pot. Return the wings and any juices on the plate to the pot. Pour in enough cold water (about 2 quarts/2 L) to cover the ingredients by 1 inch (2.5 cm). Bring everything to a simmer over high heat, skimming off the foam that rises to the surface. Add the parsley, thyme, peppercorns, and bay leaf. Reduce the heat to low and simmer, uncovered, until the stock is well flavored, 2½ to 3 hours.

3. Drain the stock through a wire sieve into a large heatproof bowl, discarding the solids in the sieve. Let it stand until tepid. (To cool it more quickly, carefully place the bowl in a sink of iced water.) Transfer the stock to airtight containers and refrigerate for up to 3 days. Remove the hardened fat on the surface of the stock before using. (The stock can be frozen for up to 3 months.)

BEEF STOCK: Substitute 2 pounds (910 g) beef bones and 1 pound (455 g) beef shanks for the chicken wings. Brown the shanks in the oil, turning occasionally, until they are nicely browned, about 10 minutes. Transfer the shanks to a plate. Do not brown the beef bones. Add the onion, carrot, and celery to the pot, cover, and cook until softened, about 5 minutes. Deglaze the pot with 2 cups (480 ml) water. Return the shanks to the pot, add the bones, and pour in enough additional water to cover the ingredients by 1 inch (2.5 cm). Proceed as directed.

VEAL STOCK: Substitute 2 pounds (910 g) veal bones and 1 pound (455 g) veal neck or shank for the chicken wings. Do not brown the veal. Heat the oil in the pot over medium heat and add the onion, carrot, and celery to the pot. Cover and cook until softened, about 5 minutes. Add the veal bones and pour in enough water to cover the ingredients by 1 inch (2.5 cm). Proceed as directed.

Seafood stock cooks quickly because fish bones are so thin and easily give up their flavor. It is becoming increasingly available in aseptic packages, but it can't compare to the fresh, clean flavor of the homemade version. When making stock, avoid oily, rich fish like salmon or mackerel, and use white-fleshed varieties. If you can't find fish bones easily, make the Quick Seafood Stock variation.

1. Using kitchen scissors, snip out and discard the dark red gills from the fish heads. Rinse the bones and heads well under cold running water. Using a sharp knife, chop the bones into manageable portions to fit the pot.

2. Heat the oil in a large pot over medium heat. Add the leek, celery, and fennel and cover. Cook, stirring occasionally, until the vegetables are softened but not browned, about 5 minutes. Add the wine and bring everything to a boil. Add the bones and heads. Pour in enough cold water (about 1¾ quarts/1.75 L) to cover the ingredients by 1 inch (2.5 cm). Bring to a simmer over high heat, skimming off the foam that rises to the surface. Add the parsley, thyme, peppercorns, and bay leaf. Reduce the heat to low and simmer, uncovered, until the stock is well flavored, 30 to 40 minutes.

3. Drain the stock through a wire sieve into a large heatproof bowl, discarding the solids in the sieve. Let it stand until tepid. (To cool it more quickly, carefully place the bowl in a sink of iced water.) Transfer the stock to airtight containers and refrigerate for up to 3 days. (The stock can be frozen for up to 3 months.)

QUICK SEAFOOD STOCK: Cook 1 small yellow onion and 1 small celery rib with leaves, both chopped, in 1 tablespoon vegetable oil in a medium saucepan over medium heat until softened but not browned, about 4 minutes. Add 2 cups (480 ml) reduced-sodium chicken broth, 2 cups (480 ml) bottled clam juice, and 1 cup (240 ml) water. If you have the shells from up to 1 pound (455 g) peeled shrimp, add them, too. Bring everything to a simmer over medium heat. Reduce the heat to low and simmer for 15 minutes. Strain and cool. Makes about 1 quart (960 ml).

SEAFOOD STOCK

CHELSEA MARKET FAMILY RECIPE

MAKES 1½ QUARTS (1.4 L)

3 pounds (1.4 kg) bones and heads from 2 cleaned, filleted white-fleshed fish, such as snapper, branzino, or porgy

1 tablespoon vegetable oil

1 small leek, white and pale green parts only, chopped, well washed, and drained (see Tips)

1 small celery rib, with leaves, chopped

½ small fennel bulb, without fronds, chopped

½ cup (120 ml) dry white wine, such as Pinot Grigio

4 sprigs fresh flat-leaf parsley

¼ teaspoon dried thyme

¼ teaspoon black peppercorns

1 bay leaf

TIPS FROM THE PROS

CLEANING LEEKS
Manhattan Fruit Exchange

Leeks are grown in sandy soil, so they always have grit between their layers. This technique is one of the most efficient ways to clean them and is guaranteed to get the dirt out. Chop the leek as needed and transfer it to a medium bowl of cold water. Agitate the leeks in the water to help loosen the grit. Let them stand for a few minutes so the grit can sink to the bottom of the bowl. Using a wire sieve, lift the floating chopped leeks out of the water, leaving the grit behind in the bowl. (Do not make the mistake of draining the entire contents of the bowl in the sieve, or the grit will be dumped back on top of the chopped leeks.) Transfer the leeks to paper towels and pat dry.

VEGETABLE STOCK

MAKES ABOUT 1½ QUARTS (1.4 L)

2 large yellow onions, chopped

4 medium carrots, chopped

2 large celery ribs with leaves, chopped

16 sprigs fresh flat-leaf parsley

½ teaspoon black peppercorns

3 bay leaves

This vegetable stock is quickly prepared from ingredients that you are likely to have in your kitchen. It has a neutral and lightly herbaceous flavor that is tasty but unobtrusive. This cannot be said of many store-bought vegetable broths, which taste of cabbage or are too salty.

1. Combine all of the ingredients in a large pot. Add 2 quarts (2 L) cold water and bring to a boil over high heat.

2. Reduce the heat to medium. Simmer briskly until the vegetables are very tender and the liquid is reduced to about 6 cups (1.4 L), 30 to 40 minutes.

3. Drain the stock through a wire sieve into a large heatproof bowl, discarding the solids in the sieve. Let the stock stand until tepid. (To cool it more quickly, carefully place the bowl in a sink of iced water.) Transfer the stock to airtight containers and refrigerate it for up to 5 days. (The stock can be frozen for up to 3 months.)

Dickson's Farmstand Meats is a unique butcher, sourcing their meats from farms with extraordinarily high standards. It is only natural (pun intended) that their chili recipe would be uncommonly good, loaded with flavor as well as detailed techniques for great results. This is not your granddaddy's chili! For example, the main meat is beef shank, a highly gelatinous cut that gives a luscious smoothness to the sauce. The meat is marinated overnight before cooking, and the seasoning gets complexity from smoky Turkish Urfa chile flakes. If you have the time, refrigerate the chili overnight before serving to mellow the flavors.

1. Prepare the beef: At least 1 day before serving the chili, cut the meat from the beef shanks. (Save the bones to make beef stock.) You should have about 3 pounds (1.5 kg) meat. Cut the meat into 1-inch (2.5-cm) cubes. Place them on a baking sheet and freeze until they are semisolid, about 1 hour. In batches, process the meat in a food processor until it is coarsely chopped. (If you are lucky to live near an artisan butcher, ask them to bone and grind the beef shank meat with the coarse "chili" blade.)

2. Mix the guajillo chile, vinegar, chile de arbol, salt, oregano, cumin, and cloves together in a nonreactive medium bowl. Add the beef and mix well. Cover tightly and refrigerate for at least 12 and up to 24 hours.

3. Prepare the beans: Put the beans in a large bowl and add enough cold water to cover by at least 3 inches (7.5 cm). Let them stand in a cool place (refrigerate if the kitchen is warm) for at least 12 and up to 16 hours.

4. Drain the beans, put them in a large saucepan, and add enough fresh cold water to cover by 3 inches (7.5 cm). Heat them, stirring often, over medium-high heat just until the water boils. Reduce the heat to medium-low and simmer until the beans are barely tender, about 1½ hours, depending on the freshness of the beans. During the last 30 minutes, add the salt to the saucepan. Drain the beans and set them aside.

5. Make the chili: Meanwhile, heat 2 tablespoons of the oil in a heavy Dutch oven over medium-high heat. In 2 or 3 batches, add the marinated beef and cook, stirring often, until it is seared, about 5 minutes. Using a slotted spoon, transfer the beef to a bowl, leaving the fat in the pot.

6. Pulse the onions and garlic together in a food processor until finely chopped but not puréed. (Or mince the onions and garlic by hand.) Add the remaining 1 tablespoon oil to the Dutch oven and heat. Add the onion mixture and cook, stirring often, until the onions are softened, about 5 minutes.

7. Return the beef to the Dutch oven. Add the tomato purée, chile flakes, oregano, thyme, and cumin and stir well. Reduce the heat to medium-low. Simmer, uncovered, for about 2½ hours, until the meat is very tender and the tomato juices thicken. Add hot water to the chili if it threatens to stick to the pot, and stir in the beans during the last hour. Season with salt and more Urfa chile flakes. If you like very spicy chili, add more ground chile de arbol. (The chili can be cooled, covered, and refrigerated for up to 2 days.) Spoon it into bowls and serve hot.

UPSTATE CHILI

DICKSON'S FARMSTAND MEATS

SERVES 8 TO 10

FOR THE BEEF:

5 pounds (2.5 kg) beef shank

½ cup (60 g) pure ground guajillo chile

⅓ cup (75 ml) cider vinegar

1 tablespoon pure ground chile de arbol

1 tablespoon kosher salt

1 tablespoon dried oregano, preferably Mexican

¼ teaspoon ground cumin

Dash of ground cloves

FOR THE BEANS:

1 pound (455 g) dried red kidney beans, rinsed and pick through for stones

1 tablespoon kosher salt

FOR THE CHILI:

3 tablespoons extra-virgin olive oil

2 large yellow onions, coarsely chopped

6 garlic cloves, crushed and peeled

2 (28-ounce/800-g) cans whole peeled tomatoes, drained, puréed in a blender

3 tablespoons Urfa Biber or Aleppo chile flakes, plus more to taste (see Tips, page 62)

2 tablespoons dried oregano, preferably Mexican

2 tablespoons dried thyme

2 tablespoons ground cumin

Kosher salt

CHILES
Spices and Tease

Chiles are actually fruits of the Capsicum plant family. (Peppercorns are the berrylike drupes of the Piper nigrum vine, dried or processed until black, white, or green.) There are hundreds of chiles, and many of them show up in our Chilifest recipes. In varying degrees, chiles have spicy heat in common, but they also have other flavor characteristics (fruitiness, sweetness, and even smokiness) that give them distinction and complexity.

Whole dried chiles are available, but ground chiles are easier to use. (Chili powder is a mixture of seasonings, formulated specifically for Texan meat stew, and usually consists of a ground mild chile and ground cumin, with oregano, dried garlic, and other ingredients often added.) Here are the most common ground chiles:

ANCHO: Processed from the dark green poblano chile after it has fully ripened to red. Relatively mild, this dark brick-red chile powder has a fruity, sweet note.

CAYENNE: Named for the city of Cayenne in French Guiana, this very hot, orange-red chile is used all over the world to give a jolt of hot spice to a dish.

CHIPOTLE: Dried and smoked jalapeño, this one is very spicy. Also popular canned in adobo sauce, a vinegary purée.

GUAJILLO: A very popular, all-purpose chile in Mexican cuisine, it is moderately spicy with a green tea–like flavor and berry undertones. On its own, it may be hot enough for some palates, but it is often augmented with spicier chile to raise its heat.

JALAPEÑO: This is a dried and ground version of the familiar fresh green chile, but, unlike the chipotle, it is not smoked.

NEW MEXICAN: You will see strings of these shiny red chiles for sale in New Mexico, but note that most of these are sprayed with a preservative and are only for decoration. The chile is sold hot or mild, and has a rounded flavor that makes it an excellent all-purpose chile for Tex-Mex cooking.

A new category of chile pepper seasonings is making its mark on the culinary scene. These Mediterranean chile flakes have a rounded, fruity flavor that is closer to paprika than cayenne. The two are similar, but not completely interchangeable, and an adventurous cook will want to have both.

URFA BIBER: Chile flakes from the Urfa region of Turkey. The chiles go through a special drying process that gives them a purplish color and smoky heat.

ALEPPO: Named for the ancient Syrian city just over the Turkish border, this pepper is brick red, with a slightly tart flavor.

It is only natural that Michael Ginsberg, a native Texan, dreamed up Chelsea Market's annual winter Chilifest. Here is his favorite recipe—one that he has served up at many a chili competition. His nickname, Metalbelly, refers not only to his gut, but the musical instrument (a kind of tricked-out washboard) that he invented and plays in a Brooklyn-based alternative rockabilly band, The Defibulators. Metalbelly/Michael firmly believes that it is the blend and variety of peppers that put his chili ahead of the pack, and he recommends (or actually insists on) refrigerating it for a day before serving so the heat can calm down.

1. Make the spice mixture: Whisk all of the spice mixture ingredients together in a medium bowl to combine.

2. Coarsely chop the bacon and cook it in a large Dutch oven or pot over medium-high heat, stirring often, until the bacon is browned, about 10 minutes. Using a slotted spoon, transfer the bacon to paper towels to drain. Pour the bacon fat into a heatproof bowl.

3. Return 2 tablespoons of the bacon fat to the pot. In batches, cook the beef, stirring occasionally, until it is browned, about 5 minutes, adding more bacon fat as needed. Transfer the beef to a platter. Add the remaining bacon fat to the Dutch oven. Add the halved onion and garlic and cook until the garlic begins to soften, about 2 minutes.

4. Return the beef and bacon to the Dutch oven, and add the jalapeños. Stir in one third of the spice mixture and mix well to coat the beef. Stir in half each of the stock, tomatoes, beer, and tomato paste. Add another third of the spice mixture, stir well, and bring the mixture to a simmer. Reduce the heat to low and cover. Simmer for 1 hour.

5. Remove the onion and jalapeños, squeezing the jalapeños against the side of the Dutch oven to release the juices, and discard. Add the remaining stock, tomatoes, beer, and tomato paste, then the remaining spice mixture. Stir well, and simmer until the meat is tender, about 2 hours more. If the chili gets too thick, stir in hot water as needed.

6. Stir in the vinegar and season the chili with salt. Remove the pot from the heat and let the chili cool until it is tepid, about 1½ hours. Cover and refrigerate it overnight.

7. To serve, reheat the chili gently over medium-low heat, stirring often, adding water to adjust the consistency as needed, and seasoning with additional vinegar and salt if needed. Spoon it into bowls and serve hot.

METALBELLY'S MARKET CHILI

CHELSEA MARKET FAMILY RECIPE

SERVES 10 TO 12

FOR THE SPICE MIXTURE:

¼ cup (30 g) pure ground chipotle chile

3½ tablespoons (25 g) ground cumin

2 tablespoons onion powder

2 tablespoons pure ground ancho chile

2 tablespoons pure ground guajillo chile

2 tablespoons pure ground New Mexican chile

2 tablespoons chili powder

2 tablespoons freshly ground black pepper

1 tablespoon plus 1 teaspoon garlic powder

1 tablespoon dried Mexican oregano

1 teaspoon pure ground dried jalapeño

1 teaspoon cayenne pepper

8 ounces (225 g) sliced bacon

4½ pounds (2 kg) boneless beef chuck, cut into 1-inch (2.5-cm) pieces

1 very large yellow onion, halved

16 whole garlic cloves, peeled

2 large whole jalapeño peppers

2 quarts (2 L) Beef Stock (page 56) or reduced-sodium beef broth

1 (28-ounce/800-g) can crushed tomatoes

2½ cups (600 ml) dark beer, chocolate beer, or stout

3 tablespoons tomato paste

1 tablespoon apple cider vinegar, plus more for seasoning

Kosher salt

CHILIFEST

CHELSEA MARKET

The ultimate celebration of chili, beer, and all things spicy, Chilifest was the brainchild of Michael Ginsberg, Jamestown's event manager. This extravaganza is held each winter inside Chelsea Market, giving ticket holders access to an enormous concourse of chili, served by dozens of New York City's best restaurants and cutting-edge chefs, all competing for the Golden Chili Mug.

Each year, Dickson's Farmstand Meats supplies each chef with 100 percent dry-aged, locally raised beef from Wrighteous Organics in Schoharie, New York, as the base for their chili. In addition to providing a level playing field for the competition, the ingredient reflects the inspiration for the event—to use meat from responsibly raised animals to create delicious food. An exclusive panel of on-site celebrity judges votes on the Chili Champ of New York City.

Ticket proceeds go to Food Systems Network NYC in support of their efforts to build a just and vibrant regional food and farm economy, that promotes human and environmental health, and prevents hunger.

CHAPTER 4

THE SALAD BOWL

MAIN COURSE & SIDE SALADS

MANHATTAN FRUIT EXCHANGE

SERVES 6

FOR THE VINAIGRETTE:

3 tablespoons fresh lemon juice

3 tablespoons fresh orange juice

2 teaspoons honey

⅓ cup plus 1 tablespoon (90 ml) extra-virgin olive oil

Kosher salt and freshly ground black pepper

FOR THE SALAD:

5 ounces (140 g) baby arugula

1 cup (40 g) loosely packed fresh mint leaves, coarsely chopped

½ small seedless watermelon, rind removed, flesh cut into about 30 (1-inch/2.5-cm) cubes

1½ cups (12 ounces/340 g) ricotta di bufala, crumbled (see Note)

½ cup (55 g) toasted and coarsely chopped pecans (see page 180)

NOTE: *Ricotta di bufala is a moist, fresh cheese made from water buffalo milk and is usually imported from Italy. It is slightly firmer than domestic cow's-milk ricotta. If you can't find it, use ricotta salata, a crumbly aged ricotta, or fresh domestic cow's-milk ricotta.*

With a palate-pleasing collection of ingredients combining spicy, crunchy, and sweet, this is a salad that you will serve again and again. It is great to serve in the summer, when watermelon is at the peak of its flavor. (See photo on previous page.)

1. Make the vinaigrette: Whisk the lemon juice, orange juice, and honey together in a small bowl. Gradually whisk in the oil. Season with salt and pepper.

2. Make the salad: Toss the arugula and mint in a large bowl with about half of the vinaigrette. Divide the salad among six dinner plates. Top each with 5 watermelon pieces and about ¼ cup (55 g) of the ricotta. Sprinkle with the pecans and serve immediately with the remaining dressing on the side.

Here's an updated version of insalata Caprese with the required tomatoes, mozzarella, and basil, but stacked for an interesting presentation. This salad especially calls for very good ingredients, with ripe tomatoes and first-class mozzarella. A fine vinaigrette, made with Champagne vinegar, smoked salt, and excellent oil, makes a major contribution, too.

1. Make the salad: Using a serrated knife, cut the rounded tops and bottoms from each of the tomatoes. Save them for another use or discard. Cut each tomato crosswise into four equal rounds. You should have 8 red tomato rounds and 4 yellow tomato rounds.

2. Make the vinaigrette: Whisk together the vinegar, basil, shallot, lemon juice, mustard, and salt. Gradually whisk in the oil. Season with the pepper.

3. To assemble the salads: For each serving, put a red tomato round on a plate and top with a mozzarella round. Drizzle with a teaspoon or so of vinaigrette. Add a yellow tomato round and another mozzarella round; drizzle with another teaspoon of vinaigrette. Finish with a final red tomato round. Drizzle about 1 tablespoon of the vinaigrette over and around the tomato-mozzarella stack, and sprinkle with the chopped basil and additional smoked salt. Serve at once.

TOMATOES & MOZZARELLA
WITH SMOKED BASIL VINAIGRETTE

THE FILLING STATION

SERVES 4

FOR THE SALAD:

2 large ripe red field or heirloom tomatoes

1 large ripe yellow field or heirloom tomato

1 pound (455 g) water-packed fresh mozzarella, drained and cut crosswise into 8 rounds

2 tablespoons finely chopped fresh basil

FOR THE VINAIGRETTE:

2 tablespoons Champagne vinegar

2 tablespoons finely chopped fresh basil

1 tablespoon minced shallot

2 teaspoons fresh lemon juice

1½ teaspoons Dijon mustard

½ teaspoon smoked alderwood salt, plus more for serving

⅓ cup plus 1 tablespoon (90 ml) extra-virgin olive oil

Freshly ground black pepper

A small counter tucked into a corner of the "new section" of the Market, One Lucky Duck specializes in delicious vegan food made with raw, organic ingredients. However, the staff emphasizes that this wonderful salad is tasty whether it is freshly mixed and crunchy or marinated and more tender. Black sesame seeds give it a striking appearance.

1. Prepare the salad: Using a large knife, cut the cabbage into thin shreds. Transfer them to a very large bowl. Using a mandoline, plastic V-slicer, or knife, cut the jicama, carrots, and beets into julienne strips about 2 inches (5 cm) long. (The exact thickness is a matter of personal choice, depending on the slaw texture that you prefer.) Transfer them to the bowl with the cabbage.

2. Make the dressing: Whisk the tamari and maple syrup together in a small bowl. Gradually whisk in the oil. Add the dressing to the salad and toss.

3. Make the topping: Stir together the cashews, sesame seeds, oil, wasabi, and salt in a medium bowl until combined. Add them to the salad and mix well. Top with the cilantro and serve. (The salad will keep, covered and refrigerated, for up to 2 days. Drain any accumulated juices and adjust the seasoning with salt, tamari, and wasabi powder before serving.)

SPICY SESAME SALAD

ONE LUCKY DUCK

SERVES 6 TO 8

FOR THE SALAD:

1 small head Savoy cabbage (1¼ pounds/570 g), cored

1 small jicama (14 ounces/400 g), peeled

2 large carrots (8 ounces/225 g), scrubbed but unpeeled

2 medium beets (12 ounces/340 g), peeled

FOR THE DRESSING:

¼ cup (60 ml) tamari or shoyu

¼ cup (60 ml) pure maple syrup

½ cup (120 ml) expeller-pressed or toasted sesame oil

FOR THE SESAME TOPPING:

2 cups (10 ounces/280 g) raw or toasted cashews, finely chopped

⅔ cup (3.5 ounces/100 g) black sesame seeds

2 tablespoons expeller-pressed or toasted sesame oil

2 teaspoons wasabi powder

¾ teaspoon fine sea salt

1 cup (40 g) loosely packed fresh cilantro leaves

Special equipment: A mandoline or plastic V-slicer

SUMMER FARRO SALAD

MARCO CANORA, GUEST CHEF

SERVES 4 TO 6

FOR THE FARRO:

2 tablespoons extra-virgin olive oil

1 small yellow onion, halved crosswise

1 small carrot, halved lengthwise

1 small celery rib, halved lengthwise

2 cups (340 g) pearled farro

1½ teaspoons kosher salt

FOR THE SALAD:

2 plum (Roma) tomatoes, seeded and cut into ½-inch (12-mm) dice

¼ seedless (English) cucumber, cut into ½-inch (12-mm) dice

½ small red onion, finely chopped

3 tablespoons red wine vinegar

⅓ cup plus 1 tablespoon (90 ml) extra-virgin olive oil

Kosher salt and freshly ground black pepper

½ cup (55 g) crumbled goat cheese, preferably Italian *caprini*

¼ cup (20 g) loosely packed chopped fresh basil

During the warm weather months, Terroir on the Porch pops up on the High Line above the Market. This alfresco establishment serves Italian-inspired fare from Marco Canora, whose other restaurants can be found around lower Manhattan. A light mixture of chewy Italian farro with summer vegetables, this grain salad is typical of Terroir's fare—rustic food perfect for enjoying with a glass of *vino* while watching the world stroll by. Enjoy it on its own, or as a side dish to grilled steak or fish.

1. Make the farro: Heat the oil in a medium saucepan over medium heat. Add the onion, carrot, and celery and cover. Cook until the vegetables begin to soften, about 5 minutes. Add the farro and stir well. Add 5 cups (1.2 L) water and bring to a boil over high heat. Reduce the heat to medium-low and cover again. Simmer for 10 minutes. Stir in the salt and continue simmering until the farro is tender, 5 to 10 minutes more. Drain well. Let cool completely. Using kitchen tongs, remove and discard the onion, carrot, and celery.

2. Make the salad: Transfer the cooled farro to a large bowl. Add the tomatoes, cucumber, and red onion and mix well.

3. Pour the vinegar into a small bowl and gradually whisk in the oil. Pour the vinaigrette over the farro mixture and mix, seasoning with salt and pepper. Add the goat cheese and basil and toss again. Serve immediately or let stand at room temperature for up to 2 hours.

TIPS FROM THE PROS

FARRO
Marco Canora, Guest Chef

Farro is an ancient grain, similar to spelt. It is especially hard, an attribute that keeps it chewy after cooking. For faster cooking, look for pearled farro, which means that its tough outer hull has been removed. (Note that this process also removes its bran and germ, so pearled farro is not considered a whole grain.)

If you prefer (or can find only) farro that has not been pearled, it must be soaked before cooking. Rinse and drain the farro in a wire sieve, then put the grains in a large bowl. Add enough cold water to cover the farro by 1 inch (2.5 cm). Let stand in a cool place or the refrigerator for 8 hours. Drain in a large wire sieve. To cook, simmer the farro with the vegetables and water for 1 hour, adding more hot water to the saucepan as needed to keep the farro covered. Using kitchen tongs, remove the vegetables from the saucepan. Stir in the salt and continue cooking, adding hot water as needed, until the farro is tender, 30 minutes to 1 hour more.

This dish has its roots in the vibrant cuisine of Turkey, and the rich flavors in this salad deepen if chilled overnight. It is the perfect addition to a buffet, or can be the centerpiece of a summer lunch. Try it with grilled lamb.

1. Bring the lentils, 4½ cups (1 L) water, and the smashed garlic clove to a boil in a medium saucepan over high heat. Reduce the heat to low and simmer until the lentils are tender, adding hot water to the saucepan as needed if the water cooks away, about 40 minutes. Drain, rinse the lentils under cold water, and drain again. Let them cool.

2. Meanwhile, stir the bulgur and boiling water together in a medium heatproof bowl. Let them stand until the bulgur is tender, about 20 minutes. Drain well in a fine-mesh wire sieve. Press on the bulgur to extract excess water, and transfer the bulgur to a large bowl. Add the lentils and parsley and mix together.

3. Whisk together the lemon juice, oil, mustard, tomato paste, vinegar, and cumin in a medium bowl to dissolve the tomato paste. Stir into the lentil mixture and mix well. Season generously with salt and pepper. Cover and refrigerate for at least 2 hours, preferably overnight. (The salad can be refrigerated for up to 5 days.)

4. To serve, spread the lettuce on a deep serving platter. Taste and season the lentil salad again with lemon juice, oil, salt, and pepper. Heap the lentil salad on the lettuce, and top with the tomato wedges. Serve chilled or at room temperature.

TURKISH LENTIL & BULGUR SALAD

SPICES AND TEASE

SERVES 6 TO 8

1½ cups (285 g) brown lentils, rinsed

3 garlic cloves, 1 peeled and smashed, and 2 minced

½ cup (80 g) bulgur

1 cup (240 ml) boiling water

1 cup (95 g) finely chopped fresh flat-leaf parsley

¼ cup (60 ml) fresh lemon juice, plus more for serving

2 tablespoons extra-virgin olive oil, plus more for serving

2 tablespoons Dijon mustard

1 tablespoon tomato paste

1 tablespoon white wine vinegar

2 teaspoons ground cumin

Kosher salt and freshly ground black pepper

1 head romaine lettuce, cored and coarsely chopped

2 tomatoes, cut into thin wedges

OLD SCHOOL POTATO SALAD

RUTHY'S

SERVES 8

3 pounds (1.5 kg) red-skinned potatoes, peeled and cut into 1-inch (2.5-cm) pieces

¾ cup (170 g) mayonnaise-style salad dressing, such as Miracle Whip

3 tablespoons drained sweet pickle relish

2 tablespoons prepared yellow mustard

1 tablespoon sugar

2 celery ribs, cut into ½-inch (12-mm) dice

1 yellow onion, finely chopped

3 large eggs, hard-boiled (see page 34)

Kosher salt and freshly ground black pepper

2 tablespoons drained chopped pimiento

Sweet paprika, for garnish

It is virtually impossible to get a consensus on what makes the perfect potato salad, but this version will come pretty close. It uses three elements that many cooks consider essential—sweet pickle relish, hard-boiled eggs, and pimientos—to create an iconic, picnic-ready salad that will make everyone happy.

1. Bring a large saucepan of salted water to a boil over high heat. Add the potatoes and cook until they are just tender when pierced with the tip of a sharp knife, 10 to 15 minutes. Drain them well. Spread the potatoes on a large baking sheet and let them cool to room temperature.

2. Whisk together the salad dressing, relish, mustard, and sugar in a large bowl. Add the potatoes, celery, and onion. Chop 2 of the hard-boiled eggs into ½-inch (12-mm) pieces and add them to the bowl; mix the salad well. Season with salt and pepper. Transfer the salad to a serving bowl.

3. Thinly slice the remaining hard-boiled egg and arrange it on top of the salad. Sprinkle the top with the pimientos, followed by the paprika. Cover tightly with plastic wrap and refrigerate until chilled, at least 2 hours. (The salad can be made up to 1 day ahead.) Serve chilled.

BEET SALAD

WITH PICKLED GREEN GARLIC & TARRAGON-YOGURT DRESSING

JESSE SCHENKER, GUEST CHEF

SERVES 6

FOR THE ROASTED BEETS:

8 medium assorted beets (red, golden, and candy-striped), greens removed, scrubbed

Kosher salt

FOR THE PICKLED GREEN GARLIC:

½ cup (120 ml) sherry vinegar

2 tablespoons sugar

¼ teaspoon kosher salt

8 ounces (225 g) green garlic, cut into thin rounds

FOR THE DRESSING:

½ cup (120 g) plain Greek yogurt

2 tablespoons sherry vinegar

Freshly grated zest of 1 lemon

2 tablespoons fresh lemon juice

2 tablespoons extra-virgin olive oil

2 tablespoons finely chopped fresh tarragon

Kosher salt and freshly ground black pepper

5 ounces (140 g) baby arugula

The restaurant Recette is just a couple of blocks from the Market, at the northernmost edge of Greenwich Village. Chef/owner Jesse Schenker served this beautiful salad—with magenta roasted beets cloaked in an ivory-colored yogurt dressing—at our annual springtime Sunday Supper event. You'll find green garlic, which looks like scallions, during its late spring season before the farmers allow the shoots to grow into mature, round bulbs. This not-too-common ingredient gives the salad an element of surprise that will be sure to spark dinner-table conversation.

1. Roast the beets: Preheat the oven to 400°F (200°C).

2. Place 4 of the beets on a large square of heavy-duty aluminum foil, season well with salt, and wrap them in the foil. Repeat with the remaining beets. Place the foil packages on a baking sheet. Roast until the beets are tender, about 1 hour.

3. Unwrap the beets and let them cool. Slip off the skins and cut the beets into bite-size chunks.

4. Make the pickled green garlic: Bring the vinegar, ½ cup (120 ml) water, the sugar, and salt to a boil in a medium nonreactive saucepan over high heat, stirring to dissolve the sugar. Put the green garlic in a small bowl. Pour the vinegar mixture over the green garlic and mix to be sure the garlic is evenly covered. Refrigerate for 1 hour.

5. Make the dressing: Mix the yogurt, vinegar, lemon zest, lemon juice, oil, and tarragon in a small bowl. Season with salt and pepper. Let stand at room temperature for 1 hour to blend the flavors.

6. When ready to serve, drain the green garlic. Combine the beets and green garlic in a medium bowl and season with salt and pepper. Divide the beet mixture evenly among six plates and top each with a handful of arugula. Drizzle with the yogurt dressing and serve.

This cured salmon is a member of the gravlax school, coated with sugar, salt, and lots of fresh dill, and chilled. The three-day cure gives the fish a lush, silky texture that is nicely accented by the lime and tequila. Alex, who is often seen shopping at the Market with her daughter, Ava, in tow, likes serving it with an elegant little salad garnished with red trout caviar and striped radish, but it is also good as part of a brunch buffet served with bagels or toast. This is a special dish that deserves the very best wild salmon.

1. Make the salmon: Line a rimmed baking sheet with a large sheet of plastic wrap, letting the extra hang over the sides of the baking sheet. Cut the salmon fillet in half crosswise. Place the salmon pieces, flesh-side up, on the baking sheet.

2. Mix the dill, sugar, salt, peppercorns, lime zest, and mustard together in a small bowl. Sprinkle the mixture evenly over the salmon flesh. Drizzle with the tequila. Sandwich the two salmon pieces together, cut sides facing each other. Wrap them in the plastic. Place a second rimmed baking sheet on top of the salmon, and weigh it down with heavy cans. Refrigerate for 3 days (it will develop a curing liquid, which should not yet be discarded), occasionally turning the salmon over and replacing the top baking sheet and weights.

3. To serve, unwrap the salmon and discard the curing liquid. Using a wet towel or the dull side of a knife, scrape off any clinging curing mixture. Place one piece of salmon on a carving board. Using a sharp thin knife held at a slight angle, carve the salmon off the skin into thin, wide slices; discard the skin.

4. Place the lemon juice in a large bowl. Gradually whisk in ¼ cup (60 ml) of the oil. Add the mâche and toss well. Season with salt and pepper. Mix the remaining 1 tablespoon oil with the salmon roe in a small bowl. Divide the salmon among eight dinner plates. Top with equal amounts of salad and a sprinkling of the radishes. Spoon the roe around each plate and serve immediately.

CURED SALMON
WITH MÂCHE SALAD

ALEXANDRA GUARNASCHELLI, GUEST CHEF

SERVES 8

FOR THE SALMON:

1 (2½-pound/1-kg) center-cut wild salmon fillet

½ cup (50 g) chopped fresh dill

½ cup (100 g) sugar

⅓ cup (80 g) kosher salt

1½ teaspoons black peppercorns, cracked with a mortar and pestle or under a heavy saucepan

Freshly grated zest of 2 limes

1½ teaspoons dry mustard powder

¼ cup (60 ml) silver tequila

2 tablespoons fresh lemon juice

¼ cup (60 ml) plus 1 tablespoon extra-virgin olive oil

8 ounces (225 g) mâche (lamb's lettuce) or mixed baby greens

Kosher salt and freshly ground black pepper

6 ounces (170 g) fresh salmon roe

4 large radishes, preferably 'Easter Egg' variety, thinly sliced

Here is a salad where the result is truly greater than the sum of its parts. It is a variation on the Greek salad, but with extra-large gigantes beans, grilled salmon, and a dressing that is truly good enough to serve as a dunk for bread. You can serve this in individual portions, as directed, or assemble the salad on a big platter, with the salmon arranged on top.

1. Make the dressing: Put the uncracked egg in a small bowl and add enough hot tap water to cover; let it stand for 5 minutes to warm the egg.

2. Crack the egg into a blender and add the cucumber, dill, yogurt, lemon juice, garlic, salt, and pepper. Blend until combined. With the blender running, gradually pour the oil through the hole in the lid to make a creamy dressing. Transfer it to a covered container and refrigerate until ready to serve. (The dressing can be stored in the refrigerator for up to 2 days.)

3. Make the beans: Put the beans in a medium saucepan and add enough cold water to cover by 1 inch (2.5 cm). Bring to a boil over high heat. Cook for 2 minutes. Remove the pan from the heat, cover, and let it stand for 1 hour. (Alternatively, soak the beans in cold water to cover for at least 4 and up to 12 hours.) Drain.

4. Return the beans to the saucepan. Add the oil, garlic, and thyme and enough cold water to cover the beans by 1 inch (2.5 cm). Bring to a boil over high heat. Reduce the heat to medium-low and simmer until the beans are tender, about 1 hour, adding the salt during the last 20 minutes. Drain well, discarding the garlic and thyme. Let the beans cool completely. Transfer them to a covered container and refrigerate until chilled, at least 2 hours. (The beans can be refrigerated for up to 2 days.)

5. Make the salmon: Position a rack in the center of the oven and preheat the oven to 200°F (90°C). Heat a large ridged grill pan over medium-high heat.

6. Brush the salmon on both sides with oil and season with the salt and pepper. In batches, place the salmon in the grill pan and cook until the underside is seared with grill marks, about 3 minutes. Turn the salmon over and cook until the other side is seared and the salmon is rosy pink when flaked in the center with the tip of a small knife, 3 to 4 minutes more. Transfer the cooked fillets to a baking sheet and keep warm in the oven while cooking the remaining salmon.

7. Toss the beans, romaine, cucumber, carrots, onion, olives, and feta together in a large bowl. Divide the salad among six large, wide soup bowls. Top each with a salmon fillet and serve immediately, with the dressing passed on the side.

GRILLED SALMON SALAD
WITH WHITE BEANS & DILL DRESSING

FRIEDMAN'S LUNCH

SERVES 6

FOR THE DRESSING:
1 large egg

½ cup (70 g) diced seedless (English) cucumber

¼ cup (25 g) packed fresh dill leaves

¼ cup (60 g) plain low-fat Greek yogurt

2 tablespoons fresh lemon juice

1 small garlic clove

½ teaspoon kosher salt

¼ teaspoon freshly ground black pepper

1 cup (240 ml) canola oil

FOR THE BEANS:
1¼ cups (225 g) dried gigantes or cannellini beans, picked over for stones

¼ cup (60 ml) extra-virgin olive oil

3 garlic cloves, smashed and peeled

3 sprigs fresh thyme

1 teaspoon kosher salt

FOR THE SALMON:
6 (5- to 6-ounce/140- to 170-g) skinless salmon fillets, pinbones removed

Extra-virgin olive oil, for brushing

1 teaspoon kosher salt

½ teaspoon freshly ground black pepper

2 heads romaine hearts, coarsely chopped

½ seedless (English) cucumber, thinly sliced

2 carrots, shredded

1 small red onion, thinly sliced

1 cup (140 g) pitted and coarsely chopped kalamata olives

1 cup (120 g) crumbled feta cheese

SUNDAY SUPPER

CHELSEA MARKET

Each year, Chelsea Market and the James Beard Foundation welcome more than 250 guests for a family-style dining experience in the Chelsea Market concourse, celebrating some of the nation's finest culinary talent, while raising funds for a worthy cause. Traditionally, the event supports the Robert Fulton Houses in Chelsea by benefitting the Fulton Youth of the Future's culinary scholarships and the James Beard Foundation's scholarship funds, helping promote youth culinary arts and farming initiatives with deserving residents of the neighborhood. With dozens of critically acclaimed chefs preparing a multicourse dinner of their best dishes, Sunday Supper attracts widespread attention from the media and the food-loving public.

CHAPTER 5

FROM THE BUTCHER

RED MEATS

CARNE ASADA TACOS

LOS TACOS NO. 1

MAKES 24 TACOS

FOR THE CARNE ASADA:

¼ cup (40 g) chopped white onion

¼ cup (15 g) finely chopped fresh cilantro

2 tablespoons canola oil, plus more for brushing

2 tablespoons fresh lemon juice

2 teaspoons kosher salt

1 teaspoon garlic salt

1 teaspoon onion salt

1 teaspoon freshly ground black pepper

¼ teaspoon cayenne pepper

3½ pounds (1.6 kg) skirt steak, cut into 3 or 4 manageable portions

FOR THE TORTILLAS:

5 cups (630 g) unbleached all-purpose flour

½ cup (110 g) vegetable shortening, cut into chunks

½ teaspoon fine sea salt

⅛ teaspoon baking powder

1½ cups (360 ml) warm water

FOR THE SALSA RANCHERA:

⅓ cup (50 g) coarsely chopped white onion

¼ cup (10 g) packed fresh cilantro

1 or 2 dried chiles de arbol, seeded, stemmed, and coarsely chopped

1 jalapeño chile, seeded, stemmed, and coarsely chopped

(continued)

Los Tacos No. 1 has proudly shared one of their very best recipes with us, and we should all be grateful for their generosity. Making these beefy soft tacos from scratch, right down to the tortillas, is a very enjoyable accomplishment. Don't let the long ingredient list daunt you: Each one of the components is easy to prepare, and the surprisingly simple tortillas can be made ahead and warmed just before serving. Another option is to turn the tortilla making into part of a dinner party, letting friends help with the rolling and griddling. If need be, skip the outdoor grilling and broil them indoors (see Note). The bottom line: Make these tacos! (See photo on previous page.)

1. Make the carne asada: Whisk ¼ cup (60 ml) water, the onion, cilantro, oil, lemon juice, salt, garlic salt, onion salt, black pepper, and cayenne together in a large nonreactive bowl. Put the steak in a 1-gallon (3.8-L) zip-tight plastic storage bag, and add the marinade. Close the bag and refrigerate, turning the bag occasionally, for at least 12 and up to 24 hours.

2. Make the tortillas: Combine the flour, shortening, salt, and baking powder in a large bowl. Stir in the water. Knead the mixture in the bowl until it forms a smooth dough, about 1 minute. Shape it into a ball. Cover the bowl with a kitchen towel and let the dough stand for 20 minutes.

3. Divide the dough into 24 equal pieces, and shape each into a ball. One at a time, on a lightly floured surface, roll out the dough balls into 6-inch (15-cm) rounds. Stack the tortillas, separated by sheets of waxed paper.

4. Heat a large griddle or skillet over medium heat. Working in batches, add the tortillas in a single layer and cook until the undersides have golden brown splotches, about 1½ minutes. Turn and cook until the other sides look the same, about 1½ minutes more. Stack the cooked tortillas (no need to separate them) on a baking sheet. (The tortillas can be cooled, covered with plastic wrap, and stored at room temperature for up to 8 hours.)

5. Make the salsa ranchera: Pulse the onion, cilantro, chiles de arbol, jalapeño, and garlic in a food processor until combined and chopped a bit more finely. Add the tomatoes and pulse to make a coarse salsa. Season with salt. Transfer the salsa to a serving bowl. Let it stand at room temperature for at least 30 minutes or up to 8 hours.

6. Make the avocado sauce: Purée the avocados in a food processor, adding enough milk to give the sauce the consistency of yogurt. Season with salt. Transfer it to a bowl and cover it with plastic wrap pressed directly on the surface of the sauce. Refrigerate it until ready to serve. (The sauce can be refrigerated for up to 8 hours.)

7. Prepare an outdoor grill for cooking over direct high heat. For a gas grill, preheat it to at least 500°F (240°C). Place a disposable foil smoker pan directly on the heat source. For a charcoal grill, let the coals burn until they are covered with white ash and you can hold your hand just above the cooking grate for only 1 or 2 seconds.

8. Meanwhile, remove the steaks from the marinade and shake off the excess marinade. Lightly brush the steaks with oil. Let them stand for 15 minutes.

9. Sprinkle the drained wood chips into the heated smoker pan in the gas grill, or directly onto the coals of the charcoal grill. Wait until the chips begin to give off smoke. Place the steaks on the grill. Cook, with the lid closed as much as possible, until the undersides are well browned, about 2½ minutes. Turn over the steaks and grill until the other sides are browned and the meat is medium-rare (when it feels somewhat soft with a bit of resilience when the top is pressed with a fingertip; see Tips, below), about 2½ minutes more. Remove the steaks from the grill. Transfer the steaks to a carving board and let them stand for 5 minutes.

10. Make the grilled scallions: Brush the scallions with the oil. Place them on the grill, perpendicular to the cooking grate. Cook, with the lid closed as much as possible, rolling the scallions on the grill to turn them, until they are seared with grill marks and wilted, about 3 minutes. Remove them from the grill. Cut each scallion into thirds and transfer them to a serving bowl.

11. To serve, warm the tortillas on the grill until heated through, about 1 minute per side. Transfer them to a towel-lined basket or bowl and cover to keep warm. Cut the steaks across the grain into thin strips and transfer them, with any carving juices, to a serving bowl. Serve the tortillas, steak strips, and scallions with bowls of the salsa, avocado sauce, onion, cilantro, lime, and cucumber. Let each guest build a taco, filling a tortilla with the desired ingredients and folding it in half before eating.

1 garlic clove, coarsely chopped

2 pounds (910 g) ripe tomatoes, cored and seeded

Kosher salt

FOR THE AVOCADO SAUCE:

3 ripe avocados, peeled, pitted, and coarsely chopped

⅓ cup (75 ml) whole milk, as needed

Kosher salt

FOR THE GRILLED SCALLIONS:

8 whole scallions, trimmed

1 tablespoon canola oil

1 medium white onion, finely chopped

1 cup (40 g) packed fresh cilantro

4 limes, cut into wedges

1 medium cucumber, peeled and thinly sliced

Special equipment: 1 large handful mesquite wood chips, soaked in water for 30 minutes, drained

NOTE: *To make the tacos indoors, position the broiler rack about 6 inches (15 cm) from the heat source and preheat the broiler on high. Place the oiled steaks on the broiler rack and grill, turning once, until they are browned and medium-rare (see Tips at left), 5 to 6 minutes. Transfer them to a carving board and let them stand for 5 minutes before carving.*

Heat the tortillas according to the package directions and wrap them in a clean towel to keep warm.

Brush the scallions with oil and broil until they are lightly browned and wilted, about 3 minutes. Chop them into thirds. Serve the tortillas as directed with the toppings.

TIPS FROM THE PROS

TESTING STEAK FOR DONENESS
Los Tacos No. 1

Skirt steak is too thin to test with a meat thermometer, but you can tell the doneness level by touch, as the steak loses water and toughens as it cooks. Rare to medium-rare steak will feel a bit firmer than raw steak; medium, resistant; and well-done, firm. In any case, skirt steak is a tough cut and should never be cooked beyond medium-rare, or it will make chewy, unpleasant eating.

FLATIRON STEAKS

WITH A BERRY, PORT
& WINE REDUCTION

MARC FORGIONE, GUEST CHEF

SERVES 4

FOR THE GARLIC BUTTER:

¼ cup (60 ml) extra-virgin olive oil

5 garlic cloves, peeled

6 tablespoons (¾ stick/85 g) unsalted butter, at room temperature

2 tablespoons chopped fresh parsley, preferably curly

Kosher salt

FOR THE PORT WINE REDUCTION:

1 tablespoon canola oil

2 shallots, sliced

4 white button mushrooms, sliced

1½ teaspoons coarsely cracked black peppercorns (use a mortar and pestle or crush under a heavy saucepan)

1 tablespoon sugar

2 cups (480 ml) ruby port

1 (750-ml) bottle hearty red wine, such as Shiraz

1½ cups (360 ml) Veal Stock (page 56)

2 sprigs fresh thyme

1 small bay leaf

½ cup fresh huckleberries, blueberries, or blackberries

FOR THE STEAKS:

4 (10- to 12-ounce/280- to 340-g) flatiron steaks, about ¾ inch (2 cm) thick

Kosher salt and freshly ground black pepper

(continued)

In this fantastic steak recipe, Marc Forgione, whose eponymous downtown restaurant is a magnet for food lovers, shows the skills that made him a favorite on the Food Network's *The Next Iron Chef*. Layers of flavors build up to enhance flatiron steak (which gets its name from its elongated triangular appearance), a cut that is currently coming back into vogue on restaurant—and dinner party—menus. The garlic butter and port wine reduction can both be made well ahead, so all the cook has to do is sauté the steaks just before serving. Steak and potatoes are a partnership of long standing, and for a side dish, you can't do better than Potato Mille-Feuille (page 162). Add a simple vegetable dish, such as sautéed spinach, and you have a terrific steak dinner to serve with your best bottle of Cabernet.

1. Make the garlic butter: Heat the oil and garlic together in a small saucepan over medium heat just until the garlic is golden brown, 3 to 5 minutes. Strain it through a sieve into a heatproof bowl. (Reserve the garlic oil for another use, such as garlic bread.) Let the garlic cool. Coarsely chop the garlic and transfer it to a small bowl. Add the butter and parsley, season with salt, and stir well to combine. (The garlic butter can be covered with plastic wrap and refrigerated for up to 2 days. Bring it to room temperature before using.)

2. Make the port wine reduction: Heat the oil in a large nonreactive pot over medium-high heat until it is hot but not smoking. Add the shallots, mushrooms, and peppercorns. Reduce the heat to medium and cook, stirring occasionally, until the shallots and mushrooms are browned and the juices have browned into a thin layer (called a *fond*) on the bottom of the pot, about 5 minutes. Stir in the sugar. Add the port and stir to scrape up the brown layer on the bottom of the pot. Add the wine and bring to a boil over high heat. Cook until the mixture is reduced to about 2 cups (960 ml), about 30 minutes. Stir in the stock, return the mixture to a boil, and cook, skimming off any foam that forms on the surface, until it is reduced to 2 cups (960 ml), about 15 minutes more.

3. Pour the reduction into a heatproof bowl. Add the thyme and bay leaf and cover tightly with plastic wrap. Let them infuse (condensation will form on the inside of the wrap) for 1 hour. Strain the liquid through a wire sieve into another bowl, pressing hard on the solids. Discard the solids. (The port wine reduction can be covered and refrigerated for up to 2 days.)

4. About 10 minutes before cooking the steaks, pour the reduction into a small nonreactive saucepan. Bring it to a boil over high heat and cook until it is reduced to about ½ cup (120 ml), about 10 minutes. Reduce the heat to low, stir in the berries, and cook just until they are heated but not bursting, about 1 minute. Remove the pan from the heat and cover, with the lid ajar, to keep the reduction warm.

5. Prepare the steaks: Season the steaks liberally on both sides with salt and pepper. Let them stand at room temperature for 10 to 15 minutes.

6. Heat two large heavy skillets over high heat. Add 1 tablespoon of the oil to each skillet. Add 2 steaks to each skillet and cook, without turning the steaks, until the undersides are well browned, about 5 minutes. Turn the steaks over and cook for 1 minute more. Add 2 tablespoons of the butter, 3 thyme sprigs, and 3 garlic cloves to each skillet. Cook, letting the butter melt and spooning the mixture over the steaks, and adding a splash of additional oil if the mixture threatens to burn, until the meat feels somewhat soft with some resilience when pressed with a fingertip for medium-rare, about 1 minute. Transfer the steaks to a platter and let them stand for 3 minutes before serving.

7. For each serving, place a steak on a dinner plate and top it with a dollop of the garlic butter. (Save any remaining garlic butter for another use, such as a spread for toasted bread.) Spoon a couple of tablespoons of the port wine reduction and its berries over and around each steak, and top with a sprinkling of the blue cheese. Serve immediately.

2 tablespoons canola oil, plus more as needed

4 tablespoons (½ stick/110 g) unsalted butter, cut into tablespoons

6 sprigs fresh thyme

6 garlic cloves, peeled and smashed

½ cup (2 ounces/55 g) crumbled blue cheese, preferably Maytag

Special equipment: 2 large heavy skillets

Tuck Shop, which makes down-home cooking from Down Under, stakes its reputation on handsome, golden brown pies. They offer many fillings, but the robust stout, beef, and mushroom version is an especially good choice for cold-weather entertaining. Note that the meat marinates for a few hours, and that the cooked filling and pastry must be cold before making the pies, so allow for these preparation times.

1. Make the filling: Combine the steak and stout in a medium bowl. Mix well, cover, and refrigerate for 2 to 4 hours.

2. Strain the steak in a sieve over a bowl, reserving the stout. Pat the steak dry with paper towels. Season the beef with 1½ teaspoons of salt and ½ teaspoon of pepper. Heat 2 tablespoons of the oil in a large Dutch oven over medium-high heat. In three batches, add the beef to the saucepan and cook it for about 3 minutes, turning occasionally to brown lightly on all sides, adding more oil as needed. Adjust the heat as needed to keep the pan juices from burning. Transfer the browned beef to a bowl.

3. Add 2 more tablespoons of the oil to the Dutch oven and reduce the heat to medium. Add the onion and garlic and cook, stirring often, until softened, about 3 minutes. Add the reserved stout and bring it to a simmer, scraping up the browned bits in the pan with a wooden spoon. Return the beef to the Dutch oven and add the rosemary. Add enough water (about 1 quart/1 L) to cover the beef by 1 inch (2.5 cm) and bring it to a simmer. Reduce the heat to medium-low and cover. Simmer until the beef is tender, about 1¼ hours. Strain the meat mixture through a wire sieve into a bowl, reserving the cooking liquid and beef separately. Discard the rosemary. Measure and reserve 3¼ cups (780 ml) of the cooking liquid, and discard the rest. Let it stand for 5 minutes, then skim off the fat from the surface of the liquid.

4. Meanwhile, heat the remaining 2 tablespoons oil in a large skillet over medium-high heat. Cut the mushrooms into quarters. Add the mushrooms to the skillet and cook, stirring occasionally, until they are lightly browned, about 8 minutes. Remove them from the heat.

5. Return the empty Dutch oven to medium heat. Add the butter and let it melt. Whisk in the flour and let it bubble for 1 minute. Gradually whisk in the reserved cooking liquid and bring it to a simmer. The gravy will be quite thick. Add the beef and onion mixture, mushrooms, peppercorns, and horseradish and stir. Simmer for 10 minutes to blend the flavors.

6. Transfer the filling to a large bowl and let it cool. Cover and refrigerate until it is chilled, at least 3 hours. (To speed cooling, place the bowl in a larger bowl of well-iced water, and let stand, stirring occasionally, until it is chilled, about 45 minutes.) The filling must be chilled when used, or it will melt the raw pastry dough and the baked pie won't be crisp.

7. Meanwhile, make the pastry: Mix the flour and sea salt together in the bowl of a heavy-duty standing mixer. Add the butter and toss with your hands to coat the butter with flour. Place the bowl on the mixer and

(continued)

TUCK SHOP

SERVES 6

FOR THE FILLING:

1½ pounds (680 g) hanger steak (see Tip), cut into ¾-inch (2-cm) cubes

1 (22-ounce/615-ml) can Guinness Stout

Kosher salt and freshly ground black pepper

6 tablespoons (90 ml) vegetable oil, plus more as needed

1 large yellow onion, chopped

3 garlic cloves, smashed and peeled

2 sprigs fresh rosemary

12 ounces (340 g) white button mushrooms, quartered

6 tablespoons (¾ stick/85 g) unsalted butter

½ cup (65 g) all-purpose flour

2 tablespoons bottled green peppercorns, rinsed and drained

2 tablespoons peeled and freshly grated horseradish

FOR THE PASTRY:

4⅓ cups (560 g) unbleached all-purpose flour

1 teaspoon fine sea salt

1½ cups (3 sticks/345 g) cold unsalted butter, cut into ½-inch (12-mm) cubes

½ cup (120 ml) ice water, plus more as needed

1 large egg

1 tablespoon whole milk

Special equipment: 6 individual pot-pie pans, 5 inches (12 cm) in diameter, 1⅝ inches (4 cm) deep

fit the mixer with the paddle attachment. Mix on low speed until the mixture resembles coarse crumbs with some pea-size pieces of butter. Pour in the water and mix until the dough clumps together. If the dough seems too dry, add more water, 1 tablespoon at a time.

8. Gather up the dough in the bowl. Divide it into six equal portions (if you have a scale, they will weigh about 5.35 ounces/150 g each). Wrap each in plastic wrap and refrigerate them for at least 30 minutes or up to 2 hours. (The dough can be made up to 2 days ahead. If the dough is chilled hard, let it stand at room temperature for 10 minutes before rolling it out.)

9. Working with one portion of the dough at a time, cut off one-third of the dough and set it aside for the top crust. Roll out the remaining dough on a floured work surface into an 8-inch (20-cm) round. Fit the dough into a potpie pan, being sure it fits snugly into the corners and letting the excess dough hang over the edges of the pan. Fill it with one-sixth of the chilled filling. Lightly brush the edges of the dough in the pan with water. Roll out the reserved piece of dough into a 6-inch (15-cm) round. Center the dough over the filling and press the top and bottom crusts together. Using a paring knife, trim the excess dough at the edge of the pan. Using a fork, press around the edge of the crust to seal it. Pierce the top crust with the tip of a knife to allow steam to escape. Transfer the potpie to the refrigerator. Repeat with the remaining dough and filling. Refrigerate until the dough is chilled, about 30 minutes and up to 2 hours.

10. Preheat the oven to 400°F (205°C).

11. Whisk the egg and milk together in a small bowl until well combined. Arrange the potpies on a large rimmed baking sheet. Brush the tops lightly with the egg mixture. Bake for 10 minutes. Reduce the oven temperature to 350°F (175°C). Continue baking until the pies are golden brown, about 30 minutes more. Remove them from the oven and let them stand for 10 minutes. Serve them hot, in their pans or removed (see Note).

TIPS FROM THE PROS

HANGER STEAK
Tuck Shop

Hanger steak has lots of beefy flavor and is cut from the underside of the steer. It is a tough steak, like flank and skirt steak, and is usually marinated and grilled medium-rare. Here it is braised to make the potpie filling. This long, cylinder-shaped steak isn't always easy to find at the supermarket because it has become a popular wholesale item for restaurants. (You will sometimes see it on French restaurant menus as onglet.) Chuck steak is a good substitute, but increase the cooking time to 1¾ hours so it can become appropriately tender.

OLD-FASHIONED BEEF STEW

WITH WILD MUSHROOMS

DICKSON'S FARMSTAND MEATS

SERVES 6 TO 8

6 tablespoons (90 ml) grapeseed or olive oil, plus more as needed

3 pounds (1.5 kg) beef chuck, cut into 1-inch (2.5-cm) pieces

Kosher salt and freshly ground black pepper

4 carrots, 1 coarsely chopped and 3 cut into ½-inch- (12-mm-) thick rounds

4 celery ribs, 1 coarsely chopped and 3 cut into ½-inch- (12-mm-) thick pieces

1 yellow onion, coarsely chopped

1 tablespoon tomato paste

1 cup (240 ml) hearty red wine, such as Shiraz

2 quarts (2 L) Beef Stock (page 56) or reduced-sodium beef broth

2 sprigs fresh thyme

1¼ pounds (570 g) baking potatoes, such as russets or Burbanks, peeled and cut into 1-inch (2.5-cm) chunks

1 pound (455 g) wild or cultivated mushrooms, such as chanterelle, oyster, stemmed shiitake, and cremini, sliced or quartered according to size

4 tablespoons (½ stick/60 g) unsalted butter

⅓ cup (40 g) all-purpose flour

Chopped fresh flat-leaf parsley, for garnish

Dickson's takes a seasonal approach to their version of beef stew—that icon of the comfort-food canon. As the local produce changes, so can the basic stew, incorporating appropriate vegetables into the traditional mix of carrots, celery, and potatoes. Just cook the vegetables of your choice accordingly and add them to the stew to warm through before serving. While this cold-weather version uses wild mushrooms, try peas or artichoke hearts in the spring or corn kernels and fava beans in the summer.

1. Heat 2 tablespoons of the oil in a Dutch oven over medium-high heat. Season the beef with 2 teaspoons salt and 1 teaspoon pepper. In batches, add the beef to the Dutch oven and cook, turning occasionally and adding more oil as needed, until it is browned on all sides, about 5 minutes. Using a slotted spoon, transfer the beef to a bowl.

2. Add 2 more tablespoons of the oil to the Dutch oven and reduce the heat to medium. Add the coarsely chopped carrot, celery, and onion and cook, occasionally stirring and scraping up the browned bits in the bottom of the pan with a wooden spoon, until the vegetables soften, about 5 minutes. Move the vegetables to one side of the Dutch oven. Add the tomato paste to the empty side of the Dutch oven and cook until it turns a darker shade of red around the edges, about 2 minutes. Stir the tomato paste into the vegetables. Add the wine and bring it to a boil.

3. Return the beef and any juices to the Dutch oven. Add the stock. Bring it to a boil over high heat, skimming off any foam that rises to the surface. Add the thyme. Reduce the heat to low and cover. Simmer until the beef is tender, about 2 hours.

4. Strain the beef and vegetables in a colander set over a large bowl, reserving the cooking liquid. Discard the chopped carrot, celery, onion, and thyme stems. Tent the beef with aluminum foil. Let the cooking liquid stand for 5 minutes. Skim off the fat that rises to the surface of the liquid. Return the liquid to the Dutch oven. Add the raw carrots, celery, and potato and bring the mixture to a simmer over high heat. Reduce the heat to medium and cook at a brisk simmer until the vegetables are barely tender, about 20 minutes.

5. Meanwhile, heat the remaining 2 tablespoons oil in a large skillet over medium-high heat. Add the mushrooms and cook, stirring occasionally, until their juices evaporate and they begin to brown, about 10 minutes. (Some mushrooms give off more juices than others, so be flexible with the cooking time, or pour off the liquid if it is excessive. This often happens with chanterelles.) Season the mushrooms with salt and pepper. Remove them from the heat. Set aside.

6. Melt the butter in a medium saucepan over medium-low heat. Whisk in the flour to make a roux, and let it bubble without browning for about 2 minutes. Measure 2 cups (480 ml) of the cooking liquid from the Dutch oven, and whisk it into the roux. Stir this sauce back into the stew and bring it to a simmer. Reduce the heat to medium-low and simmer, stirring often, until the stew is slightly thickened, about 5 minutes.

7. Add the beef to the stew. Add the mushrooms and simmer just until the beef and mushrooms are heated through, about 5 minutes. Sprinkle the stew with the parsley and serve hot.

These authentic meatballs, *polpette al ragù*, with their a few ingredients and leisurely simmering, will remind many cooks of recipes from their Italian heritage. Pine nuts give these meatballs their special quality. Buon'Italia sells these without pasta as part of their extensive delicatessen selection, but add spaghetti and a topping of Parmigiano-Reggiano at will.

1. Put the bread in a small bowl and add enough water to moisten it. Let the bread soak for 5 minutes.

2. Drain the bread in a wire sieve, pressing hard to extract the excess water. Transfer the bread to a large bowl. Add the ground round, eggs, Parmigiano-Reggiano and Pecorino Romano cheeses, pine nuts, parsley, garlic, and 1½ teaspoons salt. Using your hands, knead the ingredients together just until combined. Shape the mixture into 18 equal balls. Transfer the meatballs to a large rimmed baking sheet.

3. Bring the tomato purée, 1 cup (240 ml) water, and ¼ cup (60 ml) of the oil to a simmer in a large saucepan over medium heat. Reduce the heat to very low and let it simmer. Season with salt.

4. Heat the remaining ½ cup (120 ml) oil in a large skillet over medium heat. In batches, add the meatballs and cook, turning them occasionally, until they are lightly browned, about 6 minutes. As they are browned, use a slotted spoon to transfer them to a large plate.

5. When the meatballs have all been browned, add them to the simmering sauce. Cook, stirring occasionally and adjusting the heat as needed to keep the sauce simmering, until the meatballs are cooked through, about 30 minutes. Serve hot.

MEATBALLS
IN RED SAUCE

BUON'ITALIA

SERVES 6

2 cups (110 g) packed bite-sized pieces day-old crusty bread

2 pounds (910 g) ground beef round

4 large eggs, beaten

¾ cup (75 g) freshly grated Parmigiano-Reggiano cheese

¾ cup (75 g) freshly grated Pecorino Romano cheese

¾ cup (105 g) pine nuts

2 tablespoons chopped fresh flat-leaf parsley

1 garlic clove, minced

Kosher or fine sea salt

1 (28-ounce/800-g) can puréed tomato

¾ cup (180 ml) extra-virgin olive oil

BOBOTIE

MARCUS SAMUELSSON, GUEST CHEF

SERVES 4 TO 6

1¼ pounds (570 g) ground beef round

1 medium red onion, finely chopped

2 garlic cloves, minced

1 tablespoon curry powder

½ teaspoon ground cumin

½ teaspoon crushed coriander seeds (use a mortar and pestle or crush under a heavy skillet)

2 ripe tomatoes, chopped, or 1 cup (240 ml) drained and chopped canned plum tomatoes

Kosher salt and freshly ground black pepper

¼ cup (30 g) unseasoned dried bread crumbs

¼ cup (65 g) finely chopped peanuts or natural unsweetened peanut butter

Softened butter, for the baking dish

FOR THE TOPPING:

1 cup (240 ml) whole milk

2 large eggs plus 2 large egg yolks

½ teaspoon salt

Pinch of freshly grated nutmeg

Marcus Samuelsson, a chef perhaps best known for his high-style cuisine, shares this casserole that exemplifies the very best of home cooking. Bobotie, a beloved dish in South Africa, is a curried meat mixture baked with a custard topping for an easy, warming meal. If you wish, serve it with basmati rice, and perhaps mango chutney.

1. Heat a Dutch oven or large, heavy saucepan over medium-high heat. Add the beef, onion, and garlic and cook, stirring occasionally and breaking up the meat with the side of the spoon, until the meat is browned, about 5 minutes. Stir in the curry powder, cumin, and coriander, and cook until fragrant, about 30 seconds. Stir in the tomato and reduce the heat to low. Cook, stirring occasionally, until the tomatoes are very tender, about 10 minutes. Season the mixture with salt and pepper.

2. Stir in ½ cup (120 ml) water, the bread crumbs, peanuts, and 1½ teaspoons salt. Bring to a simmer and cook, stirring often, until the stew is thick, about 5 minutes more. Using a slotted spoon, transfer the beef mixture to paper towels to drain briefly. Spread the beef mixture on a plate and refrigerate it until tepid, about 20 minutes.

3. Position a rack in the center of the oven and preheat the oven to 350°F (175°C). Generously butter a 2-quart (2-L) baking dish.

4. Make the topping: Whisk the milk, eggs, egg yolks, salt, and nutmeg together in a medium bowl.

5. Spread the beef mixture in the bottom of the dish and press it down to pack it well. Place the baking dish in a larger roasting pan. Pour enough hot water into the larger pan to come halfway up the sides of the baking dish. Pour the topping over the beef mixture. Cover the larger pan with a large sheet of aluminum foil.

6. Bake for 25 minutes. Remove the foil and continue baking until a wooden toothpick inserted into the topping comes out clean, about 20 minutes more. Let stand for 5 minutes. Remove the baking dish from the pan and serve.

Francesco Realmuto, owner of L'Arte del Gelato, says that his mamma, Rosa, would often make this substantial dish as the centerpiece of an after-church lunch. With layers of meat, eggplant, and cheese, it is a mountain of a meal. Francesco makes it with the traditional Sicilian anelletti pasta and caciocavallo cheese, but we've suggested substitutes.

1. Make the sauce: Heat the oil in a large saucepan over medium heat. Add the onion and cook, stirring occasionally, until golden, about 6 minutes. Add the ground beef and pork and increase the heat to medium-high. Cook, stirring and breaking up the meat with the side of a spoon, until it loses its raw look, about 10 minutes. Pour off the excess fat in the saucepan. Add the wine and cook until it is absorbed by the meat, about 5 minutes. Add the tomato paste and mix well. Stir in the tomatoes and 1 cup (240 ml) water and bring to a simmer. Reduce the heat to medium-low. Cook, stirring occasionally and adding more water as needed if the sauce gets too thick, for about 45 minutes. During the last 5 minutes, stir in the peas. Season the sauce with salt and pepper. (The sauce can be cooled, covered, and refrigerated for up to 1 day.)

2. Make the pasta: Meanwhile, pour in enough oil to come halfway up the sides of a large, deep skillet. Heat it over medium-high heat until very hot but not smoking. In batches, add the eggplant and fry, turning as needed, until it is golden brown, about 3 minutes. Transfer the eggplant to paper towels to drain.

3. Preheat the oven to 350°F (175°C). Lightly oil a deep 13-by-9-by-3-inch (33-by-23-by-8-cm) lasagna pan.

4. Spread the bread crumbs on a large rimmed baking sheet. Bake, stirring occasionally, until they are golden brown, about 10 minutes. Let them cool. Leave the oven on.

5. Bring a large pot of salted water to a boil over high heat. Add the anelletti and cook according to the package directions, until it is just short of al dente. (The anelletti will continue to cook when baked.) Drain the anelletti well and return it to the cooking pot.

6. Add the sauce to the anelletti and mix well. Stir in the cheeses.

7. Spread one-third of the pasta mixture in the prepared pan. Layer it with half of the eggplant and sprinkle with one-third of the bread crumbs. Repeat with half of the remaining pasta, the remaining eggplant, and half of the remaining bread crumbs. Finish with the remaining pasta and top with the remaining bread crumbs. Dot the top with the butter. Place the pan on a large rimmed baking sheet.

8. Bake until the topping is golden brown, about 35 minutes. Remove the pan from the oven and let the pasta stand for 10 minutes. Serve hot.

PASTA AL FORNO

L'ARTE DEL GELATO

SERVES 12

FOR THE SAUCE:

⅓ cup (75 ml) extra-virgin olive oil

1 yellow onion, finely chopped

18 ounces (500 g) ground beef round

18 ounces (500 g) ground pork

1 cup (240 ml) hearty red wine, such as Shiraz

2 (6-ounce/170-g) cans tomato paste

1 (28-ounce/800-g) can Italian whole plum tomatoes in juice, preferably San Marzano, drained and coarsely chopped

2⅓ cups (400 g) thawed frozen peas

Kosher salt and freshly ground black pepper

FOR THE PASTA:

Vegetable oil for frying, plus more for the baking dish

4 medium eggplants, trimmed, peeled, and cut into ½-inch (12-mm) rounds

Kosher salt

3 cups (165 g) fresh bread crumbs, made in a food processor from day-old crusty bread

1¾ pounds (800 g) anelletti or other tube-shaped pasta

11 ounces (310 g) un-aged provolone cheese, cut into ½-inch (12-mm) dice

1¼ cups (150 g) shredded caciocavallo or Greek kasseri cheese

2 tablespoons cold unsalted butter, diced

Special equipment: 13-by-9-by-3-inch (33-by-23-by-8 cm) lasagna pan

Glen Siegel of Belvedere Capital is one of the Market's lead investors, and he is as famous throughout the office for his hamburgers as he is for his business skills. He shrugs it off, and attributes the deep beefy flavor to using a cast-iron skillet to get a crusty exterior. The wine-soaked mushrooms don't hurt, either.

1. Season the ground sirloin with 1 teaspoon salt and ½ teaspoon pepper and mix it gently but thoroughly. Shape it into four 4-inch (10-cm) patties. Let them stand while cooking the mushrooms.

2. Heat the oil in a large heavy skillet (preferably cast iron) over medium heat. Add the mushrooms and cook, stirring occasionally, until their juices evaporate and they begin to brown, 8 to 10 minutes. Stir in the shallots and garlic and cook until the shallots are tender, about 2 minutes. Season the mushroom mixture with salt and pepper. Transfer the mixture to a bowl. Wipe out the skillet with paper towels.

3. Return the skillet to medium-high heat. Do not add more oil to the skillet. Add the patties and cook, without moving the burgers, until the undersides are well browned, about 3 minutes. Flip the patties and cook, moving the burgers as little as possible, until the other sides are well browned and they feel somewhat soft with a little resilience when pressed on top for medium-rare, about 3 minutes more. Transfer the burgers to a plate. Pour out the fat in the skillet.

4. Return the mushroom mixture to the skillet. Add the wine and thyme. Bring the mixture to a boil, scraping up the browned bits in the skillet with a wooden spoon. Cook until the wine has reduced to a glaze, about 2 minutes. Season with salt and pepper.

5. Meanwhile, preheat the broiler to high.

6. Broil the brioche buns, cut-sides up, until they are lightly toasted, about 30 seconds.

7. For each burger, spread the bun with 1 tablespoon of the mustard. Place a patty on a bun bottom and top with one-quarter of the mushrooms, a handful of arugula, and a tomato slice. Add the brioche tops and serve immediately.

GLEN'S BOURGUIGNON BURGERS

CHELSEA MARKET FAMILY RECIPE

SERVES 4

1½ pounds (680 g) ground beef sirloin

Kosher salt and freshly ground black pepper

1 tablespoon extra-virgin olive oil

10 ounces (280 g) sliced cremini mushrooms

2 tablespoons minced shallots

1 small garlic clove, minced

½ cup (120 ml) hearty red wine, such as Shiraz

½ teaspoon chopped fresh thyme leaves

4 brioche rolls or hamburger buns, split

4 tablespoons (60 ml) Dijon mustard

2 ounces (55 g) baby arugula

4 large tomato slices

MONGOLIAN RACK OF LAMB

WITH CRYSTALLIZED GINGER CRUST

BUDDAKAN

SERVES 4

FOR THE SPICED BREAD CRUMBS:

½ cup (30 g) panko (Japanese bread crumbs)

1 tablespoon finely chopped crystallized ginger

1 teaspoon ground juniper berries (use a spice grinder or a mortar and pestle)

Pinch of kosher salt

FOR THE GINGER GLAZE:

1 tablespoon hot water

1 teaspoon Chinese hot mustard powder

⅓ cup (50 g) finely chopped crystallized ginger

2 tablespoons unseasoned rice vinegar

2 tablespoons plum (umeboshi) vinegar

FOR THE LAMB:

2 (8-rib) racks of lamb (about 1¾ pounds/800 g each), trimmed and frenched

2 teaspoons kosher salt

1 teaspoon freshly ground black pepper

2 tablespoons vegetable oil

FOR THE BOK CHOY:

8 heads baby bok choy

1 small fresh hot red chile, cut into very thin rounds

1 teaspoon toasted sesame oil

Kosher salt

Buddakan built its reputation as a white-hot food destination with luxurious dishes like this one—seared rack of lamb baked with a spiced crust and served with tender baby bok choy. It is surprisingly easy to re-create at home.

1. Make the spiced bread crumbs: Combine the panko, ginger, juniper berries, and salt together in a small bowl; set aside.

2. Make the ginger glaze: Whisk the water and mustard powder together in a small bowl. Transfer the mixture to a blender. Add the ginger and vinegars and purée until smooth. Transfer the glaze to a bowl and set aside. (The bread crumbs and glaze can be covered and stored at room temperature for up to 8 hours.)

3. Make the lamb: Position a rack in the center of the oven and preheat the oven to 400°F (205°C).

4. Season the lamb with the salt and pepper. Heat the oil in a large oven-proof skillet over high heat. Using kitchen tongs, add the lamb racks and cook, turning and holding the racks as needed, until the meaty areas are lightly browned, about 2 minutes. Remove them from the heat and transfer the lamb to a plate. Brush the meaty top of each rack with the glaze. Sprinkle and coat the glazed area with the bread crumbs, patting to help them adhere. Return the lamb racks, crusted-side up, to the skillet.

5. Put the skillet into the oven and roast the lamb until an instant-read thermometer inserted in the thickest part of a rack reads 125°F (50°C) for medium-rare, 15 to 20 minutes. Transfer the lamb to a carving board and let it stand for 5 minutes.

6. Meanwhile, prepare the bok choy: Bring a medium saucepan of salted water to a boil over high heat. Add the baby bok choy and cook until they turn a brighter shade of green, about 1 minute. Drain them in a colander and gently squeeze excess water from each bok choy. Pat them dry with paper towels.

7. Heat the sesame oil and chile in a large nonstick skillet over medium heat just to warm the oil. Add the bok choy and season it with salt. Cook, turning the bok choy occasionally, until it is heated through, about 2 minutes.

8. Carve each lamb rack between the bones to yield 16 chops. For each serving, arrange 4 chops and 2 baby bok choy on a dinner plate. Serve at once.

The vibrant flavors of New York's Cuban community come alive in these marinated pork chops. *Mojo* is the essential marinade of the island, with a base of sour orange juice. This fruit is easy to find at Latino markets, or you can use a mixture of fresh orange and lime juices. Take care not to marinate the pork chops for longer than two hours, or the acidic marinade will toughen the meat. We give instructions for indoor cooking, but the chops can be grilled outdoors over medium heat for about 15 minutes. Serve the chops with the Cuban Black Beans with Bacon & Sofrito on page 168.

1. Make the *mojo*: Purée the onion, garlic, juice, salt, cumin, oregano, herbes de Provence, pepper, vinegar, and pepper flakes in a food processor. With the machine running, gradually add the oil.

2. Place the pork chops in a 1-gallon (3.8-L) zip-tight plastic storage bag. Pour in the *mojo* and close the bag. Refrigerate, turning the bag occasionally, for at least 1 hour but no more than 2 hours.

3. Position a rack in the center of the oven and preheat the oven to 350°F (175°C).

4. Heat an ovenproof ridged grill pan over medium-high heat. Lightly oil the pan. Remove the pork chops from the *mojo* and shake off the excess marinade. Add the pork chops to the grill pan and cook until the undersides are seared with grill marks, about 2 minutes. Rotate the chops 45 degrees, and cook for another 2 minutes to create a cross-hatch pattern. Turn the pork chops over. Transfer the pan to the oven and bake until the chops show just a bare sign of pink when pierced at the bone with the tip of a small sharp knife, about 15 minutes. Transfer them to a platter and let them stand for 5 minutes before serving.

PORK CHOPS
WITH MOJO MARINADE

SPICES AND TEASE

SERVES 4

FOR THE MOJO:

1 large yellow onion, coarsely chopped

8 garlic cloves, coarsely chopped

½ cup (120 ml) fresh sour orange juice (from 3 sour oranges), or ⅓ cup fresh orange juice and 3 tablespoons fresh lime juice

1 teaspoon kosher salt

1 teaspoon ground cumin

1 teaspoon dried oregano

1 teaspoon herbes de Provence

1 teaspoon freshly ground black pepper

1 teaspoon distilled white vinegar

¼ teaspoon hot red pepper flakes

½ cup (120 ml) olive oil, plus more for the pan

4 (8-ounce/225-g) center-cut pork loin chops on the bone, about 1 inch (2.5 cm) thick

THE KNIFE LADY

SAMURAI SHARPENING SERVICE

The official name of Margery Cohen's company is Samurai Sharpening Service, but she is affectionately known at the Market as "The Knife Lady." Every Wednesday and Saturday, she can be found at her sharpening table outside of Bowery Kitchen, whetting knives from market vendors and neighborhood home cooks alike. She tells her story:

I began my sharpening career at a very early age, when I discovered I could sharpen a popsicle stick on the pavement. Although I was trained as an artist, I worked at fish markets on the New Jersey shore, a job where you have to learn how to keep your knives sharp. I ended up working with a master woodworker who also had a knife sharpening business in Berkeley, California, and he taught me the Japanese way to care for knives—by hand with sharpening stones, and not by machine. When he returned to his native Hawaii, I took over the business. In 1996, I moved to New York City for a one-year sublet, and when I acquired my space at Chelsea Market, there was no turning back.

Customers bring me quite a variety of knives, from expensive Japanese sashimi knives to inferior dollar-store ones. It's no secret that a good knife can attain and hold an edge better than a cheap one. Shopping in a store with an educated salesperson who allows you to hold and test a knife is the best way to go.

Sharpening a knife is a fairly simple task. At least to me . . . but I have sharpened thousands and thousands of knives in my life. The basic concept of sharpening is to sculpt each side of the blade until it comes to a fine tapered edge. Each knife is different and needs to be sharpened accordingly. There's no set angle, and some knives are beveled only on one side. A thick knife usually has a steeper bevel and is less flexible than a long, thin knife that narrowly tapers, which is best for slicing lox or a roast.

I sharpen all knives by hand. I usually get started by sharpening the knife on a diamond stone, which is abrasive enough to cut through metal but fine enough to give the knife a smooth edge. Some people use oil to lubricate the stone, but I prefer water, which cools the stone from friction-generated heat and helps gather the microscopic metal particles. The stones need care too, and must be flattened regularly before they become concave from use.

Rubbing the knife against the stone in small circular motions, I carefully work down the length of the knife until I can feel that I have formed a rough edge (called a burr) on the other side of the blade. Then I turn the knife around to sharpen and form a burr on the other side. The burr is removed in one single action by sweeping the knife on the stone. This is a much-simplified version of my 2½-hour sharpening workshop! With the many different knives appearing on the Market, there is a lot to learn, even for me. It is a continuous process, and part of the reason why I love what I do.

Bringing your knife to a professional sharpener who will be able to determine how to best sharpen the knife is my recommendation, especially at first. But the right upkeep can help. Hone your knife on a sharpening steel to keep the edge sharp. Never store knives in a drawer, where they can knock up against each other and nick and dull the blades and handles. If you must store them in a drawer, slip each knife into a plastic sheath. If you use a countertop knife holder, the slits should go horizontally to

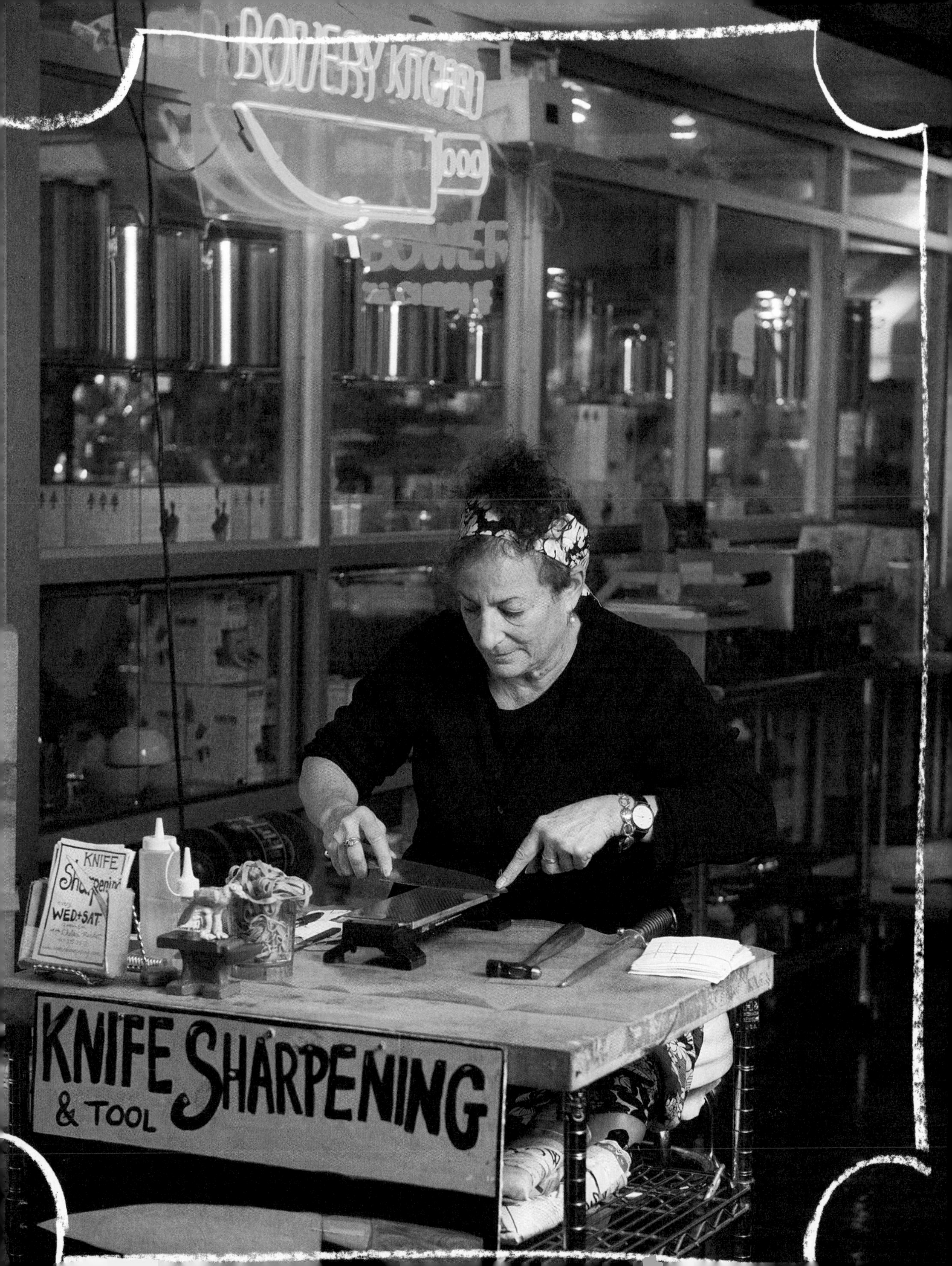
KNIFE
Sharpening
WED+SAT
KNIFE SHARPENING
& TOOL

remove excess weight on the knife edge. And it may go without saying, but never wash the knife in a dishwasher. The handles will crack, and if the blade has an iron component, it will rust. It takes longer to put a knife in a dishwasher than it does to take a few seconds to wash it by hand.

From my sharpening table in the corridor of Chelsea Market, I watch hundreds of people pass by and I am asked dozens of questions a day. This can be overwhelming when I have dozens of knives to sharpen. I love to talk to children and often ask if they want to inherit my business when I retire. The answer is yes more often than no! There's never a "dull" moment at Samurai Sharpening Service.

CHAPTER 6

FEASTS OF FOWL

POULTRY

BUTTERMILK FRIED CHICKEN

WITH HONEYED HOT SAUCE & KOHLRABI SLAW

HUGH ACHESON, GUEST CHEF

SERVES 4

FOR THE SLAW:

2 medium kohlrabi, pared

Kosher salt

2 tablespoons fresh lime juice

1 tablespoon cider vinegar

1 jalapeño, seeded and minced

FOR THE CHICKEN:

1 (3½-pound/1.6-kg) chicken, giblets discarded

1 teaspoon kosher salt

2 cups (480 ml) buttermilk

Pinch of cayenne pepper

Pinch of freshly ground black pepper

2 cups (410 g) lard

2 cups (240 ml) peanut oil

1 cup (130 g) unbleached all-purpose flour

FOR THE SAUCE:

¼ cup (60 ml) honey

2 tablespoons cider vinegar

½ cup (120 ml) hot red pepper sauce, preferably a Louisiana brand, such as Crystal

2 tablespoons cold unsalted butter, cut into ½-inch (12-mm) cubes

Special equipment: A mandoline or plastic V-slicer

Hugh Acheson flew up from Atlanta to cook for our second Sunday Supper event. He is justifiably famous for his fried chicken, which is a masterpiece of simplicity (see photo on previous page). While his recipe is as basic as can be, his accompaniments are contemporary, kind of like matching the Southern sensibilities of a Stephen Foster song with those from the Dixie Chicks. Kohlrabi, a relative of cabbage, makes a mean slaw, and wait until you taste what honey can do for hot sauce (or vice versa)!

1. Make the slaw: Using a mandoline, a V-slicer, or a large sharp knife, cut the kohlrabi into thin strips. Transfer them to a medium bowl and toss them with ¼ teaspoon of salt. Let them stand for 1 hour. Stir in the lime juice, vinegar, and jalapeño and mix well. Cover and refrigerate until the slaw is chilled, at least 1 and up to 8 hours. Season it with salt.

2. Prepare the chicken: Using poultry shears or a large heavy knife, cut along both sides of the chicken backbone and remove the backbone. Cut the chicken into two thighs, two drumsticks, two wings, and two breasts. Then cut each breast in half lengthwise; you should have four breast pieces in total.

3. Season the chicken with the salt. Transfer it to a medium bowl and pour in the buttermilk. Add the cayenne and black pepper. Cover and refrigerate for at least 1 hour and up to 1 day.

4. Place a wire rack over a rimmed baking sheet near the stove. Heat the lard and peanut oil together in a large, deep cast-iron skillet, until it reaches 350°F (175°C) on a deep-frying thermometer. Put the flour in a heavy brown paper bag. One piece at a time, leaving the breast pieces for last, remove the chicken from the buttermilk, letting the excess drip back into the bowl. Add the chicken to the bag and shake until it is coated with flour. Transfer each piece to the skillet, skin-side down, until all the chicken pieces are in the skillet. Fry, adjusting the heat as needed to maintain 350°F (175°C), until the underside of the chicken is nicely crisped and browned, about 10 minutes. Turn the chicken over and continue frying for about 10 minutes more, until the other side is browned and the chicken is cooked through. Remove the lean breast pieces a few minutes sooner than the dark meat. Transfer them to the wire rack to drain.

5. Meanwhile, make the sauce: Cook the honey in a medium saucepan over medium heat until it boils and caramelizes slightly, about 2 minutes. Stir in the vinegar and cook until the mixture is reduced by half, about 2 minutes more. Stir in the hot sauce. Reduce the heat to very low. Add the butter and whisk until it is melted and the sauce is slightly thickened. Pour it into a gravy boat.

6. Divide the kohlrabi slaw among four dinner plates. Top each with two pieces of chicken, saving the wings for seconds. Serve hot, with the sauce passed on the side.

CHOOSING YOUR CHICKEN

Hugh Acheson, Guest Chef

Over the last couple of decades, chickens have grown to oversize proportions. Before then, chickens were smaller, averaging three pounds, and a four-pounder was considered a monster. Cut into pieces, a chicken could easily fit into a skillet for a great fried supper. Big chickens burn on the outside before they get a chance to cook through, so pay attention to the size in the recipe—any chicken larger than 3½ pounds (1.6 kg) will not fry properly.

These days, you may have to do a little searching to find a chicken small enough to fry in a single batch. One might say a small chicken is scarcer than hen's teeth. Most of today's diminutive birds are raised by old-fashioned methods with grain feed (some commercially raised birds are fed meat by-products to fatten them up) and tend to be organic. Look for them at natural foods stores or in the organic section of the supermarket meat case.

BRINING POULTRY

Dickson's Farmstand Meats

Poultry is leaner than red meat, so it tends to dry out during cooking, especially from dry-heat cooking methods such as roasting or grilling. Soaking poultry in a brine to add moisture and flavor has become a very popular technique, embraced by both chefs and home cooks. When brining, it seems that the heavier salted water displaces the natural juices in the poultry. When the poultry is removed from the brine, the salty liquid stays trapped inside the meat, seasoning it from the inside out. (Red meat, with its intramuscular fat, is rarely brined; lean cuts of pork are brined with good results.)

Kosher salt has fewer additives (such as anti-caking agents) than other types and is preferred for making the brine. Some cooks prefer fine sea salt, which works well, but use about 1 tablespoon less than the kosher salt called for in the chicken brine on the opposite page. (Sea salt crystals are finer and measure differently than kosher salt.)

When it comes to brining time, longer does not mean better. Extended contact with the brine only makes the poultry saltier and can affect the meat texture, too. In general, allow about 1 hour for every pound of meat.

The poultry must be well chilled during brining. One way to do this is to make ice-cold brine. The ice cubes must be clean tasting, without any "freezer flavor," so it is best to make a fresh tray the night before using them. If you have an ice dispenser, use only the fresh cubes on the top of the container.

Dickson's cooks their brined birds on a rotisserie, but you can get very good results by turning the roasting bird while it's cooking to expose all of the skin to the oven heat for even browning. Like many chefs, Dickson's likes brining because it seasons the bird from the inside out and adds extra moisture. With this version, you can easily mix the brine in the morning and soak the bird for a few hours for an evening meal. Dickson's recommends serving the chicken with a simply dressed green salad.

1. Make the brine: Briskly whisk the hot water, salt, soy sauce, rice wine, and sugar together until the salt is dissolved. Add the bay leaves and let the brine stand until cooled. Add the ice water and stir to melt the ice and chill the brine.

2. Put the chicken, breast-side down, in a deep nonreactive bowl. Add enough of the brine to cover the chicken. Don't worry if the back isn't covered with brine. Refrigerate it for at least 3 hours and up to 5 hours.

3. Make the spice paste: Coarsely grind the coriander, fennel, and peppercorns together in an electric spice grinder or with a mortar and pestle. Transfer them to a bowl and add the garlic, rosemary, paprika, and oregano. Add the oil and wine and stir, adding more oil if needed, until the spice paste is moist and spreadable.

4. Remove the chicken from the brine and drain it well. Discard the brine. Using paper towels, pat the chicken dry, inside and out. If desired, using kitchen twine, tie the wings to the bird with a loop of twine, and tie the ends of the drumsticks together. Rub the spice paste all over the bird. Let it stand for 15 minutes.

5. Position a rack in the center of the oven and preheat the oven to 300°F (150°C). Choose a roasting pan just large enough to hold the chicken and fit it with an oiled roasting rack.

6. Put the chicken, breast-side up, on the rack in the pan. Roast it for 15 minutes. Using a wooden spoon inserted in the body cavity, turn the chicken breast-side down to roast for 15 minutes more. Then increase the oven temperature to 425°F (220°C). Turn the chicken breast-side up and baste with the pan juices. Roast, turning the chicken every 10 to 15 minutes and basting occasionally, leaving the chicken breast-side up for the final 20 minutes, until the chicken is deeply browned and an instant-read thermometer inserted in the thickest part of the thigh reads 165°F (75°C), about 1 hour more. Transfer the chicken to a carving board and let it stand for 10 minutes. Taste the pan juices; if they haven't burned, pour them into a glass bowl and set them aside.

7. Carve the chicken and transfer it to a serving platter. Skim the yellow fat from the surface of the pan juices. Pour the carving juices and pan juices over the chicken and serve it hot.

BRINED & RUBBED CHICKEN

DICKSON'S FARMSTAND MEATS

SERVES 4

FOR THE BRINE:

1½ quarts (1.5 L) hot tap water

1 cup (160 g) kosher salt

½ cup (120 ml) soy sauce

½ cup (120 ml) Shaoxing rice wine or dry sherry

2 tablespoons sugar

2 bay leaves

1½ quarts (1.5 L) ice water

1 (4½-pound/2-kg) organic chicken, tail fat and giblets discarded

FOR THE SPICE PASTE:

1 teaspoon coriander seeds

1 teaspoon fennel seeds

1 teaspoon black peppercorns

4 garlic cloves, minced

2 teaspoons minced fresh rosemary

1 teaspoon sweet paprika

¼ teaspoon dried oregano

2 tablespoons grapeseed or olive oil, as needed

1 tablespoon dry white wine

This dish, *pad gra prow*, excites the palate with spicy chiles, fragrant Thai basil, and funky fish sauce. Once the bell pepper, chiles, and garlic are chopped, it comes together in just a few minutes. Thai basil (or its cousin, holy basil) has an anise-like scent, but you can use standard Italian basil if the Asian kind is unavailable. Saruj Nimkarn, Chelsea Thai's owner, says that the fiery condiment *nam-pla prik* goes with *pad gra prow* just like ketchup and a hot dog.

1. Make the *nam-pla prik*: Combine the fish sauce and chiles in a small serving bowl. Set aside at room temperature for at least 30 minutes to blend the flavors.

2. Mix the fish sauce, dark soy sauce, and soy sauce together in a small bowl. Set aside.

3. Heat a wok or large skillet over high heat. Add the oil, swirl the wok to coat the inside with oil, and heat until the oil is very hot but not smoking. Add the bell pepper and stir-fry until it begins to soften, about 1 minute. Stir in the garlic and chiles and cook until they are softened, about 15 seconds. Add the chicken and stir-fry until the chicken loses its raw look, about 3 minutes. Add the soy sauce mixture and stir-fry until the sauce has reduced slightly, about 1 minute. Add the basil and stir-fry until it is wilted and the chicken is cooked through (it should look opaque when pierced with the tip of a small sharp knife), about 1 minute.

4. Serve the *pad gra prow* hot over the rice, with the *nam-pla prik* passed on the side for seasoning as desired.

THAI CHICKEN
WITH HOLY BASIL
(PAD GRA PROW)

CHELSEA THAI

SERVES 4

FOR THE NAM-PLA PRIK:

½ cup (120 ml) Thai or Vietnamese fish sauce (nam pla or nuoc mam)

2 small hot red chiles, preferably Thai bird chiles, thinly sliced into rounds

¼ cup (60 ml) Thai or Vietnamese fish sauce (nam pla or nuoc mam)

1 tablespoon dark (black) soy sauce

1 tablespoon soy sauce

2 tablespoons vegetable oil

1 large red bell pepper, cored and cut into ½-inch (12-mm) dice

4 garlic cloves, minced

2 small hot red chiles, preferably Thai bird chiles, seeded and chopped

2 pounds (910 g) boneless skinless chicken breast, cut across the grain into ¼-inch- (6-mm-) thick slices

1½ cups (60 g) packed fresh Thai or Italian basil leaves

Cooked jasmine rice, for serving

CHICKEN CACCIATORE PASTA

BILL TELEPAN, GUEST CHEF

SERVES 4 TO 6

2 tablespoons olive oil

4 (9-ounce/255-g) chicken leg quarters

Kosher salt and freshly ground black pepper

1 large red bell pepper, cored and cut into ¼-inch- (6-mm-) wide strips

1 small yellow onion, cut into thin half-moons

6 garlic cloves, thinly sliced

1 tablespoon finely chopped fresh oregano

1 teaspoon dried thyme

1 (28-ounce/800-g) can crushed plum tomatoes

1 (15-ounce/430-g) can cannellini beans

1 pound (455-g) fusilli or rotini

2 tablespoons red wine vinegar

Bill Telepan travels downtown about fifty blocks from his popular eponymous Upper West Side restaurant to cook at our annual Sunday Supper event. He says that this is the kind of dish that he makes at home for his wife and daughter, and although its name is familiar, it has unique touches that you would expect from a chef—such as a dash of vinegar to heighten the flavor.

1. Position a rack in the center of the oven and preheat the oven to 325°F (165°C).

2. Heat the oil in a large ovenproof skillet over medium-high heat. Season the chicken with 1 teaspoon salt and ½ teaspoon pepper. Add the chicken to the pan, skin-side down, and cook until the skin is browned, about 4 minutes. Turn and cook until the other side is browned, about 3 minutes more. (If necessary, brown the chicken in batches. If it is crowded in the skillet, it won't brown properly.) Transfer the chicken to a plate.

3. Pour out all but 2 tablespoons of the fat from the skillet. Return the skillet to medium heat. Add the bell pepper and onion and cook, stirring occasionally, until they are tender, 6 to 8 minutes. Stir in the garlic and cook until it is fragrant, about 1 minute. Stir in the oregano and thyme, followed by the tomatoes. Return the chicken and any juices on the plate to the skillet and bring to a simmer. Cover tightly.

4. Transfer the skillet to the oven and cook until the chicken shows no sign of pink when pierced at the bone with the tip of a knife, about 40 minutes.

5. Remove the skillet from the oven. Transfer the chicken to a carving board and let it cool slightly. Add the beans to the sauce in the skillet and bring the sauce to a simmer over medium heat. Cook until the beans are warmed, about 3 minutes. Remove the sauce from the heat and cover the skillet to keep it warm.

6. Meanwhile, bring a large pot of salted water to a boil over high heat. Add the fusilli and cook according to the package directions, until it is al dente.

7. While the pasta is cooking, carve the chicken meat off the bones and cut it into bite-size pieces. Stir the chicken and vinegar into the sauce. Season with salt and pepper. Cover the sauce again to keep it warm.

8. Drain the fusilli well in a colander, and return the pasta to its cooking pot. Add the sauce and mix well. Serve hot.

Dominick Coyne, the talented designer of Jamestown's Chelsea Market offices, has made this his go-to roast chicken. The honey and balsamic vinegar give the skin a dark brown, almost black, sheen, and its crisp texture is utterly irresistible. You will keep going back to the platter for bits of the juicy meat and sweet skin.

1. Position a rack in the center of the oven and preheat the oven to 450°F (230°C). Rinse the chicken under cold running water and pat it dry with paper towels.

2. Combine the basil, rosemary, thyme, and sage in a small bowl. Mix the salt and pepper together in another small bowl. With a fork, mix the honey and vinegar together in a third small bowl.

3. Slip your fingers under the chicken skin at the breast area. Loosen the skin around the breast and thighs without tearing the skin. Distribute half the herb mixture under the chicken skin on the breast and thigh meat. Rub the outside of the chicken with the oil. Season the chicken cavity with half of the salt and pepper. Put one onion quarter in the chicken cavity.

4. Separate the remaining onion quarters into layers and place them in a roasting pan to make a "rack" for the chicken. Put the chicken on the onion pieces. Pour the honey mixture evenly over the chicken and rub it in, letting the excess drip into the pan. Sprinkle the chicken all over with the remaining herb and salt mixtures.

5. Roast for 10 minutes. Reduce the oven temperature to 400°F (205°C) and continue roasting, opening the oven door as little as possible, until an instant-read thermometer inserted in the thickest part of the thigh reads 165°F (75°C), about 1¼ hours more. The chicken skin will look lacquered and almost black.

6. Let the chicken stand at room temperature for 10 to 15 minutes before carving. Skim the fat from the surface of the pan juices and discard it. Carve the chicken and serve it with the pan juices.

ROAST CHICKEN
WITH BALSAMIC GLAZE

CHELSEA MARKET FAMILY RECIPE

SERVES 4 TO 6

1 (5½-pound/2.5-kg) roasting chicken, giblets discarded

1½ teaspoons coarsely chopped fresh basil

1½ teaspoons coarsely chopped fresh rosemary

1½ teaspoons coarsely chopped fresh thyme

1½ teaspoons coarsely chopped fresh sage

2 teaspoons kosher salt

½ teaspoon freshly ground black pepper

2 tablespoons honey

2 tablespoons balsamic vinegar

2 tablespoons olive oil

1 large yellow onion, quartered lengthwise

ROASTED TURKEY

WITH JALAPEÑO–SAGE–ORANGE BUTTER & RED CHILE–BERRY GRAVY

BOBBY FLAY, GUEST CHEF

SERVES 8 TO 10

FOR THE ENRICHED CHICKEN STOCK:

5 pounds (2.3 kg) raw chicken carcasses (or backs)

2 pounds (910 g) chicken wings

3 tablespoons canola oil

2 medium yellow onions, unpeeled, quartered

2 large celery ribs, coarsely chopped

2 large carrots, coarsely chopped

2 teaspoons black peppercorns

10 sprigs fresh dill

10 sprigs fresh flat-leaf parsley

1 bay leaf

2 jalapeños, roasted (see Tips)

FOR THE JALAPEÑO-SAGE-ORANGE BUTTER:

2 cups (480 ml) fresh orange juice

1 cup (2 sticks/220 g) unsalted butter, at room temperature

Freshly grated zest of 1 orange

¼ cup (15 g) whole fresh sage leaves

3 jalapeños, roasted (see Tips), peeled, and seeded

Kosher salt and freshly ground black pepper

1 (16-pound/7.2-kg) fresh turkey

(continued)

Bobby Flay—restaurateur, cookbook author, and television personality—has spent plenty of time at the Market, as the Food Network is one of our tenants. This holiday turkey recipe, with a sensational jalapeño-orange-sage butter rub and an out-of-the-ordinary red chile and cranberry gravy, is Bobby at his best, with bold, vibrant flavors. The Wild Rice & Goat Cheese Dressing on page 166 was designed to go with this beauty of a Thanksgiving entrée.

1. Make the enriched chicken stock: Position a rack in the center of the oven and preheat the oven to 375°F (190°C).

2. Toss the chicken carcasses and wings with the oil in a large roasting pan. Roast, turning the chicken after 15 minutes, until it is deep golden brown, about 25 minutes.

3. Transfer the chicken to a large stockpot. Add the onions, celery, carrots, peppercorns, dill, parsley, and bay leaf. Add 3½ quarts (3.3 L) cold water and bring it to a boil over high heat. Reduce the heat to medium-low and simmer, skimming the surface often, until the stock is full-flavored, about 2 hours.

4. Strain the stock through a cheesecloth-lined strainer into a large saucepan, discarding the solids. Using a small paring knife, make a slit in the side of each jalapeño. Add the jalapeños to the stock, bring it to a boil over high heat, and cook until it is reduced by half to about 6 cups (1.4 L), about 30 minutes.

5. Strain the stock through a wire sieve into a large bowl, discard the jalapeños, and let the stock cool to room temperature. Refrigerate it until chilled, at least 8 hours or overnight. Remove the layer of fat from the surface. (The stock can be covered and refrigerated for up to 2 days or frozen for up to 3 months.)

6. Make the jalapeño-sage-orange butter: Bring the orange juice to a boil in a small nonreactive saucepan over high heat. Cook until it is syrupy and reduced to about ¼ cup (60 ml), about 10 minutes. Let it cool completely.

7. Process the cooled orange syrup, butter, orange zest, sage, and jalapeños together in a food processor until smooth. Season the mixture with salt and pepper. Transfer the mixture to a small bowl. (The butter can be covered and refrigerated for up to 2 days. Bring it to room temperature before using.)

8. Roast the turkey: Position a rack in the lower third of the oven and preheat the oven to 450°F (230°C).

9. Remove the turkey neck, giblets, and yellow fat pads from the tail and discard them. Rinse the turkey well with cold water and pat it dry with paper towels. Rub the turkey all over with about half of the jalapeño-sage-orange butter, reserving the remaining butter. Season the turkey well, inside and out, with salt and pepper. Using kitchen twine, tie the drumstick ends together. Tie the wings to the body with a loop of twine. Place the turkey on a rack in a large roasting pan.

10. Roast the turkey for 30 minutes. Reduce the oven temperature to 375°F (190°C). Continue roasting, brushing the turkey with the remaining sage–orange butter every 15 minutes, until an instant-read thermometer inserted in the thickest part of the thigh, not touching a bone, reads 165°F (75°C), 2 to 2½ hours. Remove the turkey from the oven and let it stand for at least 20 minutes before carving.

11. Meanwhile, make the red chile–berry gravy: Place the ancho and New Mexico chiles in a heatproof bowl and add enough boiling water to cover. Let them stand until they soften, about 30 minutes. Purée the chiles and ¼ cup (60 ml) of the soaking liquid in a blender.

12. Heat the butter and oil together in a medium saucepan over high heat. Add the shallots and cook, stirring often, until they are tender, about 4 minutes. Stir in the garlic and cook until it is fragrant, about 30 seconds. Add the wine and port and bring them to a boil. Cook until they are reduced to a syrup, 7 to 10 minutes.

13. Add 1 quart (960 ml) of the enriched stock (reserve the remaining stock for another use), the chile purée, and sugar and bring the mixture to a boil. Cook, stirring often, until it is reduced to about 3 cups (720 ml), about 20 minutes. Add the cranberries and cook, stirring often, until they are popped and tender and the gravy is thick enough to coat the spoon, 10 to 15 minutes more. (The gravy can be stored at room temperature for up to 2 hours. Reheat it before proceeding.) Remove the gravy from the heat and stir in the blackberries, parsley, and sage. Season with salt and pepper.

14. Carve the turkey and serve it with the gravy.

FOR THE RED CHILE–BERRY GRAVY:

2 dried ancho chiles, seeded and stemmed

1 dried New Mexico chile, seeded and stemmed

3 cups (720 ml) boiling water, as needed

2 tablespoons unsalted butter

1 tablespoon canola oil

2 large shallots, finely chopped

3 garlic cloves, minced

1 cup (240 ml) dry white wine

½ cup (120 ml) ruby or tawny port

3 tablespoons light brown sugar

1 cup (3½ ounces/100 g) fresh cranberries

½ cup (3 ounces/85 g) gently crushed fresh blackberries

¼ cup (25 g) coarsely chopped fresh flat-leaf parsley

2 tablespoons finely chopped fresh sage

TIPS FROM THE PROS

ROASTING CHILES
Bobby Flay, Guest Chef

Fresh chiles have a thin skin that can be bitter, so it should be removed. The best way to do this is to broil the chile to char the skin for easier peeling (the charring adds flavor, too). If your skin is sensitive, wear latex gloves while handling the chiles.

Position a broiler rack about 6 inches (15 cm) from the heat source and preheat the broiler to high. Place the chiles on a broiler pan. Broil, turning them occasionally, just until the skins are blackened and blistered (being sure not to burn through the skin into the flesh), about 10 minutes. Transfer the chiles to a heatproof bowl and cover it with plastic wrap. Let them cool for about 20 minutes. Using a paring knife as an aide, peel the chiles. If the recipe requires seeded chiles, split open the chiles and remove the seeds and ribs with the tip of the knife, and discard the stem.

DUCK BREASTS

WITH FIVE SPICES & GRAPES

ANITA LO, GUEST CHEF

SERVES 4

FOR THE DUCK:

2 (14-ounce/400-g) boneless duck breasts

¾ teaspoon kosher salt

½ teaspoon freshly ground black pepper

1 tablespoon unsalted butter

¼ teaspoon Chinese five-spice powder

FOR THE SAUCE:

32 red or green (or a combination) seedless grapes

¼ cup (60 ml) Chinese black vinegar (see Tips)

2 tablespoons balsamic vinegar

Duck breast is an indulgence for most cooks, making it a good choice for a dinner party entrée that will treat your guests to something out of the ordinary. This recipe, contributed by Anita Lo, another one of our Sunday Supper chefs with a restaurant located nearby in the West Village, is very easy, and can be prepared in minutes. Have the Dandelion Sauté with Onion & Fennel on page 169 ready to warm up as a side dish.

1. Make the duck: Heat a large skillet over medium-high heat. Using a sharp knife, score the duck skin in a cross-hatch pattern, cutting through the thick skin but not into the flesh. Season the duck all over with the salt and pepper. Transfer the duck, skin-side down, to the skillet and immediately reduce the heat to very low.

2. Cook, spooning off and discarding the fat as it accumulates in the skillet, until most of the fat has rendered and the skin is deep brown, about 15 minutes. Turn the duck over and increase the heat to medium. Cook until the underside is browned and an instant-read thermometer inserted horizontally through the side of a breast into the center reads 125°F (50°C), about 5 minutes more. During the last 2 minutes, add the butter and the five-spice. Let the butter melt, and spoon it over the duck (the butter will brown, but it should not burn). Transfer the duck to a carving board and pour off the fat in the skillet. Let the duck stand for 5 minutes.

3. Make the sauce: Return the skillet to high heat. Add the grapes, black vinegar, and balsamic vinegar. Cook, stirring up the browned bits in the skillet with a wooden spoon, until the grapes are hot and the liquid reduces to about 2 tablespoons, about 2 minutes. Remove it from the heat.

4. Using a sharp knife, cut each breast across the grain into thin slices. Divide the slices among four dinner plates. Spoon the grapes and sauce over the duck, drizzle with the carving juices, and serve.

TIPS FROM THE PROS

BLACK VINEGAR
Anita Lo, Guest Chef

With a complex taste from the combination of fermented rice and malt, black vinegar (sometimes called Chinkiang vinegar) brings flavor to Chinese and Asian-inspired dishes. It is sometimes compared to balsamic vinegar, which is made from wine grapes and is entirely different. So different, in fact, that this duck recipe uses both for an interesting blend.

THE WEIGHT OF THE MATTER:
A TACTILE GUIDE TO WINE PAIRING

CHELSEA WINE VAULT

Wine and food pairing can be daunting, even to the most avid wine lover. The easiest way to pair wine with a dish is to sidestep the idea of flavors and consider the body of the wine. The "body" of a wine is its overall texture—how it feels in your mouth, independent of flavor. A wine's body is made up of several components: tannins, acids, sugar, and alcohol. In wine pairing, you always want to serve bold wines with hearty foods, and subtle wines with milder foods so neither overwhelms the other. Below is a checklist with good examples of wines that really exemplify a specific part of wine body. This guide will help you find pairings for your favorite foods in a very tactile way.

TANNINS: These are the compounds in a wine that make it feel astringent, or bitter, but also smooth and round. There are lots of different types of tannins in wine, but to keep this simple, we'll just talk about them as a group. Some tannins come directly from the grape skins themselves, especially in wines made from red grapes, and others come from the oak barrels some wines are aged in.

If you're new to wine and you're not sure what tannins feel like, think of a cup of black tea. When it's perfectly brewed, the tannins make it feel clean and precise. When it's over-brewed, the tea releases more tannins, resulting in a bitter, mouth-puckering feeling. That's the same kind of drying feeling you get from a tannic wine, though not as extreme. Sometimes the tannins feel silky smooth, other times they are aggressive and rough-edged, but it's always a "feeling" in your mouth rather than an aroma or taste.

Tannins interact with food by cutting through fat. When you have a steak, for instance, you want a big-bodied red with enough tannic grip to hold its own against that beefy goodness, like a California Cabernet or an Italian Primitivo. On the other hand, a delicate dish of sautéed morels with thyme and butter needs a gentler dose of tannin, from an Oregon Pinot Noir or a light-bodied red Burgundy, for instance.

A side note about oak: Many wines, whether red, white, or pink, are aged in oak barrels. Contact with wood can introduce more tannins into a wine, and it can also react with the tannins already there. Barrel aging can soften a wine and mellow its tannins, and it can add color, richness, and flavors of vanilla, spice, and caramel.

ACID: All wines have some degree of natural acidity, as they're made of fruit. Much easier to grasp than tannins, acid is another important facet of wine to consider for food pairing. You know acid from the squeeze of a lemon, a tangy cup of yogurt, or a juicy apple. Different kinds of acid produce subtly different flavors in wine, but for now we'll just group all acids together. When you take a sip of wine, and it makes your mouth water, that's the work of the acid. This is one of the most crucial parts of a balanced wine. Without enough acid, a wine can taste flabby or flat. The right amount of acid perks up a wine, brings out all of its flavors, and gives it a longer finish. Wines with high acid content pair well with rich

but not-too-heavy foods. Serve a bright Muscadet with oysters, pair Vermentino with rabbit, and serve Cabernet Franc with duck breast.

SWEETNESS: Just as all wines have acid, they all have some residual sugar that comes from the grapes. When we describe a wine as "dry," we mean it doesn't have enough residual sugar to taste outright sweet. Most wines are dry, so if you pick one at random, your chances are good it'll be dry. Other wines range from off-dry to semisweet to full-on dessert sweet. For dessert pairings, Vin Santo picks up the creamy, caramel flavors of a crème brulée, Brachetto highlights delicate berry tarts, and Port is perfect for all kinds of chocolate.

But wines with a bit of residual sugar aren't meant to pair only with desserts. A touch of sweetness helps counteract spice in foods, so for your most tongue-tingling tandoori, you'll want a lightly sweet Gewürztraminer or Riesling. That extra sugar can also help tame a really strong flavor that would clash with a tannic, dry wine. For example, a ripe blue cheese is delightful with a glass of sweet Vouvray or Canadian icewine, but it can taste bitter and waxy with a red Bordeaux.

ALCOHOL: All wines include alcohol; it's created during the fermentation process when hungry yeast cells metabolize the sugar in the grapes. Without alcohol, you just have juice. In terms of food pairing, a wine with a higher alcohol content (above 14 percent) will feel warmer, richer, and overall bigger than a low-alcohol-content wine. And since many of the chemicals that we detect as aromas are alcohol-soluble, a higher-proof wine can pack more flavor. That makes it a good match for hearty, rustic foods that need a spirited partner. Try an Australian Shiraz with pulled pork sandwiches, a Valpolicella with pepperoni pizza, a California Chardonnay with macaroni and cheese, and a Fino Sherry with oil-cured olives and manchego.

Once you get the hang of measuring up a wine by its body, you'll find it much easier to pick out a partner for your dinner. If you're ever really stuck for a pairing, almost any food matches with sparkling wine. Champagne, Cava, Prosecco, and Crémants are great with everything from crostini to soup to entrées. Remember: There is no wrong pairing as long as it tastes good to you. So get out there and experiment with your food and wine pairings, because the best way to learn about wine is to keep tasting new things.

CHAPTER 7

FROM THE FISHMONGER

SEAFOOD

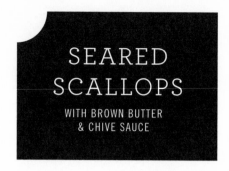

SEARED SCALLOPS

WITH BROWN BUTTER & CHIVE SAUCE

THE LOBSTER PLACE

SERVES 4

12 very large sea scallops, patted dry on paper towels

Kosher salt and freshly ground black pepper

1 tablespoon olive oil

3 tablespoons clarified butter (see Tips)

⅓ cup (75 ml) dry white wine, such as Pinot Grigio

1 teaspoon finely chopped fresh chives

1 teaspoon fresh lemon juice

For a quick weeknight supper, scallops are a wonderful choice because they must be cooked quickly. Look for such designations as "dry" (meaning that they were not soaked in preservatives before shipping), "diver" (indicating that they were harvested by hand by divers), or "day-boat" (to show that the boat returned to shore the same day it fished its fresh, unfrozen catch). For a deliciously browned exterior, be sure that they are dried well before adding them to the skillet. Serve them with steamed chard and some couscous for a simple but elegant dinner. (See photo on previous page.)

1. Season one side of the scallops with salt and pepper. Heat the oil in a very large nonstick skillet over medium-high heat until it is very hot but not smoking. Add the scallops, seasoned-side down, and season their tops with salt and pepper. So they develop that all-important seared surface, cook the scallops without moving them until the underside is well browned, about 5 minutes.

2. Flip the scallops over. Add 2 tablespoons of the butter to the skillet. When it melts, constantly spoon the butter over the scallops, letting them turn a deeper shade of brown, about 1 minute. Transfer them to a platter.

3. Reduce the heat to medium. Stir in the wine and bring it to a boil. Remove from the heat. Add the remaining 1 tablespoon butter, the chives, and lemon juice and stir well. Pour the sauce over the scallops and serve them immediately.

TIPS FROM THE PROS

CLARIFIED BUTTER
The Lobster Place

Chefs love clarified butter because it can be heated to high temperatures without burning. During the clarification process, the lactose-rich dairy solids, which are the first element to burn in regular butter, are removed. It is easiest and most efficient to clarify at least 8 ounces (2 sticks/225 g) of butter at a time, but note that the clarified butter keeps for up to 6 months in the refrigerator and can be used for any sauté.

Melt unsalted butter in a small saucepan over medium heat until it is boiling and foamy. Reduce the heat to medium-low and boil for 1 minute. Remove the pan from the heat and let it stand for 5 minutes, letting the beige milk solids sink to the bottom of the saucepan. Skim any foam from the surface of the melted butter and discard it. Carefully pour the clear yellow liquid into a small covered container, leaving the milk solids behind in the saucepan. The clarified butter is now ready to use. Discard the solids.

For longer storage, cover the container and refrigerate it for at least 8 hours, until the clarified butter is firm. Using a dinner knife as an aide, remove the firm butter in one piece from the container and wipe away any white clinging liquid (this is the remains of the dairy solids) on the butter with a paper towel. Set the butter aside. Pour out any liquid from the container; wash and dry the container. Replace the butter in the container, cover, and refrigerate it for up to 3 months.

Friedman's Lunch is renowned for its comfort food, and sometimes its specialties hail from the Left Coast and not the Big Apple. Fish tacos of this quality, with layers of texture and flavor, are not common on the East Coast. With so many components, these are a bit of a production to make, but the steps are easy. Pollack is Friedman's fish of choice, but just about any firm-fleshed fish, such as haddock or cod, will do.

1. Whisk the mayonnaise, Sriracha, and lime juice together in a serving bowl. Cover and refrigerate (for up to 1 week) until ready to serve.

2. Make the tomatillo salsa: Position the broiler rack about 6 inches (15 cm) from the heat source and preheat the broiler.

3. Combine the tomatillos, onion, garlic, and jalapeño in a large bowl. Drizzle them with the oil and mix to coat. Spread them in a broiler pan. Broil, stirring occasionally, until the ingredients are lightly charred and the juices begin to run, but the tomatillos are not bursting, about 10 minutes. Return everything to the bowl and add the lime juice and cilantro. Working in batches, in a food processor or blender, process the tomatillo mixture into a coarse purée and transfer it to a serving bowl. Season it with salt and pepper. Let the salsa cool completely. Cover and refrigerate it until ready to serve. (The salsa can be refrigerated for up to 1 week.)

4. Make the citrus-fennel slaw: Core the cabbage. Using the slicing blade of a food processor, thinly slice the cabbage and fennel. (Or slice by hand with a large knife or a mandoline.) Transfer the vegetables to a large bowl.

5. Using a serrated knife, cut away the thick peel from an orange where it meets the flesh. Working over a bowl to catch the juices, cut between the membranes to release each orange segment, letting the segments fall into the bowl. Repeat with the remaining orange and grapefruits.

6. Add the citrus segments and their juices to the cabbage mixture. Add the vinegar, cilantro, and coriander and mix. Season the slaw with salt and pepper. Transfer it to a serving bowl. Cover and refrigerate it for at least 1 hour. (The slaw can be refrigerated for up to 8 hours.)

7. Make the fish: Mix the paprika, 1 teaspoon kosher salt, ½ teaspoon black pepper, the thyme, oregano, garlic, onion, and cayenne in a small bowl. Sprinkle them over the pollack. Heat the oil in a large nonstick skillet over medium-high heat until very hot but not smoking. Add the fish and cook until the underside is golden brown, about 3 minutes. Flip the fish over and cook until it looks barely opaque when flaked in the thickest part, about 3 minutes. Transfer the fish to a serving bowl and break it into bite-size pieces.

8. Serve the bowls of fish, Sriracha mayonnaise, salsa, and slaw with the tortillas, lime wedges, and cilantro leaves. Let the guests build the tacos, filling a tortilla with fish, topped with slaw and salsa, followed by a drizzle of mayonnaise, and adding a squeeze of lime juice and cilantro leaves, if desired.

FISH TACOS

WITH CITRUS-FENNEL SLAW & TOMATILLO SALSA

FRIEDMAN'S LUNCH

SERVES 8

1 cup (225 g) mayonnaise
¼ cup (60 ml) Sriracha
1 tablespoon fresh lime juice

FOR THE TOMATILLO SALSA:
2 pounds (910 g) fresh tomatillos, husked
1 yellow onion, thinly sliced
3 garlic cloves, peeled
1 jalapeño chile, seeded and chopped
3 tablespoons canola oil
¼ cup (60 ml) fresh lime juice
¼ cup (10 g) packed fresh cilantro leaves
Kosher salt and freshly ground black pepper

FOR THE CITRUS-FENNEL SLAW:
½ head green cabbage (1¼ pounds/570 g)
2 small fennel bulbs, cored
2 navel oranges
2 ruby grapefruits
¼ cup (60 ml) cider vinegar
¼ cup (10 g) packed fresh cilantro leaves
2 teaspoons ground coriander

FOR THE FISH:
2 teaspoons sweet paprika
1 teaspoon dried thyme
1 teaspoon dried oregano
½ teaspoon granulated garlic
½ teaspoon granulated onion
¼ teaspoon cayenne pepper
1½ pounds (680 g) skinless pollack fillets
2 tablespoons canola oil
24 (6-inch/15-cm) warm white corn tortillas
Lime wedges and cilantro leaves, for serving

BRAISED BLACK COD

WITH VEGETABLE RAGOUT

MORIMOTO

SERVES 6

FOR THE VEGETABLE RAGOUT:

1 carrot, sliced crosswise on an angle

1 whole bamboo shoot (about 8 ounces/ 225 g), rinsed and diced (see Note)

1 (8-inch/20-cm) piece burdock root, peeled and diced on an angle

2 tablespoons toasted sesame oil

6 dried shiitake mushrooms, rehydrated in hot water to cover for 30 minutes, stemmed, drained, and quartered

7 ounces (195 g) Japanese yam cake, diced

1½ cups (360 ml) Chicken Stock (page 56)

½ cup (120 ml) soy sauce

⅓ cup (65 g) sugar

¼ cup (60 ml) sake

FOR THE COD:

2 cups (480 ml) sake

6 (⅛-inch-/3-mm) slices fresh ginger

6 (6- to 7-ounce/175- to 200-g) black cod fillets, with skin on

1½ cups (300 g) sugar

1 cup (240 ml) soy sauce

1½ teaspoons tamari

3 tablespoons mirin

Julienned Tokyo scallion or standard scallion, for garnish

Julienned ginger, for garnish

Sprigs of *kinome* (ash tree leaves), for garnish

You have probably seen this modern classic or tasted it before. The biggest secret of success here is finding pristinely fresh black cod, also known as sablefish or butterfish. It is an oil-rich, firm-textured fish with white flesh that takes well to a dark sweet sauce. Native to the Pacific Northwest, it is a luxury item on the East Coast, but the preparation also works well with just about any thick fish fillets. Yam cake, burdock root, dried shiitake mushrooms, and *kinome* (ash tree leaves) are sold at Japanese grocers.

1. Make the vegetable ragout: Bring a large pot of water to a boil. Set a large bowl of iced water next to the stove. Blanch the carrots for 2 minutes, lift them out of the water, and transfer them to the iced water. Repeat with the bamboo shoots, then the burdock roots. Drain well. (The vegetables can be prepared several hours in advance.)

2. Heat the oil in a large skillet over medium heat. Add the carrots, bamboo shoots, burdock, mushrooms, and yam cake. Cook, stirring occasionally, until the carrots are lightly browned, about 3 minutes.

3. Add the stock, soy sauce, sugar, and sake. Simmer, stirring occasionally, until the vegetables are just tender, 20 to 30 minutes.

4. Make the cod: Pour the sake into a large, deep skillet or flameproof casserole. Add the ginger, followed by the fish fillets, skin-side up. Cover and cook them over high heat for 2 minutes. Add the sugar and cook, covered, over medium-high heat for 2 minutes more.

5. Pour the soy sauce and tamari over the fish fillets. Cook over medium-high heat, covered, for 2 minutes. Add the mirin and cook, uncovered, basting the fish often with the thickening glaze and reducing the heat as needed to keep the fish from burning, until the fish is barely opaque when pierced in the thickest part with the tip of a knife, about 2 minutes more.

6. With a slotted spatula, carefully transfer the fillets to a platter. Check the fish to make sure it has no bones hidden in it. If the braising liquid is not syrupy, keep cooking it over high heat until it thickens.

7. For each serving, place a cod fillet, skin-side down, on a dinner plate. Garnish it with the julienned scallion and ginger and sprigs of kinome. Drizzle it with the braising liquid. Using a slotted spoon, add the vegetable ragout. Serve hot.

NOTE: *Whole bamboo shoots are available, sold from tubs, in the refrigerated section of most Asian markets. Their flavor and texture is much better than those of canned sliced bamboo shoots.*

This updated classic begins with beautiful fresh fish from local waters (and that is the only kind you will find served by Mary Cleaver and her staff at The Green Table), and continues with a light, artful mix of ingredients that enhances the fish. Cooking the fish in an "envelope" of parchment traps the aromas and flavors, and releases them when the paper is opened in front of each guest. Preserved lemons, an essential ingredient of Moroccan cuisine, can be purchased at specialty food stores. If necessary, substitute the grated zest of 1 lemon and 2 teaspoons of its juice for the preserved lemon and brine.

1. Make the preserved lemon butter: Heat the oil in a medium skillet over medium heat. Add the shallots and cook, stirring often, until the shallots are tender but not browned, about 3 minutes. Transfer them to a medium bowl to cool completely.

2. Add the butter, parsley, preserved lemon, brine, Aleppo pepper, and salt to the cooled shallots and mix well to combine. (The butter can be covered and refrigerated for up to 2 days. Remove it from the refrigerator 1 hour before using.)

3. Use a mandoline, V-slicer, or large sharp knife to cut the carrot and fennel into julienne. Slice the onion into thin half-moons. Heat 1 tablespoon of the oil in a large skillet over medium heat. Add the carrot, fennel, onion, and leek and cook, stirring often, until the carrots are just tender, about 5 minutes. Transfer the vegetables to a bowl.

4. Stem the mushrooms and cut them into thin strips. Add the remaining 2 tablespoons oil to the skillet over medium-high heat. Add the mushrooms and cook, stirring often, until they are lightly browned and tender, about 8 minutes. Add them to the bowl of vegetables and season the mixture lightly with salt and pepper. Let cool completely.

5. For each serving, place a parchment rectangle on the work surface in front of you. Place a fish fillet on the parchment, about 3 inches (8 cm) from the bottom, and season it lightly with salt and pepper. Top it with one-sixth of the vegetable mixture and about 2 tablespoons of the lemon butter. Drizzle it with 1 tablespoon of the vermouth. Fold the top half of the parchment down to meet the bottom edge. Tightly roll up and crimp the parchment paper on all sides to enclose the fish and vegetable mixture. Transfer the packets to two large rimmed baking sheets. (The fish packets can be refrigerated for up to 3 hours.)

6. Position racks in the center and top third of the oven and preheat the oven to 425°F (220°C).

7. Bake the packets on the baking sheets until the parchment is lightly browned, about 10 minutes. Transfer each packet to a dinner plate. Serve, allowing each person to cut open his or her packet with a sharp knife or scissors, being careful to avoid the escaping steam.

STRIPED BASS EN PAPILLOTE
WITH PRESERVED LEMON BUTTER

THE GREEN TABLE

SERVES 6

FOR THE PRESERVED LEMON BUTTER:

1 tablespoon olive oil

⅓ cup (50 g) finely chopped shallots

½ cup (1 stick/115 g) unsalted butter, at room temperature

1 tablespoon finely chopped fresh flat-leaf parsley

1 tablespoon finely chopped drained preserved lemon

2 teaspoons preserved lemon brine

1 teaspoon Aleppo pepper (see page 62), or ½ teaspoon hot red pepper flakes

½ teaspoon fine sea salt

1 medium carrot

½ small fennel bulb

1 small red onion

3 tablespoons canola oil

1 leek, white and green parts only, cut into thin strips, well rinsed to remove grit

8 ounces (225 g) fresh shiitake mushrooms

Fine sea salt and freshly ground black pepper

6 (6-ounce/170-g) wild-caught skinless striped bass fillets

6 tablespoons (90 ml) dry vermouth or dry white wine

Special equipment: A mandoline or plastic V-slicer; 6 (18-by-13-inch/46-by-33-cm) pieces of parchment paper

Great crab cakes, no matter who makes them, all share a few characteristics. Yes, the inside should be bursting with crab flavor and not too much filler, but let's not forget about the crispy, crunchy exterior. Panko (which are really Japanese bread flakes more than they are bread crumbs) do the trick. Don't be afraid to use a substantial amount of oil and high heat to cook the crust to golden brown perfection. Enjoy these on their own with a squirt of lemon and your favorite tartar sauce, or in a sandwich, perhaps with a couple of slices of bacon.

1. Make the tartar sauce: Mix the mayonnaise, pickles, scallion, parsley, lemon juice, mustard, Worcestershire sauce, and hot sauce in a medium bowl until combined. Cover the bowl and refrigerate for 30 minutes to blend the flavors.

2. Make the crab cakes: Mix the mayonnaise, parsley, mustard, lemon juice, and Old Bay in a large bowl until combined. Add the panko and mix again. Add the crabmeat and mix, taking care not to crush the crab meat. Shape the crab mixture into eight equal patties, about 3 inches (7.5 cm) in diameter. Place them on a baking sheet, cover, and refrigerate them for 15 to 30 minutes.

3. Preheat the oven to 200°F (90°C). Line a large baking sheet with a clean brown paper bag or a double thickness of paper towels.

4. Pour in enough oil to come ½ inch (12 mm) up the sides of a large skillet and heat it over medium-high heat until the oil is hot but not smoking. In batches, add the crab cakes and cook them until the undersides are golden brown, about 2 minutes. Flip over the crab cakes and continue cooking until the other sides are golden brown, about 2 minutes more. Transfer the cakes to the lined baking sheet and keep them warm in the oven while cooking the remaining crab cakes. Serve them hot with the tartar sauce and lemon wedges.

CRISPY CRAB CAKES
WITH TARTAR SAUCE

THE LOBSTER PLACE

SERVES 4

FOR THE TARTAR SAUCE:

1 cup mayonnaise, preferably Hellmann's

⅓ cup (45 g) chopped dill pickles

1½ tablespoons finely chopped scallion

1 tablespoon finely chopped fresh parsley

2 teaspoons fresh lemon juice

1 teaspoon Dijon mustard

½ teaspoon Worcestershire sauce

½ teaspoon hot red pepper sauce, such as Tabasco

FOR THE CRAB CAKES:

1 cup (240 g) mayonnaise, preferably Hellmann's

2 tablespoons finely chopped fresh flat-leaf parsley

2 tablespoons Dijon mustard

2 tablespoons fresh lemon juice

2 teaspoons Old Bay Seasoning

1½ cups (90 g) panko (Japanese bread crumbs)

2 pounds (910 g) lump crabmeat, sorted through for cartilage and shells

Vegetable oil, for frying

Lemon wedges, for serving

LOBSTER, LEEK & BRUSSELS SPROUTS GRATIN

MICHELLE BERNSTEIN, GUEST CHEF

SERVES 6

3 lobsters (1¼ pounds/570 g each)

FOR THE STOCK:

2 tablespoons olive oil

1 small yellow onion, chopped

1 celery rib, chopped

½ cup (120 ml) dry white wine

4 sprigs fresh flat-leaf parsley

¼ teaspoon dried thyme

¼ teaspoon black peppercorns

FOR THE SAUCE:

2 tablespoons olive oil

2 tablespoons unsalted butter

½ cup (80 g) minced shallots

1 garlic clove, minced

4 large leeks, white and pale green parts only, split lengthwise, cut crosswise into ½-inch (12-mm) slices, washed and drained

¼ cup (30 g) all-purpose flour

1 cup (240 ml) heavy cream

Freshly grated zest of 1 lemon

Kosher salt and freshly ground black pepper

1 pound (455 g) Brussels sprouts, trimmed and quartered lengthwise

1 cup (60 g) panko (Japanese bread crumbs)

(continued)

A James Beard Foundation Award winner in the Best Chef: South category, Michelle Bernstein has come up from Miami and her restaurant Michy's to share her delightful cuisine at a Sunday Supper. Michelle, a former ballerina, nimbly combines elegant and humble ingredients in this satisfying dish, which can also be baked in a 13-by-9-inch (33-by-23-cm) baking dish for a very special buffet entrée.

1. Fill the sink with iced water. Bring a very large pot of salted water to a boil over high heat. Using tongs, plunge a lobster, head first, into the boiling water and cover the pot. (If you have a very large pot, you may be able to fit two lobsters in the water at once.) Cook until the lobster shell is bright red, 8 to 10 minutes. The meat will not be fully cooked. Using the tongs, transfer the lobster to the iced water to cool until it is easy to handle. Repeat with the remaining lobsters.

2. Working over a bowl to save any juices, use poultry shears to cut through the lobster shells as needed and remove the claw, knuckle, and tail meat, reserving the shells and feelers. Discard the viscera, including the sac in the head, but save the green tomalley and red coral, if desired. Using the shears, snip the shell and feelers into 2-inch (5-cm) pieces and set them aside with the juices. Cut the lobster meat into bite-size pieces, transfer them to a bowl, cover, and refrigerate until ready to use.

3. Make the stock: Heat the oil over medium heat in a large saucepan. Add the onion and celery and cover. Cook, stirring occasionally, until they are softened, about 3 minutes. Add the wine and bring it to a boil. Stir in the reserved shells and feelers with the lobster juices in the bowl. Add enough water to barely cover the shells, about 1½ quarts (1.5 L). Bring it to a boil over high heat, skimming off any foam from the surface. Add the parsley, thyme, and peppercorns. Reduce the heat to low and simmer until the stock is fully flavored, about 30 minutes. Strain it, reserving the liquid and discarding the solids. Return the stock to the saucepan and boil until it is reduced to 1 quart (960 ml). Reserve 2 cups (480 ml) of the stock and save the remainder for another use.

4. Make the sauce: Heat the oil and butter together in a medium saucepan over medium heat. Add the shallots and garlic and cook until they are softened, about 2 minutes. Add the leeks and cook, stirring often, until they are tender, about 10 minutes. Sprinkle them with the flour and stir well. Gradually whisk in the reserved stock and cook, stirring almost constantly, until it comes to a simmer. Whisk in the cream and bring the mixture to a boil. Reduce the heat to low and simmer gently, whisking often, until no raw flour flavor remains and the sauce has thickened slightly, about 5 minutes. Remove it from the heat. Stir in the zest and season with salt and pepper.

5. Bring a large saucepan of lightly salted water to a boil over high heat. Add the Brussels sprouts and cook until they are barely tender, about 5 minutes. Drain and rinse them well under cold running water. Drain them again and pat them dry with paper towels.

6. Position a rack in the top third of the oven and preheat the oven to 400°F (205°C). Lightly oil 6 individual gratin dishes or ovenproof casseroles.

7. Mix the panko, cheese, tarragon, parsley, and oil together in a small bowl. Spread the Brussels sprouts in the baking dishes, and top them with the lobster meat. Pour the leek sauce on top and spread it evenly. Sprinkle each gratin generously with the bread crumb mixture.

8. Bake until the topping is browned and the sauce is bubbling, 15 to 20 minutes. Serve the gratins hot.

¼ cup (25 g) freshly grated Pecorino Romano cheese

2 tablespoons finely chopped fresh tarragon

2 tablespoons finely chopped fresh flat-leaf parsley

2 tablespoons olive oil, plus more for the gratin dishes

Special equipment: 6 individual (about 2 cups/480 ml each) gratin dishes or ovenproof casseroles

PROVENÇAL FISH STEW

CHELSEA MARKET FAMILY RECIPE

SERVES 4 TO 6

1½ pounds (680 g) skinless cod, snapper, or other firm, white-fleshed fish fillets, cut into 1-inch (2.5-cm) pieces

Kosher salt and freshly ground black pepper

¼ cup (60 ml) olive oil

1 small yellow onion, chopped

1 leek, white and pale green parts only, cut into ½-inch (12-mm) pieces and washed well

½ small fennel bulb, cut into ½-inch (12-mm) cubes

2 celery ribs, cut into ½-inch (12-mm) dice

1 carrot, cut into ½-inch (12-mm) dice

1 large baking potato, peeled and cut into 1-inch (2.5-cm) cubes

2 garlic cloves, minced

¼ cup (60 ml) anise-flavored aperitif, such as Pernod or Ricard, or dry white wine

1 quart (960 ml) Seafood Stock or Quick Seafood Stock (page 57), or reduced-sodium fish, chicken, or vegetable broth

3 sprigs fresh thyme

1 bay leaf

¼ cup (25 g) chopped fresh flat-leaf parsley

2 tablespoons fresh lemon juice

4 to 6 slices day-old crusty bread, toasted

Lemon wedges, for serving

Ori Cosentino is a caterer (and life partner of Michael Ginsberg, Jamestown's Events Manager) who has long depended on the Market for sourcing the freshest seafood for this stew. She loves its versatility, and adds whatever the guys at The Lobster Place recommend for cooking that night's dinner. It has its roots in Provençal cooking, and is actually quite close to authentic bouillabaisse, which usually has potatoes but does not always include tomatoes.

1. Season the fish with 1 teaspoon salt and ½ teaspoon pepper. Cover and refrigerate it while preparing the stew.

2. Heat the oil in a large Dutch oven over medium heat. Add the onion, leek, fennel, celery, and carrot and season them lightly with salt and pepper. Cook, stirring occasionally, until they are softened but not browned, about 8 minutes. Add the potato and garlic and cook, stirring often, until the garlic is tender, about 3 minutes more.

3. Add the aperitif and bring it to a boil. Stir in the stock, thyme, and bay leaf and bring everything to a simmer. Reduce the heat to medium-low. Simmer until the mixture is well flavored and the potato pieces are almost tender when pierced with the tip of a small knife, about 10 minutes.

4. Add the cod and simmer until the fish is opaque when pierced with the tip of a small knife, about 10 minutes. Remove the thyme stems and bay leaf. Stir in the parsley and lemon juice and season with salt and pepper.

5. For each serving, place a toasted bread slice in a deep soup bowl. Ladle in the soup and serve it hot with the lemon wedges.

SHRIMP & SAUSAGE CIOPPINO

GIADA DE LAURENTIIS, GUEST CHEF

SERVES 4

¼ cup (60 ml) extra-virgin olive oil

1 large fennel bulb, chopped into ½-inch (12-mm) pieces

½ cup (80 g) chopped shallots

4 garlic cloves, smashed and peeled

1 teaspoon kosher salt

½ teaspoon freshly ground black pepper

1 pound (455 g) spicy Italian turkey sausage, casings removed

2 cups (480 ml) dry white wine, such as Pinot Grigio

¼ cup (65 g) tomato paste

3 cups (720 ml) Chicken Stock (page 56) or low-sodium chicken broth

1 bay leaf

1 pound (455 g) large (26 to 31 count) shrimp, peeled and deveined

1 (15-ounce/420-g) can cannellini beans, drained and rinsed

1 cup (40 g) chopped fresh basil

1 tablespoon finely chopped fresh thyme leaves

Crusty sourdough bread, for serving

Giada (no last name required) is one of the Food Network's brightest stars, and she is no stranger to Chelsea Market. Her take on Italian food—updated, but with every delicious traditional flavor intact—is exemplified by this variation of cioppino, a seafood stew that some say originated with Italian fishermen in San Francisco. As wonderful as it is alone, this dish seems incomplete without crusty sourdough bread.

1. Heat the oil in a Dutch oven or soup pot over medium-high heat. Add the fennel, shallots, garlic, ½ teaspoon of the salt, and ¼ teaspoon of the pepper. Cook, stirring occasionally, until the vegetables soften slightly, about 4 minutes. Add the sausage and break it into ½-inch (12-mm) pieces with a wooden spoon. Cook until it is browned, about 5 minutes. Add the wine and scrape up the browned bits in the bottom of the pan with a wooden spoon. Stir in the tomato paste, followed by the stock and bay leaf. Bring to a simmer and reduce the heat to medium-low. Cover and simmer for 10 minutes.

2. Uncover the pan and add the shrimp, beans, basil, and thyme. Simmer, uncovered, until the shrimp are pink and cooked through, about 4 minutes. Remove the bay leaf and discard it. Season the stew with the remaining ½ teaspoon salt and ¼ teaspoon pepper. Ladle it into soup bowls and serve it with crusty sourdough bread.

Everyone needs a pasta recipe that can be prepared quickly for a weeknight dinner. Italian tuna, packed in olive oil, has a more lush texture than regular tuna, and is worth having in your pantry for this dish (and upgraded tuna salad). The sauce is made in minutes with sweet cherry tomatoes.

1. Bring a large pot of salted water to a boil over high heat.

2. Meanwhile, drain the tuna in a wire sieve, reserving the oil. Add enough additional oil to make ¼ cup (60 ml). Flake the tuna.

3. Heat the oil mixture in a medium skillet with the garlic and pepper flakes, if using. Cook over medium heat until the garlic is softened but not browned, about 2 minutes. Add the tomatoes and cook, stirring occasionally, until they are hot, about 2 minutes. Stir in the tuna and parsley and cook just until heated through, about 2 minutes. Season with salt. Remove from the heat and cover to keep warm.

4. Meanwhile, add the broccoli to the boiling water and cook just until it is tender, about 5 minutes. Using a wire skimmer or sieve, remove the broccoli from the water and transfer it to a bowl. Return the water to a boil. Add the farfalle to the water and cook according to the package directions, until it is al dente. During the last minute, return the broccoli to the boiling water to heat it through. Drain the farfalle and broccoli in a colander, then return the farfalle mixture to the pot.

5. Add the cherry tomato mixture and stir well to combine. Serve the pasta hot, drizzling each serving with extra olive oil.

PASTA WITH TUNA, BROCCOLI & CHERRY TOMATOES

BUON'ITALIA

SERVES 4 TO 6

1 (5.5-ounce/155-g) can imported tuna in olive oil

Extra-virgin olive oil

1 garlic clove, thinly sliced

½ teaspoon hot red pepper flakes (optional)

10 ounces (1 dry pint / 280 g) cherry tomatoes, halved

1 tablespoon finely chopped fresh flat-leaf parsley

Fine sea salt

1 pound (455 g) broccoli, cut into bite-size florets

1 pound (455 g) farfalle (bow-tie) pasta

OUR FAVORITE COOKBOOKS

POSMAN BOOKS

At Posman Books, like any bookseller, cookbooks are a big part of our business. When we compiled this list of our favorites, we were surprised to see that we didn't rely on the old standards. This is probably because we have a constant stream of new, beautifully produced books to consider, and each one vies for our attention by being more visually attractive than the last. Of course, the proof of the pudding is in the cooking, and we can attest to the deliciousness of the recipes in these books, too.

Before we get into the practical cooking guides, we want to recommend two books about living the life of a chef. *Kitchen Confidential*, by Anthony Bourdain, is the ultimate memoir of the genre, filled with colorful details of life in the trenches. Insightful and uproariously funny, this book sells itself. *Blood, Bones & Butter*, by Gabrielle Hamilton, is on its way to being the next classic in this vein.

In alphabetical order by author, these are our current favorites:

THE FAMILY MEAL: HOME COOKING WITH FERRAN ADRIÀ; *Ferran Adrià:* Adrià's El Bulli was long considered the most creative restaurant in the world before its recent closing. He shares his home cooking using delicious, simple recipes with beautifully instructional photos.

FISH: RECIPES FROM THE SEA; *Mark Bittman:* This extensive manual shows how to buy, gut, heighten the flavor of, and prepare more than seventy kinds of fish and seafood. It is a must for any kitchen.

MILK & COOKIES: 89 HEIRLOOM RECIPES FROM NEW YORK'S MILK AND COOKIES BAKERY; *Tina Casaceli:* This well-organized gem provides delectable variations on a staple dessert. It is a great find and perfect as a gift.

THE BACK IN THE DAY BAKERY COOKBOOK: MORE THAN 100 RECIPES FROM THE BEST LITTLE BAKERY IN THE SOUTH; *Cheryl Day and Griffith Day:* We adore this lovely cookbook for its luscious photos and vintage vibe. We have forced our resident baker bookseller to test out these recipes and we can testify to the wonderful Southern comfort these treats provide.

THE PIONEER WOMAN COOKS: RECIPES FROM AN ACCIDENTAL COUNTRY GIRL; *Ree Drummond:* Back in the store's early years, we hosted Ree at one of our first large-scale events, and it was love at first sight. How she attained her massive following is made clear with her easy-to-follow, practical writing style and hearty and delicious recipes.

THE HOMESICK TEXAN COOKBOOK; *Lisa Fain:* Another great friend to the store and local favorite, Lisa Fain combines great stories with savory Texan fare. Our often-homesick Texan manager swears by this book—particularly the soft cheese tacos.

THE RIVER COTTAGE MEAT BOOK; *Hugh Fearnley-Whittingstall:* A comprehensive and educational guide to the preparation and cooking of meat; we feel this is another cookbook essential.

FISH · MARK BITTMAN · WILEY

Sarabeth Levine · Sarabeth's Bakery · R.

FEARNLEY-WHITTINGSTALL · THE RIVER COTTAGE MEAT BOOK · TEN SPEED PRESS

75th ANNIVERSARY · Joy of Cooking · ROMBAUER · BECKER · BECKER · THE NEW YORK TIMES BESTSELLER · SCRIBNER

CHERYL DAY and GRIFFITH DAY · THE BACK IN THE DAY BAKERY COOKBOOK

The Family Meal · Home cooking with Ferran Adrià

THE BEST Simple RECIPES

OTTOLENGHI · PLENTY · CHRONICLE BOOKS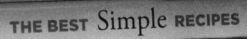

LISA FAIN · THE HOMESICK TEXAN Cookbook

THE PIONEER WOMAN COOKS · REE DRUMMOND

THE SILVER SPOON

SARABETH'S BAKERY: FROM MY HANDS TO YOURS; *Sarabeth Levine:* Our lovely neighbor across the concourse provides recipes perfect for both the novice and seasoned baker. Full of warm and sumptuous recipes, this book is a must-have. We love you, Sarabeth!

PLENTY: VIBRANT RECIPES FROM LONDON'S OTTOLENGHI; *Yotam Ottolenghi:* This proved to be one of the most anticipated cookbooks for our customers. We must have been asked every week when this UK title focusing on vegetarian fare would be released in the States. This visual delight with unexpected ingredients definitely did not disappoint.

FOOD RULES: AN EATER'S MANUAL; *Michael Pollan, illustrated by Maira Kalman:* We love the gorgeous and smart-looking gift book version that literally shows the simple truth about eating well.

SUPER NATURAL EVERY DAY: WELL-LOVED RECIPES FROM MY NATURAL FOODS KITCHEN; *Heidi Swanson:* No one can resist this exquisite and wholesome vegetarian cookbook, one of our most consistent top-selling books.

As for the standards, when someone comes in looking for a wedding or housewarming gift, we can't go wrong by recommending any one of these classics:

THE BEST SIMPLE RECIPES: MORE THAN 200 FLAVORFUL, FOOLPROOF RECIPES THAT COOK IN 30 MINUTES OR LESS; *America's Test Kitchen:* These are truly simple and inexpensive recipes that even our cooking-challenged readers can follow.

MASTERING THE ART OF FRENCH COOKING, VOLUMES 1 AND 2; *Julia Child, Simone Beck, and Louisette Bertholle (volume 1 only):* These textbooks on French cuisine are the ones that instantly made Julia Child an irreplaceable grande dame of cooking.

THE SILVER SPOON; *Editors of Phaidon Press:* The Holy Grail of Italian cookbooks, with hundreds of recipes.

THE JOY OF COOKING; *Irma S. Rombauer, Marion Rombauer Becker, and Ethan Becker:* This must-have book deserves a place in every kitchen, not just for its recipes, but as a reference.

CHAPTER 8

THE GREEN GROCER

VEGETARIAN MAIN COURSES

APPLE & BRIE CRÊPES
WITH BABY GREENS

BAR SUZETTE

SERVES 6; MAKES 6 LARGE OR 12 SMALL CRÊPES

FOR THE CRÊPE BATTER:

1⅔ cups (210 g) unbleached all-purpose flour

1½ cups (360 ml) whole milk

3 large eggs

1 teaspoon extra-virgin olive oil

1 (2-inch/5-cm) sprig fresh rosemary, leaves only

½ small garlic clove, peeled

Pinch fine sea salt

Vegetable oil, for the skillet

FOR THE FILLING:

3 tablespoons unsalted butter, melted

1 large apple, any variety, cored and very thinly sliced into 12 equal wedges

12 ounces (340 g) French double-crème Brie, with the rind, cut into 12 equal pieces

About 3 tablespoons honey, as needed, for drizzling

3 ounces (85 g) mixed baby greens

Balsamic vinegar (preferably aged 10-year balsamico), for serving

Flaky sea salt and freshly ground black pepper

Bar Suzette's owners, Peter Tondreau and Troi Lughod, make this crêpe when the local New York apples are bountiful, during the cool months of the year. It really doesn't matter which kind of apple you use, as long as it is very thinly sliced to allow the crêpe to be folded without tearing. At Bar Suzette, they make authentically large French-style crêpes on a griddle (see Tips, opposite page), but the instructions below use an average nonstick skillet. (See photo on previous page.)

1. Make the crêpe batter: Blend the flour, milk, eggs, oil, rosemary leaves, garlic, and salt together in a blender, stopping the blender to scrape down the batter as needed, until it is smooth. Transfer it to a bowl, cover, and refrigerate it for at least 2 hours.

2. Lightly oil a 7-inch (17-cm) nonstick skillet (measured across the skillet bottom) with a folded paper towel dipped in the oil. (Never spray a nonstick skillet with aerosol cooking spray, as the propellant ingredients in the spray will stick to the surface and will break the pan's warranty.) Heat the skillet over medium heat until it is hot.

3. Pour ¼ cup (60 ml) of the batter into the skillet. Immediately and quickly tilt the pan so the batter swirls into a thin layer that coats the bottom. Fill any empty spots in the crêpe with drips of the batter. Cook until the crêpe looks set and the edges are dry, about 1 minute. Using a heatproof silicone spatula, lift up an edge of the crêpe and flip it over. Cook until the other side is set and lightly browned, about 45 seconds. Transfer it to a plate. Repeat with the remaining batter, separating the crêpes with sheets of parchment or waxed paper. You should have 12 to 14 crêpes. The crêpes can be stored at room temperature for up to 2 hours. (For longer storage, let the crêpes cool completely, wrap the stack in plastic wrap, and refrigerate it for up to 2 days or freeze for up to 1 month. Thaw the frozen crêpes before using.)

4. Make the filling: Preheat the oven to 350°F (170°C). Lightly butter a large baking sheet with some of the melted butter.

5. For each crêpe, place a crêpe in front of you, spotted side up. On the bottom right quadrant of the crêpe, place 2 apple wedges and 1 piece of Brie. Drizzle them with about ¾ teaspoon honey. Fold the crêpe in quarters to enclose the ingredients. Place it on the baking sheet. Repeat with the remaining crêpes and filling. Brush all of the folded crêpes with the remaining butter.

6. Bake until the crêpes are heated and the cheese is barely beginning to melt, about 10 minutes. To serve, transfer 2 filled crêpes to a dinner plate. Top each with an equal amount of the greens, drizzle with the vinegar to taste, and season with salt and pepper. Serve at once.

CRÊPES
Bar Suzette

Bar Suzette's cast-iron griddle serves up crêpes like the ones you can buy from street vendors in France. These Big Apple–size pancakes are about 1 foot (30.5 cm) wide, and filled, folded, and eaten from the bar's signature crêpe cones. Home cooks usually make crêpes in a nonstick skillet that is about 7 inches (17 cm) in diameter. The small crêpes taste magnifique, but with the right tools, you can make large crêpes just like the "real thing."

A 12-inch (30.5-cm) diameter electric crêpe pan, available at kitchenware shops and online, allows the home cook to make French-style crêpes. The pans can be reasonably priced or very expensive, but unless you are opening up a crêpe stand, you can probably get away with a lower priced model. Most electric pans come with a T-shaped wooden tool that helps spread the batter on the griddle in a thin layer. With a large French-style crêpe maker, each crêpe is filled while it is still on the griddle. They are best hot off the griddle, but the folded crêpes can be put on large rimmed baking sheets and kept warm in a very low oven until all of the crêpes are ready to serve.

Using a paper towel, lightly oil a large electric nonstick crêpe griddle and heat it according to the manufacturer's directions. Pour a scant ½ cup (120 ml) of batter onto the griddle. Quickly use the wooden spreader to spread the batter into a thin layer to cover the griddle. Fill any gaps in the crêpe with drips of batter. Cook until the batter looks set and the edges of the crêpe are dry, about 1 minute. Using a heatproof silicone spatula, lift up an edge of the crêpe and flip it over. Cook until the other side is golden brown, about 1 minute more. Scatter (or in some cases, spread) the desired filling ingredients over the crêpe. Using the spatula as an aide, fold the crêpe in half, then lengthwise into thirds, and transfer it to a large rimmed baking sheet. Keep it warm in a 200°F (90°C) oven until all of the crêpes are cooked and filled. The amount of batter and filling ingredients in the recipe will yield 6 large crêpes.

GRILLED ARTISAN CHEDDAR & FIG JAM SANDWICH

LUCY'S WHEY

SERVES 1

1 crusty rustic roll

2 tablespoons top-quality fig jam, preferably Mitica (see Note)

2 teaspoons fragrant extra-virgin olive oil

Flaky sea salt

3 ounces (85 g) artisan American Cheddar, preferably Prairie Breeze (see Note), cut into 3 thick slices

NOTE: *The Spanish company Mitica makes a fig jam that is sweetened only with lemon blossom honey, which gives it a pure flavor. Prairie Breeze Cheddar is a sweet and tangy cheese from Iowa, made by Milton Creamery with the high-quality milk of neighboring Amish farms. Any farmstead, artisan Cheddar would be a good substitute.*

The grilled cheese sandwich at Lucy's Whey has garnered an extensive group of followers. These devotees appreciate the careful attention that goes into each bite. With so few ingredients, each one should be extraordinary. If you follow this advice at home, you will see how a humble cheese sandwich can turn heads. You can make as many sandwiches at once as you have room for on a panini press (or in a ridged grill pan weighted on top with a skillet).

1. Heat a panini press according to the manufacturer's instructions. Alternatively, heat a ridged grill pan or large skillet over medium heat.

2. Using a serrated knife, cut the roll in half horizontally. Spread each cut side of the roll with 1 tablespoon of the fig jam, drizzle the jam with 1 teaspoon of the oil, and season it with the salt. Arrange the Cheddar pieces closely on the bottom roll half, being sure that the cheese does not hang over the sides of the roll. Cover it with the remaining roll half, jam-side down.

3. Place the sandwich in the panini press and cook it until the roll is toasted and golden brown and the cheese is desirably melty, about 4 minutes, depending on the press. If using a ridged grill pan or skillet, place the sandwich in the pan and top it with a cast-iron skillet or heavy saucepan. Cook until the underside is toasted, about 2 minutes. Flip the sandwich over, top it with the cast-iron skillet again, and cook until the other side is toasted and the cheese is melty, about 2 minutes more.

4. Cut the sandwich in half and serve it hot.

TOMATO & OLIVE PIZZA

AMY'S BREAD

MAKES 2 (17-BY-12-INCH/40-BY-30-CM) RECTANGULAR PIZZAS

FOR THE DOUGH:

1¼ cups plus 2 tablespoons (330 ml) warm water (105° to 115°F/40° to 45°C)

1¼ teaspoons active dry yeast

3¾ cups (465 g) unbleached all-purpose flour, plus extra for rolling

2 tablespoons olive oil, plus extra for the bowl

2½ teaspoons kosher salt

FOR THE TOPPING:

4 to 5 firm but ripe plum tomatoes, cut into ¼-inch (6-mm) rounds, shaken to remove seeds

8 ounces (225 g) crumbled goat cheese

1 cup (155 g) pitted kalamata olives

½ cup (50 g) freshly grated Parmesan cheese

Olive oil for brushing

Kosher salt and freshly ground black pepper

¼ cup (25 g) coarsely chopped fresh basil or oregano (optional)

The secret to great pizza is an amazing crust and simple, fresh toppings. This is a very simple and forgiving bread dough that is easy to knead and has a short rise—so even your kids can help! The only equipment you need is a hot oven and a large baking sheet because this pizza is made in an oblong shape that doesn't require a pizza stone or baker's peel. The Mediterranean ingredients make for a flavorful but light pizza that is also perfect as an appetizer or party snack.

1. Make the dough: Combine the water and yeast in a large bowl and stir to moisten the yeast. Let them stand for 3 minutes and stir to dissolve the yeast. Add the flour, oil, and salt; mix them with your fingers or a wooden spoon to bring the wet and dry ingredients together. When the dough becomes a shaggy mass, move it to a very lightly floured surface and knead until it becomes smooth and somewhat elastic, 5 to 7 minutes. This dough should not be too dry, or it will be difficult to stretch when you're shaping the pizza, so try not to knead in any extra flour. If necessary, add water or flour 1 tablespoon at a time until you have a soft, tacky dough. Gently shape the dough into a loose ball. Put it in a lightly oiled bowl, turn to coat it with oil, and cover it with oiled plastic wrap. Let it rise in a warm place until it has doubled in volume, 45 minutes to 1 hour.

2. Position a rack in the top third of the oven and preheat the oven to 450°F (230°C). Line two 18-by-13-inch (46-by-33-cm) half-sheet pans with parchment paper.

3. When the dough has doubled, loosen it from the bowl with lightly floured hands and gently put it onto a lightly floured work surface. Divide it into two equal pieces (about 12 ounces/360 g each). Shape each piece into a tight ball, dip them in flour, place them on the work surface, and cover them with plastic wrap to rest for 10 minutes.

4. Place a dough ball on a lightly floured work surface and press down to flatten it slightly. From the center, use your fingertips to gently press the dough out to a 17-by-12-inch (40-by-30-cm) oblong, leaving it slightly thicker around the edge. Do not tear the dough; you may have to lift the edges gently and shake the dough slightly to encourage the stretching. (You can also use a rolling pin; flour the work surface and the top of the dough lightly and lift and turn the disk frequently as you roll to be sure the dough doesn't stick.) If the dough resists stretching, let it rest again for 2 to 5 minutes, or until it will let you stretch it again. Keep letting the dough rest as necessary until you achieve the size you want. Gently move the dough onto a prepared sheet pan and stretch it to fit the pan. Repeat with the remaining dough ball.

5. Make the topping: Leaving a ½-inch (12-mm) border on the dough, top it with half of the tomato slices, half of the goat cheese, half of the olives, and half of the Parmesan. Lightly brush the exposed dough on the perimeter of the pizza with oil.

6. Bake the pizza for 14 to 16 minutes, or until the crust is crisp and golden and the cheese is melting but not fully browned. You need to

(continued)

make sure the pizza is baked enough to dry out the tomatoes somewhat or the crust will be soggy. During the last few minutes of baking, top the second pizza with the remaining ingredients. Transfer the hot pizza in the pan to a wire cooling rack. Bake the second pizza for 14 to 16 minutes.

7. Let the first pizza stand for about 3 minutes. Slide the pie out of the pan onto a cutting surface, parchment and all. Season the pizza with salt and pepper and sprinkle with half of the basil or oregano, if using. Discard the parchment and use a pizza wheel or a long chef's knife to cut the pizza into 6 to 8 pieces. Serve it immediately. When the second pizza is done, let it stand on the wire rack for 3 minutes, then slice and serve.

This beautiful and delicious tart is a specialty of Dominick Coyne, Jamestown's resident designer, and he makes it often when summer tomatoes and basil are abundant. (Truth be known, it is also a good way to bring a bit of summery cheer to a winter dinner with hothouse tomatoes.) Serve it warm or at room temperature as a substantial first course (add a handful of dressed greens), as a light lunch or supper (with a larger serving of greens), or even at brunch (with scrambled eggs on the side). A colorful combination of tomatoes makes the tart even more appealing.

1. Make the dough: Pulse the flour and salt together in a food processor a few times just to combine. Add the butter and pulse about 10 times, until the mixture resembles coarse meal with some pea-size pieces of butter. (Or mix the flour and salt in a bowl, and cut in the butter with a pastry blender.) Transfer the mixture to a bowl. Gradually stir the water (start with less than the full amount; you may need more or less water) into the flour mixture until it clumps together. Gather the dough into a thick disk and wrap it with plastic wrap. Refrigerate the dough for 1 to 2 hours.

2. Unwrap the dough. On a lightly floured work surface, roll out the dough into a ⅛-inch- (3-mm-) thick round about 12 inches (30.5 cm) in diameter. Fit it into a 9-inch (23-cm) tart pan with a removable bottom, being sure that the dough fits snugly in the corners of the pan without stretching. Trim off excess dough so the dough is flush with the top of the pan. Pierce the dough all over with a fork. Freeze it for 15 to 30 minutes.

3. Position a rack in the center of the oven and preheat the oven to 400°F (205°C).

4. Meanwhile, make the roasted garlic: Cut the garlic head in half crosswise, without breaking up the clusters of cloves. Place the halves, cut-side up, on a piece of aluminum foil and drizzle them with the oil. Reshape the garlic into its original head and wrap it in the foil.

5. Remove the dough from the freezer and line the dough in the pan with a 15-inch (38-cm) round of parchment paper. Top the paper with pastry weights or dried beans to fill the pastry shell. Place the pan on a rimmed baking sheet and transfer it to the oven. Place the foil-wrapped garlic directly on the oven rack.

6. Bake until the visible edges of the dough look set and are beginning to brown, about 20 minutes. Lift off the paper with the weights. Pierce the dough again and continue baking until the dough is lightly browned, about 5 additional minutes. Remove it from the oven and let it cool on the baking sheet.

7. Continue baking the garlic until the flesh is very tender and deep beige (open the foil to check), 20 to 30 minutes more. Remove it from the oven, unwrap, and let it cool until it is easy to handle. Squeeze the garlic flesh out of its peels into a small bowl, discarding the peels. Mash the flesh with a fork. Season it with salt and pepper.

(continued)

SUMMER TOMATO TART

CHELSEA MARKET FAMILY RECIPE

SERVES 6 AS A MAIN COURSE; 8 AS AN APPETIZER

FOR THE DOUGH:

1⅔ cups (210 g) unbleached all-purpose flour, plus extra for rolling

½ teaspoon fine sea salt

10 tablespoons (1¼ sticks/140 g) cold unsalted butter, cut into ½-inch (12-mm) cubes

⅓ cup (75 ml) ice water, as needed

FOR THE ROASTED GARLIC:

1 large head garlic

1 tablespoon extra-virgin olive oil

Kosher salt and freshly ground black pepper

FOR THE TART:

2 large or 4 small red and yellow heirloom tomatoes (about 1¾ pounds/570 g)

1 cup (120 g) shredded fontina cheese

1 tablespoon extra-virgin olive oil

2 tablespoons finely chopped fresh basil

Special equipment: 9-inch (23 cm) tart pan with removeable bottom; dried beans or pie weights

8. Make the tart: Increase the oven temperature to 425°F (220°C). Slice the tomatoes into ½-inch- (12-mm-) thick slices. Spread them on paper towels and let them drain briefly on both cut sides.

9. Using a small offset spatula or the back of a spoon, spread the mashed garlic evenly in the bottom of the tart shell. Sprinkle it with ¾ cup (90 g) of the fontina. Arrange the alternating colors of the tomato slices in overlapping concentric circles in the shell. Season them with salt and pepper. Sprinkle them with the remaining fontina, and then drizzle them with the oil. Return the tart to the oven and bake until the tomatoes are lightly browned and the cheese is melted, 20 to 25 minutes. Let it cool in the pan for 10 minutes. Remove the tart pan. Sprinkle the top with the basil. Cut the tart into wedges and serve hot or warm.

Like pasta, risotto can be a blank canvas for a seemingly endless array of variations. Ronnybrook's contribution to the risotto canon can be served as a vegetarian entrée or in smaller portions as a first course to a special dinner. The selection of mushrooms in the recipe is just a suggestion; use whatever assortment you prefer, keeping in mind that some give off more liquid and therefore take longer to cook.

1. Make the mushrooms: Melt the butter in a large skillet over medium-high heat. Add the mushrooms and cook, stirring occasionally, until their juices evaporate and they begin to brown, about 8 minutes. Stir in the shallots and cook until they are tender, about 2 minutes. Season them with salt and pepper. Remove the pan from the heat. Cover to keep the mushrooms warm.

2. Meanwhile, make the risotto: Bring the stock to a boil in a medium saucepan over high heat. Reduce the heat to very low to keep the stock hot, but not simmering.

3. Heat the oil in a large, heavy-bottomed saucepan over medium heat. Add the shallots and cook, stirring often, until they are softened, about 1 minute. Add the rice and cook, stirring almost constantly, until it turns chalky white and feels heavy in the spoon, about 3 minutes. Do not let the rice brown. Stir in about ¾ cup (180 ml) of the hot stock and adjust the heat to keep the mixture cooking at a steady, but not too fast, simmer. Cook, stirring almost constantly, until the rice has absorbed almost all of the stock, about 1½ minutes. Stir in another ¾ cup (180 ml) of stock and stir until it is absorbed. Repeat adding and stirring the stock until the rice is barely tender, about 20 minutes in total. With the last addition of stock, the risotto should be loose and flowing. If you run out of stock before the rice is cooked, use very hot water. Stir in the cream and butter, followed by the cheese. Season the risotto with salt and pepper.

4. Divide the risotto among shallow soup bowls. Top each with the warm mushrooms and a sprinkle of chives. Serve immediately.

TIPS FROM THE PROS

RISOTTO RICE
Buon'Italia

Arborio is the most common rice variety for risotto, but it isn't the only one. Vialone Nano and Carnaroli also make excellent risottos. These medium-grain varieties contain a high level of starch. Vialone Nano has the highest, followed by Arborio and Carnaroli. The more starch, the creamier the risotto. Home cooks often shy away from risotto because they think it needs constant attention. The rice does need to be stirred a lot, but you can leave the stove every now and then.

BLUE CHEESE RISOTTO
WITH WILD MUSHROOMS

RONNYBROOK FARM DAIRY

SERVES 4 AS A MAIN COURSE; 6 AS AN APPETIZER

FOR THE MUSHROOMS:

2 tablespoons unsalted butter

8 ounces (225 g) fresh shiitake mushroom caps, sliced

4 ounces (115 g) fresh cremini mushrooms, sliced

¼ cup (40 g) finely chopped shallots

Kosher salt and freshly ground black pepper

FOR THE RISOTTO:

5 cups (1.2 L) Vegetable Stock (page 58) or reduced-sodium vegetable broth

2 tablespoons extra-virgin olive oil

½ cup (80 g) finely chopped shallots

1¼ cups (225 g) Arborio rice (see Tips)

¼ cup (60 ml) heavy cream

1 tablespoon unsalted butter

½ cup (60 g) crumbled firm blue cheese

Kosher salt and freshly ground black pepper

Finely chopped fresh chives, for serving

BROWN RICE BOWL

WITH ASIAN VEGETABLES & SESAME-LIME DRESSING

FRIEDMAN'S LUNCH

SERVES 4 TO 6

FOR THE BROWN RICE:

2 cups (370 g) long-grain brown rice

1½ teaspoons kosher salt

FOR THE SESAME-LIME DRESSING:

4 garlic cloves, peeled

2 tablespoons peeled and chopped fresh ginger

1 large scallion, white and green parts, coarsely chopped

¼ cup (60 ml) tamari or soy sauce

¼ cup (60 ml) fresh lime juice

¼ cup (60 ml) unseasoned rice vinegar

¼ cup (60 ml) Thai sweet chile sauce

2 tablespoons honey

1 tablespoon toasted sesame oil

¼ cup (60 ml) canola oil

FOR THE ASIAN VEGETABLES:

2 long Japanese eggplants (about 1½ pounds/680 g total), trimmed and cut into ½-inch (12-mm) rounds

4 tablespoons (60 ml) canola oil

Kosher salt and freshly ground black pepper

1 pound (455 g) baby bok choy

2 large carrots, cut into julienne

1 pound (455 g) fresh bean sprouts

1 cup (185 g) thawed frozen edamame beans (without pods)

2 scallions, white and green parts

The ingredient list for this healthful dish looks long, but the concept is simple: Serve your favorite stir-fried vegetables over brown rice, and top them with a zesty dressing. Eggplant tends to soak up a lot of oil during frying, so to keep the dish light, Japanese eggplant is roasted before being added to the stir-fry. Protein is supplied by the edamame.

1. Make the brown rice: Combine the rice, 4 cups (960 ml) water, and the salt in a medium heavy-bottomed saucepan. Bring to a boil over high heat. Reduce the heat to low and cover tightly. Simmer until the rice is tender and the liquid is absorbed, about 40 minutes. Remove the pan from the heat and let it stand, covered, for 5 minutes.

2. Make the sesame-lime dressing: Pulse the garlic, ginger, and scallion together in a blender until they are finely chopped. Add the tamari, lime juice, vinegar, chile sauce, honey, and sesame oil and pulse until they are combined. With the blender running, pour the canola oil through the hole in the lid and blend until the dressing is smooth and emulsified. Set aside.

3. Make the Asian vegetables: Position a rack in the top third of the oven and preheat the oven to 400°F (205°C).

4. Toss the eggplant with 2 tablespoons of the oil, 1 teaspoon salt, and ½ teaspoon pepper in a large bowl. Spread it on a large rimmed baking sheet. Bake, flipping occasionally, until the eggplant is lightly browned and tender, about 20 minutes. Remove it from the oven and let it cool.

5. When the rice is ready to serve, stir-fry the remaining vegetables: Coarsely chop the bok choy. Heat a wok or large skillet over high heat. Pour in the 2 remaining tablespoons oil and swirl to coat the wok with the oil. Add the bok choy and stir-fry until it is softened, about 2 minutes. Add the carrots and stir-fry until softened, about 1 minute. Add the roasted eggplant, bean sprouts, and edamame and stir-fry until they are heated through, about 1 minute. Season them with salt and pepper. Remove the pan from the heat.

6. Slice the scallions into thin rounds. Divide the rice among four to six deep soup bowls and top it with equal amounts of the Asian vegetables. Sprinkle with the sliced scallions. Serve immediately, with the sesame-lime dressing passed on the side.

PASTA WITH CREAMY ROASTED TOMATO SAUCE

RONNYBROOK FARM DAIRY

SERVES 4 TO 6

4 pounds (1.8 kg) red heirloom or beefsteak tomatoes, halved crosswise

Extra-virgin olive oil

Kosher salt and freshly ground black pepper

½ cup (80 g) sliced shallots

4 garlic cloves

½ cup (120 ml) Vegetable Stock (page 58) or reduced-sodium vegetable broth, as needed

1 cup (40 g) packed fresh basil leaves

¼ cup (60 ml) heavy cream

1 pound thin pasta, such as angel hair (capellini) or vermicelli

Coarsely chopped fresh basil leaves, for garnish

Freshly grated hard cheese, preferably local, or Parmigiano-Reggiano, for serving

Many tomato sauces simmer on top of the stove for hours, a time-honored and reliable technique. But the folks at Ronnybrook have discovered that cooking the tomatoes in a charcoal grill concentrates the tomato juices, imparting a smoky flavor in the bargain, and finishing the dish with their famous heavy cream adds a luscious richness. The recipe will also work in a gas grill, and we've provided an oven-roasted variation as well. This meatless sauce is best savored with thin pasta, such as angel hair or vermicelli.

1. Prepare an outdoor grill for cooking over indirect high heat. A charcoal grill fueled with hardwood charcoal is preferred for this recipe, as it will impart the most flavor, but a gas grill will work, too. For a charcoal grill, build a fire on one side of the grill, leaving the other side empty. Let the coals burn until they are covered with white ash and you can hold your hand just above the cooking grate for only 2 to 3 seconds. For a gas grill, preheat the grill to high, then turn off half of the burners. Adjust the thermostats to medium (400°F/205°C).

2. Brush the tomatoes with oil and season them with salt and pepper. Arrange them, cut-side up, on the empty (unignited) side of the grill. Cook, with the lid closed as much as possible, until the tomatoes are lightly charred and juicy, about 30 minutes. Carefully transfer the tomatoes to a bowl, reserving as much juice as possible.

3. Heat 2 tablespoons of oil in a large saucepan over medium heat. Add the shallots and garlic and cook, stirring often, until they are softened, about 3 minutes. Add the roasted tomatoes and bring to a simmer. Reduce the heat to medium-low. Simmer, stirring often and breaking up the tomatoes with the side of a wooden spoon, until the juices thicken, 20 to 30 minutes. If the sauce gets too thick, thin it with the stock as needed. Stir in the basil and cream.

4. In batches, transfer the sauce to a food processor. Pulse the mixture a few times into a coarse purée (do not pulverize the tomato seeds). If desired, pass it through a food mill or wire mesh sieve to remove the seeds and skins. Return the sauce to the saucepan and keep it warm over low heat.

5. Meanwhile, bring a large pot of salted water to a boil over high heat. Add the pasta and cook according to the package directions, until it is al dente. Drain it well and return it to the pot. Add the tomato sauce to the pasta and mix well. Spoon it into deep bowls and top each with a sprinkle of basil leaves. Serve hot with the grated cheese on the side.

VARIATION: Roasted Tomato Sauce: To cook the tomatoes indoors, preheat the oven to 400°F (205°C). Oil a large rimmed baking sheet. Place the tomatoes, cut-side up, on the baking sheet. Drizzle them with 2 tablespoons olive oil and season them with salt and pepper. Roast until the tomatoes are tender and their edges are lightly charred, about 45 minutes. Proceed as directed.

Tonarelli cacio e pepe is a super-simple Roman specialty of pasta in a light cheese sauce with plenty of cracked pepper. Giovanni Rana Pastificio & Cucina gives it a "green" touch with the addition of fresh artichokes, garlic, and vegetable stock. Trimming an artichoke and its stem down to the fleshy base is an essential technique of Italian cuisine. You'll master it in no time with a little practice and a sharp paring knife. This dish is sensational with fresh pasta—just like the kind you'll find at Rana's beautifully rustic restaurant on the Ninth Avenue side of the Market.

1. Squeeze the juice of one lemon half into a medium bowl and add 2 quarts (2 L) cold water. Working with one artichoke at a time, pull off and discard the tough, olive green outer leaves to reach the pale green, tender leaves in the shape of an upside-down cone. Cut off and discard the cone of leaves at the indentation where it meets the firm, bulbous artichoke bottom. Cut the base in half lengthwise through the stem. Using the tip of the knife, dig out and discard the "hairy" choke. Rinse the artichoke bottoms under cold running water. Rub the cut areas with the remaining lemon half. Using the knife, pare away the dark green skin from the bottom of the heart and the stem. Put the trimmed artichokes in the bowl of lemon water. Repeat with remaining artichokes. (The artichokes can be prepared through this step up to 2 hours ahead.)

2. When ready to cook, drain the trimmed artichokes. Using a large knife, slice each artichoke, with the stem, lengthwise into slices about ¼-inch (6-mm) thick, then cut the slices into strips about ⅛-inch (3-mm) wide. The strips will be of varying lengths.

3. Pour the oil into a very large skillet, large enough to hold the drained pasta, and add the artichoke strips and garlic. Cook over medium heat, stirring often, until the artichoke begins to soften without coloring, about 3 minutes. Add the vegetable stock and season lightly with salt and pepper. Bring to a boil over high heat, then reduce the heat to medium-low and cover, with the lid ajar. Cook at brisk simmer until the artichokes are just tender and the stock has evaporated, about 15 minutes, adding a few tablespoons of water to the skillet if the liquid evaporates before the artichokes are done. Season lightly again with salt and pepper. Remove from the heat, cover, and keep warm.

4. Meanwhile, bring a large pot of lightly salted water to a boil over high heat. Add the *tonarelli* to the water and cook according to the package instructions, until al dente. Reserve ¾ cup (180 ml) of the cooking water. Drain the *tonarelli* well.

5. Add the drained *tonarelli* and the ½ cup (120 ml) of the reserved pasta cooking water to the artichoke mixture in the skillet. Cook over medium-low heat, using kitchen tongs to thoroughly combine the *tonarelli* and artichoke mixture. Remove the skillet from the heat and add the Pecorino Romano and parsley. Mix well, adding the remaining ¼ cup (60 ml) pasta water as needed to make a clinging and creamy sauce. Season generously with additional pepper, and add more salt, if needed. Transfer to bowls and serve immediately.

TONARELLI

WITH ARTICHOKES & PECORINO ROMANO

GIOVANNI RANA PASTIFICO & CUCINA

SERVES 4 TO 6

1 lemon, halved

4 large artichokes with stems, about 2½ pounds (1.2 kg) total

3 tablespoons extra-virgin olive oil

1 garlic clove, minced

1 cup (240 ml) Vegetable Stock (page 58) or water

Kosher salt and freshly ground black pepper

1 pound (450 g) *tonarelli*, spaghetti, or linguine, preferably fresh

1⅓ cups (160 g) freshly grated Pecorino Romano

3 tablespoons finely chopped fresh flat-leaf parsley

Lasagna is often thought of as a carnivore's dish, but this vegetarian recipe has been in the Ruthy's family for over fifty years. Ruthy's only uses the very best organic vegetables to make this, and you can follow suit. If you prefer to broil the vegetables instead of grilling them outdoors, go ahead. The lasagna will fill its pan to the brim, but it will shrink a bit during baking, so don't be alarmed—just be sure to put a baking sheet under the pan to catch any drips. Because the lasagna itself doesn't have tomatoes, serve it with your favorite tomato sauce. The Creamy Roasted Tomato Sauce on page 150 is an especially good option.

1. Make the pesto oil: Pulse the pine nuts, Parmesan, and garlic in a food processor until the pine nuts are minced. Add the basil and pulse until it is finely chopped. With the machine running, gradually pour in the oil. Transfer the pesto oil to a bowl. Season it with salt. Cover the pesto oil with plastic wrap and set it aside.

2. Make the grilled vegetables: Prepare an outdoor grill for cooking over direct medium heat. For a charcoal grill, let the coals burn until they are covered with white ash, and you can hold your hand just above the cooking grate for only 2 to 3 seconds. For a gas grill, preheat it to high. Adjust the thermostats to medium-high (450°F/230°C). Brush the cooking grates clean. (Alternatively, position an oven broiler rack about 6 inches/15 cm from the heat source and preheat the broiler.)

3. Whisk the oil and vinegar together. Arrange the zucchini, squash, eggplants, and onions on baking sheets. Brush the vegetables on both sides with the oil mixture. Don't worry if the onions separate into rings.

4. In batches, place the vegetables on the grill and cover them with the grill lid. Cook, flipping the vegetables over halfway through cooking, until they are lightly browned and barely tender. Transfer the vegetables to a large bowl as they are done. Cook the zucchini, squash, and onions for 6 to 8 minutes (taking care that the onions don't fall through the grate); cook the eggplants for 8 to 10 minutes.

5. Put the peppers on the grill with the skin-side down (or under the broiler skin-up). Cook (if grilling), covered, until the skins are blistered and blackened, about 10 minutes; transfer them to a small bowl, cover with plastic wrap, and let stand for 5 minutes. Peel off and discard the blackened skin. Coarsely chop the vegetables and transfer to a large bowl. Season with salt and pepper.

6. Bring a large pot of salted water to a boil over high heat. Add the lasagna noodles and cook just until they are almost but not quite tender, about 7 minutes. Drain, rinse them under cold running water, and drain again.

7. Assemble the lasagna: Lightly oil a 15-by-10-by-2-inch (38-by-25-by-5-cm) baking dish. Spread ½ cup (120 ml) of the pesto oil in the bottom of the dish. Stir the ricotta and ½ cup (120 ml) of the pesto oil together in a large bowl and season with the coarse salt and pepper.

(continued)

GRILLED VEGETABLE & PESTO LASAGNA

RUTHY'S

SERVES 12

FOR THE PESTO OIL:

¼ cup (35 g) pine nuts

¼ cup (25 g) freshly grated Parmesan

2 garlic cloves, minced

2½ cups (100 g) packed fresh basil leaves

1¼ cups (300 ml) extra-virgin olive oil

Coarse salt, preferably Himalayan pink salt or kosher salt

FOR THE GRILLED VEGETABLES:

⅓ cup (75 ml) extra-virgin olive oil

1 tablespoon balsamic vinegar

2 zucchini, halved lengthwise

2 yellow squash, halved lengthwise

2 globe eggplants (about 3 pounds/1.5 kg), cut into ¼-inch- (6-mm-) thick rounds

2 large yellow onions, cut into ¼-inch- (6-mm-) thick rounds

4 red or yellow bell peppers, cored and quartered lengthwise

Freshly ground black pepper

1 pound (455 g) lasagna noodles

Extra-virgin olive oil, for the baking dish

1 (32-ounce/1-L) container whole milk or part-skim ricotta cheese

2 cups (240 g) shredded mozzarella

2 cups (200 g) finely grated Parmesan

8. Arrange 6 lasagna noodles in the dish (4 horizontally and 2 vertically), trimming them to fit. Spread them with one-third of the ricotta mixture. Arrange half of the grilled vegetables closely together on top of the ricotta mixture. Sprinkle them with one-third each of the mozzarella and Parmesan, then drizzle them with 3 tablespoons of the pesto oil. Repeat with 6 more noodles, half of the remaining ricotta, and the remaining grilled vegetables, topped with half of the remaining mozzarella and Parmesan and another 3 tablespoons of pesto oil. Finish with the remaining lasagna noodles, spread them with the remaining ricotta, and top them with the remaining mozzarella and Parmesan. Set the remaining pesto oil aside. (The lasagna can be stored at room temperature for up to 2 hours before baking.)

9. Preheat the oven to 350°F (175°C).

10. Bake, uncovered, until a small knife inserted into the center of the lasagna for 10 seconds comes out hot and the cheese topping is golden brown, about 1¼ hours. Let it stand at room temperature for 10 to 15 minutes. Cut the lasagna into twelve equal portions and serve drizzled with the reserved pesto oil.

THE HOME COOK'S KITCHEN

BOWERY KITCHEN SUPPLY

When Bowery Kitchen Supply opened in 1996, the Chelsea Market and the New York food scenes were more low key than they are today. Even though food was on every New Yorker's mind and the Food Network was up and running, there was still a division between the home kitchen and the professional kitchen. Slowly but surely, the store began to feel the influence of the television chefs on business. When Mario Batali used a huge cleaver on the air to chop up a whole pig, phone calls poured in from viewers wanting to place orders for the same cleaver. (We didn't ask what they were going to do with it.) Producers from *Emeril Live!* would scour the store for new kitchenware items to promote on the show.

Eventually, more and more customers were asking for professional tools for their everyday cooking. They had come to realize that these knives, pans, and other equipment were made to last, and that the tools they saw their favorite chefs using on TV were more utilitarian than they were pretty. That said, there are exceptions, as our knife selection (the largest in New York) shows. It's hard to dispute the beauty of a Damascus-style knife, with its intricate wave pattern hammered into the blade. And surrounding yourself with beautiful things is one of the true pleasures of life, so why not do it when you can afford it?

Here is our list of the essential kitchen tools, utensils, and appliances that will show that you are a serious cook.

KNIVES: You really only need three knives. First, a Western-style chef's knife with a blade about 8 inches (20 cm) long. This will take care of most kitchen chores, from chopping onions to mincing herbs. (Why Western-style? Because this kind of knife is designed and weighted for chopping, while a rounded-tip knife [santoku] is really meant for slicing only.) A narrow knife with a flexible, thin 5-inch (12-cm) blade will help you bone fish, chicken, and meat, and pare vegetables and fruit. A serrated knife is necessary for cutting bread and some delicate foods, such as tomatoes.

Choose knives that fit well into your hand. One person's "just right" is another's "too big." But even more, be sure that the knife is easy to sharpen. It used to be that you had to choose between looks and efficiency with knives, but modern metals have changed all that. Some cooks still prefer the old-fashioned carbon steel blade because, even though the metal stains easily, it holds its edge well. The "perfect knife" is a matter of personal taste, and sometimes people are surprised to find that after "test driving" a few at the shop, they choose a less expensive one.

A WELL-MADE CUTTING BOARD: Some cutting boards made out of glass or hard plastic will actually dull your knives. Well, that's not good! We like cutting boards made from layered and pressed recycled paper. They are lightweight and practically indestructible.

A JAPANESE V-SLICER: If you want to really rachet up your cooking game, a V-slicer will help you make uniformly cut pieces of vegetables and fruits for salads, appetizers, and more. This tool is a lighter, more user-friendly version of an expensive mandoline, which has an adjustable blade so you can vary the width of the slices. With a few quick moves, you can make perfectly formed julienne strips of carrot or ultra-thin potato rounds. One piece of advice: The slicing guard is there for a reason, so use it.

SQUEEZE BOTTLES: For a couple of bucks, you can have a tool that will help you get your sauce to go where you want it to go, creating professional-looking drizzles and squiggles for chef-worthy garnishes.

A VEGETABLE PEELER: Get a sturdy, simple, but strong peeler with a rust-free blade because you never know when life is going to require you to peel celery root or rutabaga. These vegetables laugh at flimsy peelers.

A MICRO ZESTER: This tool looks like a carpenter's rasp, and is used to quickly remove the zest from citrus fruits. There are a variety of sizes, although most cooks like the citrus zester because it is really all-purpose, and can be used to make fine shavings of coconut and chocolate to dress up desserts, or to grate Parmesan over pasta.

A MEAT TENDERIZER: We sell an awful lot of these to restaurants, so we know that they depend on them. Get a large heavy model, with two different surfaces on the head: one flat, to help pound boneless skinless chicken breasts into even thickness, and the other spiked, to break down tough cuts of meat.

AT LEAST THREE HALF-SHEET PANS: The workhorse of the professional kitchen, an 18-by-13-inch (46-by-33-cm) half-sheet pan is much more than a baking sheet ... although it does that job admirably. (A full-sheet pan is twice as long, making it too big for the home oven.) When you are cooking a complicated recipe, prep the ingredients and use the half-sheet pan as a holding tray. Chefs use half-sheet pans as a carrying tray to transport food around the kitchen, or to hold items in the refrigerator before baking (as instructed in the Rugelach recipe on page 185).

ALUMINUM POTS AND PANS: When the neighborhood restaurants come to replace cooking utensils, they head right to the aluminum wares. Aluminum is the best conductor of heat, and can stand up to the high flames of a professional stove. Especially if you have a range with high BTUs (British Thermal Units, the unit used to measure the heat output on a stove burner), consider aluminum.

A HEAVY-DUTY STANDING MIXER: We don't know a single professional chef who uses a hand mixer. The main reason for its popularity is that it frees your hands to move on to another task. Chefs don't have the time to stand in the kitchen and hold the mixer, and you probably don't either!

CHAPTER 9

ROUNDING OUT THE MEAL

SIDE DISHES

BUTTERNUT SQUASH & POTATO GRATIN

THE GREEN TABLE

SERVES 8

2 tablespoons unsalted butter, plus more for the baking dish

2 leeks, white and pale green parts coarsely chopped and rinsed

Kosher salt and freshly ground black pepper

1 teaspoon finely chopped fresh thyme

2 cups (480 ml) heavy cream, as needed

½ teaspoon sweet paprika

⅛ teaspoon freshly grated nutmeg

1 (2-pound/910-g) butternut squash

1 pound (455 g) Yukon Gold potatoes, peeled

¼ cup (25 g) freshly grated hard cheese, preferably locally produced

This is hardly a side dish, but a gratin of epic proportions that could steal the show from a holiday turkey or roast pork. The sweet squash and leeks are balanced with the neutral potatoes, and it is all held together with a luxurious binding of cream. Note that you will be using only about half of the butternut squash, so you will have leftovers for another purpose. If you wish, make a double batch in a 4-quart (3.8-L) baking pan, and allow about 2 hours baking time. We can't recommend this gratin enough, and we often serve it with salad as a vegetarian main course. (See photo on previous page.)

1. Position a rack in the center of the oven and preheat it to 400°F (205°C). Generously butter a 2-quart (2-L) shallow baking dish that is about 2 inches (5 cm) deep.

2. Melt the butter in a large skillet over medium heat. Add the leeks, season them with salt and pepper, and cook, stirring occasionally, until they are tender but not browned, about 8 minutes. Stir in the thyme. Remove them from the heat.

3. Combine the cream, paprika, and nutmeg with 1 teaspoon salt and ½ teaspoon pepper in a medium saucepan. Bring them to a simmer over medium heat. Remove the saucepan from the heat and cover with a lid to keep warm.

4. Cut the top "neck" from the butternut squash where it meets the bulbous bottom. Set the bottom aside for another use. Peel the remaining squash and remove the seeds. You should have about 1 pound (455 g) peeled squash.

5. Using a mandoline, a plastic V-slicer, or a large sharp knife, cut the squash and potatoes into ⅛-inch- (3-mm-) thick slices. Mix the potatoes and squash together in a large bowl. Spread one third of the potato mixture in the baking dish and top with one half of the leeks. Pour one third of the warm cream mixture evenly over the vegetables. Repeat with another third of the potato mixture, the remaining leeks, and another third of the cream mixture. Finish with the remaining potato mixture. Slowly pour the remaining cream mixture evenly over the vegetables, moving them with a fork to spread them into an even layer, until they are barely covered with the cream mixture. Add more cream, if needed. Sprinkle the top with the cheese. Loosely cover the baking dish with aluminum foil and place it on a rimmed baking sheet.

6. Bake for 45 minutes. Remove the foil. Reduce the heat to 350°F (175°C). Continue baking until the gratin is golden brown and tender when pierced in the center with the tip of a small sharp knife and the cream has thickened, about 45 additional minutes. If the top becomes too brown before the vegetables are tender, tent the gratin with foil.

7. Let the gratin stand at room temperature for 10 minutes before serving.

The toasty flavor of garlic butter is almost magical in how it can enhance so many simple dishes, as it does in Ori Cosentino's take on mashed potatoes. It is worth making a double batch of the garlic butter to have extra to refrigerate and have ready for adding to grilled or steamed vegetables, popcorn, or for making fantastic garlic bread.

1. Make the garlic butter: Combine the garlic and oil in a small saucepan. Cook them over very low heat, stirring occasionally, until the garlic turns golden brown around the edges, about 15 minutes. Remove the pan from the heat and let it stand for 5 minutes. Transfer the garlic mixture to a blender. Add the butter and process it until smooth. Transfer the garlic butter to a bowl and season it with salt and pepper. (The garlic butter can be refrigerated in an airtight container for up to 5 days. Bring it to room temperature before using.)

2. Put the potatoes in a large saucepan and add enough cold salted water to cover them by 1 inch (2.5 cm). Cover the pan and bring it to a boil over high heat. Uncover and reduce the heat to medium. Cook at a brisk simmer until the potatoes are tender when pierced with the tip of a small sharp knife, about 20 minutes. Drain them well and return them to the pot.

3. Add the garlic butter to the potatoes. Using a potato masher, mash the potatoes, adding enough of the warm milk as needed to reach the desired consistency. Season the potatoes with salt and pepper. Transfer them to a serving bowl and serve them hot.

GARLIC-BUTTER MASHED POTATOES

CHELSEA MARKET FAMILY RECIPE

SERVES 4 TO 6

FOR THE GARLIC BUTTER:

10 large garlic cloves, smashed and peeled

¼ cup (60 ml) olive oil

4 tablespoons (½ stick/55 grams) unsalted butter, softened

Kosher salt and freshly ground black pepper

2 pounds (910 g) Yukon Gold potatoes, peeled and cut into 2-inch (5-cm) chunks

¼ cup (60 ml) whole milk, warmed

Kosher salt and freshly ground black pepper

POTATO MILLE-FEUILLE

WITH BLUE CHEESE & HERBS

MARC FORGIONE, GUEST CHEF

SERVES 6

2 tablespoons unsalted butter, at room temperature

1 tablespoon canola oil

5 garlic cloves, thinly sliced

½ sweet onion, preferably Vidalia, thinly sliced

1 tablespoon finely chopped fresh summer savory

2 teaspoons finely chopped fresh flat-leaf parsley

2 teaspoons finely chopped fresh rosemary

2 cups (480 ml) Veal Stock or Chicken Stock (page 56) or reduced-sodium chicken broth

2 pounds (910 g) baking (russet) potatoes

1¼ teaspoons kosher salt

½ teaspoon freshly ground black pepper

¾ cup (85 g) crumbled blue cheese, preferably Maytag

3 sprigs fresh thyme

1 small bay leaf

Special equipment: 2 (8-inch/20-cm) square baking dishes; a mandoline or plastic V-slicer

Potato gratin is one of the most beloved of all side dishes (American scalloped potatoes fall into the same category), with potato slices baked into a tender, golden brown mass. Marc Forgione's take on the classic gratin is made from paper-thin slices that give the dish a similarity to the layers in puff pastry (*mille-feuille* in French). It is cooked well before serving, then cut into portions and reheated, making it a recipe that is as useful as it is delicious.

1. At least six hours before serving, position an oven rack in the center of the oven and preheat it to 400°F (205°F). Generously butter an 8-inch (20-cm) baking dish with the butter.

2. Heat the oil in a medium skillet over medium heat. Add the garlic and cook, stirring often, until it is lightly browned, about 1 minute. Add the onion and cook, stirring often, until it is softened, about 3 minutes. Stir in the savory, parsley, and rosemary and cook until it is very fragrant, about 1 minute. Add the stock and bring it to a boil. Remove the pan from the heat.

3. Peel the potatoes. Using a mandoline, plastic V-slicer, or a large sharp knife, cut the potatoes into very thin (1/16-inch/2-mm) rounds. Mix the salt and pepper together in a small bowl. Layer one quarter of the potatoes in the prepared dish and season them with one third of the salt and pepper. Using a slotted spoon, top them with one third of the onions, garlic, and herbs in the skillet. Sprinkle the onions with one third of the blue cheese, and ladle in about one quarter of the stock. Repeat the layers twice with the remaining ingredients. Finish with the remaining potatoes and stock. Put the thyme and bay leaf on the potatoes. Cover the dish tightly with aluminum foil and place it on a rimmed baking sheet.

4. Bake it for 20 minutes. Reduce the oven temperature to 350°F (175°C) and remove the foil. Continue baking until the top is golden brown and the potatoes are very tender when pierced with the tip of small knife, about 1 hour. Remove the pan from the oven and let it cool for 30 minutes. Discard the thyme and bay leaf.

5. Place an 8-inch (20-cm) square of parchment paper on the potatoes. Top the parchment with the second baking dish. Fill the top dish with a few heavy food cans. Refrigerate the whole thing to chill and compress the *mille-feuille* for at least 5 hours and up to 1 day.

6. When you are ready to serve, preheat the oven to 350°F (175°C). Run a knife around the inside of the pan to release the *mille-feuille*. Cut it into six equal portions. Using a metal spatula, remove the portions and transfer them to a rimmed baking sheet. Bake the *mille-feuille* until it is heated through, about 20 minutes. Serve it hot.

When corn comes into season at the Market, you will sometimes see shoppers weighed down with bags of the stuff. Now, we love corn on the cob, but this creamy pudding of puréed corn spiced with smoky chipotle has become a new favorite, and the recipe (originating with coauthor Rick) has made the rounds at the Market. It goes with so many things, from ribs at a backyard barbecue to a platter of fried chicken.

1. Position a rack in the center of the oven and preheat it to 350°F (175°C). Heavily butter an 8-inch- (20-cm-) square baking dish.

2. Purée the corn in a food processor or blender. Add the chile and pulse until it is coarsely chopped. Transfer the corn mixture to a bowl. Add the milk, eggs, flour, salt, and pepper and whisk until they are smooth. Add the Cheddar and scallion and whisk until they are combined. Pour the mixture into the baking dish and sprinkle the Parmesan on top.

3. Bake until a knife inserted in the center comes out almost clean, about 30 minutes. Let the pudding stand for 5 minutes, then serve it hot.

CORN PUDDING
WITH CHEDDAR & CHIPOTLE

CHELSEA MARKET FAMILY RECIPE

SERVES 6

Softened butter, for the baking dish

2 cups (300 g) fresh corn kernels (cut from about 4 ears corn)

1 tablespoon canned chipotle chile in adobo

1½ cups (360 ml) whole milk

3 large eggs

2 tablespoons unbleached all-purpose flour

1 teaspoon kosher salt

¼ teaspoon freshly ground black pepper

½ cup (55 g) shredded sharp Cheddar cheese

1 scallion, white and green parts, finely chopped

2 tablespoons freshly grated Parmesan cheese

FRESH HERBED QUARK SPÄTZLE

KURT GUTENBRUNNER, GUEST CHEF

SERVES 4

2 cups (260 g) unbleached all-purpose flour

Fine sea salt and freshly ground black pepper

⅛ teaspoon freshly grated nutmeg

1 cup (225 g) quark cheese (see Tips)

⅓ cup (75 ml) heavy cream

2 large eggs, lightly beaten

2 tablespoons unsalted butter

2 tablespoons mixed chopped fresh herbs, such as parsley, basil, chervil, and tarragon

NOTE: *Spätzle makers come in different styles. For this recipe, use the standard spätzle maker, which consists of a graterlike perforated surface with an adjustable attachment for pressing the dough through the grater. It is easier to use than a colander and produces more uniformly shaped pasta.*

Recipes travel. Spätzle, similar in texture to gnocchi, is found all across central Europe. At Kurt Gutenbrunner's restaurants, such as Wallsé and Blaue Gans, this fresh pasta, which is boiled and then sautéed in butter until golden and crisped in spots, is easily one of the most frequently ordered side dishes. This spätzle would be great with the Old-Fashioned Beef Stew on page 88.

1. Bring a large saucepan of salted water to a boil. Meanwhile, in a large bowl, whisk the flour with ½ teaspoon sea salt, ¼ teaspoon pepper, and the nutmeg. Add the quark, cream, and eggs and beat until they are smooth.

2. Fill a large bowl with iced water. Working in batches, press the dough through a spätzle maker into the boiling water (see Note; alternatively, press the dough with a rubber spatula through a colander with large holes). Cook until the spätzle float to the surface, 2 to 3 minutes. Using a fine sieve, transfer the spätzle to the iced water for 1 to 2 minutes to cool, then remove them to a colander to drain. (At this point, the spätzle can be tossed with a teaspoon or two of olive oil and refrigerated in a plastic bag for up to 2 days.)

3. In a large skillet, melt the butter. Add the spätzle and cook them over medium-high heat, stirring occasionally, until they are lightly browned. Season them with salt and pepper, sprinkle the herbs over the top, and serve.

TIPS FROM THE PROS

QUARK
Kurt Gutenbrunner

Quark is a soft, tangy fresh cheese with a consistency similar to that of Greek-style yogurt or sour cream. You'll find it at cheese stores and many natural foods markets. In Austria and Germany, where it is known as Topfen, it is often served as a topping for fruit, smeared on bread, or incorporated into dishes such as this creamy spätzle. Although quark is greatly preferred here, you can make an acceptable substitute with equal parts all-natural (gum-free) cream cheese and ricotta, processed together in a food processor until they are combined and smooth.

WILD RICE & GOAT CHEESE DRESSING

BOBBY FLAY, GUEST CHEF

SERVES 6

¾ cup (160 g) wild rice

Kosher salt

5 tablespoons (70 g) unsalted butter, plus more for the baking dish

12 ounces (340 g) smoked Spanish-style chorizo, cut into ½-inch (12-mm) dice

1 yellow onion, chopped

1 carrot, cut into ¼-inch (6-mm) dice

1 celery rib, cut into ¼-inch (6-mm) dice

3 garlic cloves, minced

2 tablespoons finely chopped fresh thyme

12 ounces (340 g) day-old rustic bread, cut into ½-inch (12-mm) cubes (6 cups)

3 cups (720 ml) Chicken Stock (page 56) or reduced-sodium chicken broth, as needed

6 ounces (170 g) crumbled goat cheese

½ cup (20 g) finely chopped fresh flat-leaf parsley

Freshly ground black pepper

1 large egg, beaten

Your holiday turkey will be served in style with this sophisticated dressing as a side dish. It is meant to be moist, almost like a savory pudding, and it is not stuffed inside of the bird, so it acquires a golden brown, irresistible top crust.

1. Bring the rice, 1 quart (960 ml) water, and 1 tablespoon salt to a boil in a large saucepan over high heat. Cover and reduce the heat to medium. Cook at a brisk simmer until the rice is very tender and completely opened, 1¼ to 1½ hours. Be sure the rice is completely tender. Drain it well. Transfer it to a large bowl.

2. Heat 1 tablespoon of the butter in a medium skillet over medium heat. Add the chorizo and cook, stirring occasionally, until it is browned, about 5 minutes. Using a slotted spoon, transfer the chorizo to paper towels to drain, leaving the fat in the skillet.

3. Add the remaining 4 tablespoons (55 g) of the butter to the skillet and let it melt. Add the onion, carrot, and celery and cook, stirring occasionally, until they are tender, about 5 minutes. Stir in the garlic and thyme and cook until the garlic softens, about 1 minute.

4. Add the bread, vegetable mixture, and chorizo to the wild rice. Stir in 3 cups (720 ml) of the stock and mix well. The mixture should be very moist; add more stock as needed. Fold in the goat cheese and parsley. Season it with salt and pepper. Stir in the egg. Place the dressing in a casserole dish. (The dressing can be covered and refrigerated for up to 4 hours.)

5. Position a rack in the center of the oven and preheat it to 350°F (170°C). Bake the dressing, uncovered, until it is heated through and golden brown, about 30 minutes. Let it stand for 10 minutes before serving.

What makes this recipe the ultimate version of the comfort food classic? Lucy's Whey uses a careful selection of cheeses—two Cheddars and a Gouda—seasoned with Dijon mustard and anchovy paste, ingredients where a little bit goes a long way towards pumping up flavor. Also, browning the roux gives a richness that is present in every bite. Serve it as a main course for four to six, if the mood strikes, but this version's use of grown-up flavors makes it a good choice for a side dish for a buffet or dinner party.

1. Position a rack in the center of the oven and preheat it to 400°F (205°C). Butter a 13-by-9-inch (33-by-23-cm) baking dish.

2. Bring a large pot of salted water to a boil over high heat.

3. Meanwhile, melt the butter in a medium saucepan over medium heat. Whisk in the flour and cook, whisking occasionally, until it is lightly browned, about 3 minutes. Gradually whisk in the milk. Bring it to a simmer, whisking often. Remove it from the heat. Add the smooth Cheddar, Gouda, mustard, and anchovy paste and whisk until the Cheddar melts. Season it with salt and pepper. Cover it with a lid to keep the sauce from forming a skin.

4. Add the pasta to the boiling water and cook according to the package directions, just until it is short of al dente (it will cook more when baked). Drain it well. Return the pasta to its cooking pot. Add the sauce and mix well. Spread the mixture in the prepared dish. Scatter the crumbly Cheddar on top.

5. Bake until the cheese topping is melted and the sauce is bubbling, about 15 minutes. Let it stand for 5 minutes. Serve it hot.

THE ULTIMATE MACARONI & CHEESE

LUCY'S WHEY

SERVES 6 TO 8

3 tablespoons unsalted butter, plus more for the baking dish

3 tablespoons unbleached all-purpose flour

2½ cups (600 ml) whole milk, warmed

1 cup (120 g) shredded smooth-textured sharp Cheddar, such as Prairie Breeze

1 cup (120 g) shredded young Gouda, such as Marieke

2 teaspoons Dijon mustard

1 teaspoon anchovy paste

Kosher salt and freshly ground black pepper

1 pound (455 g) tube-shaped pasta, such as elbow macaroni, ziti, or penne

½ cup (60 g) shredded sharp crumbly Cheddar, such as Cabot Clothbound (this cheese will crumble more than shred)

CUBAN BLACK BEANS

WITH BACON & SOFRITO

SPICES AND TEASE

SERVES 4 TO 6

8 ounces (225 g) dried black beans, rinsed and picked through for stones

1 tablespoon olive oil

2 bacon slices, coarsely chopped

1 small red onion, chopped

1 small green bell pepper, cored and cut into ½-inch (12-mm) dice

1 small red bell pepper, cored and cut into ½-inch (12-mm) dice

3 garlic cloves, coarsely chopped

2 teaspoons ground cumin

1 teaspoon dried oregano

1 bay leaf

2 cups (480 ml) Chicken Stock (page 56) or reduced-sodium chicken broth

Kosher salt and freshly ground black pepper

Every Cuban cook has a personal recipe for black beans, a dish that is served at almost every dinner. Sofrito is the mixture of onion, bell peppers, and garlic that often gives Latino cuisine its distinctive depth of flavor. This version is made with dried beans, but if you want to speed up the process, you can use two 15-ounce (430-g) cans of black beans, drained and rinsed, instead.

1. Place the beans in a medium saucepan and add enough cold water to cover them by 2 inches (5 cm). Bring them to a boil over high heat. Cook for 2 minutes. Remove the pot from the heat and cover. Let it stand for 1 hour. Drain the beans.

2. Heat the oil in a medium saucepan over medium heat. Add the bacon and cook, stirring often, until it is browned and crisp, about 8 minutes. Add the onion, green and red peppers, and garlic. Cook, stirring occasionally, until they are softened, about 5 minutes. Stir in the cumin, oregano, and bay leaf. Add the drained beans. Pour in the stock and add enough water to barely cover the beans. Bring them to a boil over high heat. Reduce the heat to low. Simmer, uncovered, adding more hot water as needed to keep the beans moistened (but allowing the liquid to reduce somewhat), until the beans are tender, about 1 hour. During the last 10 minutes of cooking, season the beans with salt and pepper. Serve hot.

For sautéed greens, kale is a fallback, but there are countless other choices. Caterer Ori Cosentino starts with tart dandelion greens, then tames them with mellower greens like chard and spinach. The onion and fennel bring the dish together. This is also good tossed with pasta and grated Parmesan cheese for a main course, with or without some crisped pancetta mixed in.

1. Heat the oil in a large skillet over medium heat. Add the onion and fennel and season them lightly with salt and pepper. Cook, stirring occasionally, until the onion is translucent, about 6 minutes.

2. Gradually stir in the dandelion greens, letting the first batch wilt before adding more. If the mixture seems dry, add a tablespoon or two of water. Cook, stirring occasionally, until the greens are barely tender, about 7 minutes.

3. Stir in the vinegar and cook until it is absorbed into the greens, about 1 minute. Stir in the mild greens and cook just until they are tender, about 5 minutes. Season them with salt and pepper. Serve them hot.

DANDELION SAUTÉ
WITH ONION & FENNEL

CHELSEA MARKET FAMILY RECIPE

SERVES 4

1 tablespoon olive oil

1 small yellow onion, chopped

1 small fennel bulb, cored and cut into ½-inch (12-mm) dice

Kosher salt and freshly ground black pepper

1 pound (455 g) dandelion greens, tough stems discarded, rinsed well

2 tablespoons cider vinegar

4 ounces (115 g) mild cooking greens, such as spinach, watercress, or tatsoi, tough stems discarded, rinsed well

Buddakan serves this gloriously spiced cauliflower as a side dish, but it is so rich and tasty that you might want to serve it over rice as an entrée. Don't let the long list of sauce ingredients deter you, for it is exactly this combination of many flavors that gives the dish its depth. You can find these ingredients at Asian markets and online.

1. Make the chile-garlic sauce: Stir the stock, soy sauce, vinegar, *toban jan*, oyster sauce, honey, *sambal oelek*, and salt together in a medium bowl. Sprinkle the cornstarch over 1 tablespoon water in a small custard cup or ramekin and stir to dissolve it.

2. Heat 1 tablespoon of the oil in a medium saucepan over medium heat. Add the garlic and ginger and cook just until they are browned, about 30 seconds. Stir in the stock mixture and bring it to a simmer. Mix the cornstarch mixture to recombine, and stir it into the sauce. Cook until the sauce is thickened, about 1 minute. Remove it from the heat. (The chile sauce can be cooled, covered, and refrigerated for up to 5 days.)

3. Bring a large pot of salted water to a boil over high heat. Add the cauliflower and cook it until it is just tender, 1 to 2 minutes. Drain it in a colander and rinse it under cold running water. Transfer the cauliflower to a large bowl of iced water and let it cool completely. Drain it well and pat it dry with paper towels.

4. Heat a large wok or skillet over medium heat. Add the panko and cook, stirring occasionally, until it is toasted, about 1 minute. Transfer the panko to a plate.

5. Return the wok to medium-high heat. Add the remaining 2 tablespoons of oil and heat until it is hot but not smoking. Add the pork and cook, stirring often and breaking up the meat with the side of a wooden spoon, until the pork is browned, about 3 minutes. Stir in the chile sauce. Add the cauliflower and cook, stirring often, until the cauliflower is heated through and the sauce is thicker, about 2 minutes.

6. Transfer the mixture to a serving dish. Top it with the toasted panko and mint and serve it hot.

STIR-FRIED CAULIFLOWER
WITH CHILE-GARLIC SAUCE

BUDDAKAN

SERVES 4 TO 6

FOR THE CHILE-GARLIC SAUCE:

½ cup (120 ml) Chicken Stock (page 56) or reduced-sodium chicken broth

2 tablespoons soy sauce

2 tablespoons Chinese red vinegar or rice vinegar

2 tablespoons *toban jan* (chile bean sauce)

1½ teaspoons oyster sauce

1½ teaspoons honey

½ teaspoon *sambal oelek* (Indonesian chile paste)

Pinch kosher salt

1½ teaspoons cornstarch

3 tablespoons grapeseed or vegetable oil

2 garlic cloves, minced

1 teaspoon peeled and minced fresh ginger

1 head cauliflower, cut into bite-size florets

¼ cup (15 g) panko (Japanese bread crumbs)

8 ounces (225 g) ground pork

10 fresh mint leaves, cut into thin shreds

ROASTED BRUSSELS SPROUTS

TUCK SHOP

SERVES 4 TO 6

1¼ pounds (570 g) Brussels sprouts, trimmed but left whole

2 tablespoons unsalted butter, melted

Kosher salt and freshly ground black pepper

True, Tuck Shop is beloved for its savory pies (see page 85), but it is not rare to see someone sitting down to a lunch of these roasted Brussels sprouts. While most recipes for roasted sprouts use olive oil, the butter in this version encourages caramelization to give them an extra measure of irresistibility. Serve them alongside the Brined & Rubbed Chicken on page 107.

1. Position a rack in the center of the oven and preheat it to 375°F (190°C). Line a large rimmed baking sheet with parchment paper or a silicone baking mat.

2. Bring a large pot of salted water to a boil over high heat. Add the sprouts and cook just until they turn a brighter shade of green, about 2 minutes. Drain and rinse them under cold running water. Pat them dry with paper towels. Transfer the sprouts to the baking sheet and drizzle them with the butter. Toss them with your hands to coat, and season them lightly with salt and pepper. Spread the sprouts in an even layer on the sheet.

3. Bake, stirring occasionally, until the sprouts are nicely browned and barely tender, 25 to 30 minutes. Reseason them with salt and pepper. Serve them hot.

THE ART OF THE GIFT BASKET

CHELSEA MARKET BASKETS

At Chelsea Market Baskets, we have been designing gift baskets for almost twenty years. There are many reasons to give a gift basket—anniversary, birthday, housewarming, baby shower, and other milestones—but we are especially busy around the December holidays.

We put a lot of care into our baskets, ensuring that every aspect is perfect, from the basket itself to the gift card, and there is something to be said about having a professional design your gift (and ship it—no one's favorite job). On the other hand, taking the time to personalize the basket makes the gift extra special.

THE YUM FACTOR: The most important part of a gift basket is the food. It has to be mouthwateringly, perfectly, and utterly delicious. Choose the items carefully. All of the fancy wrapping in the world won't cover up cheap goods. Receiving a gift basket satisfies the need for instant gratification—open and eat.

CHOOSE YOUR THEME: We specialize in food baskets, and the possibilities are virtually endless. One of the most obvious themes is by location. It's a no-brainer to do a wine and cheese selection from California, France, or Italy, but don't forget Spain, Greece, or New York State. You can also be city-centric, and gather up goodies from your town to send, perhaps, to a homesick friend. This is pretty easy to pull

off in big cities such as New York, San Francisco, and Chicago, but you probably have local products appropriate for a gift basket wherever you live. Don't forget the chocolate! Our most popular baskets are Chelsea Market Sweets (featuring our neighbors' goods), Notable Noshables (with snacks from around the world), and the self-explanatory World Tour of Chocolate.

PICK YOUR VESSEL: Just as the food must be top-notch, the basket should ideally be a keepsake, and not disposable. If the basket is going to be mailed, then weight is an issue. Otherwise, there are many options. For a housewarming gift, consider a big bowl filled with ingredients for your favorite chocolate chip cookie recipe (recipe included, of course), or a colander brimming with excellent sauce and imported pasta for a spaghetti dinner.

WRAP IT UP: Go to your local crafts store and be inspired by the possibilities for enclosing the basket. You'll find long rolls of cellophane that can act as wrapping, held in place with clear tape. Fill in empty spaces between the items with excelsior or even paper streamers from a party shop.

TOP IT OFF: A jaunty bow is often in order to set off the basket, but if the ribbon is above average—wide grosgrain ribbon in an attractive color and design from a craft store or fabric shop—you could get away with a very simple overhand knot. Wired French ribbon is ideal because the extra support holds the bow's curves in place.

THE CARD SAYS IT ALL: A trip to the stationer will provide the perfect card for the basket. You might even find appropriate postcards, recipe cards, or stationery at an antique shop or second-hand store.

CHAPTER 10

WARM FROM THE OVEN

BREADS & SWEET BAKED GOODS

SALTED CARAMEL-NUT TART

THE NUT BOX

SERVES 8

FOR THE TART DOUGH:

1 cup plus 1 tablespoon (140 g) all-purpose flour

3 tablespoons granulated sugar

¼ teaspoon salt

6 tablespoons (¾ stick/85 g) unsalted butter, chilled and cut into ½-inch (12-mm) cubes, plus extra for the pan

1 large egg yolk

2 tablespoons ice water

FOR THE FILLING:

¾ cup (180 ml) heavy cream

1 cup (200 g) granulated sugar

3 tablespoons unsalted butter, melted

1 large egg, beaten

1 teaspoon pure vanilla extract

2¼ cups (8 ounces/225 grams) unsalted roasted whole mixed nuts

FOR THE WHIPPED CREAM:

¾ cup (80 ml) heavy cream

1 tablespoon confectioners' sugar

½ teaspoon pure vanilla extract

¼ teaspoon flaky sea salt, preferably Cyprus Flake or fleur de sel

Special equipment: 9-inch (23-cm) round tart pan with removeable bottom; pie weights or dried beans

More and more cooks are discovering how a judicious amount of salt can add an unexpected complexity to some desserts. Salt and caramel are old friends, and the pairing is especially advantageous in this nutty, buttery tart. Look for a deluxe brand of mixed nuts, one with plenty of variety, or mix your own with peanuts, cashews, almonds, hazelnuts, Brazil nuts, and pistachios. A couple of other tips: Be careful when adding the cream to the caramel, because it bubbles alarmingly. And let the caramel cool before adding the egg, or the filling could curdle. (See photo on previous page.)

1. Position a rack in the center of the oven and preheat it to 400°F (205°C). Lightly butter a 9-inch (23-cm) round tart pan with a removable bottom.

2. Make the tart dough: Pulse the flour, sugar, and salt in a food processor to combine. Add the butter and pulse about 10 times, until the mixture resembles coarse crumbs with some pea-sized pieces of butter. Mix the yolk and ice water in a custard cup or ramekin. With the machine running, add the yolk mixture and process just until the dough is moistened. It will look crumbly, but should hold together when pressed between your thumb and forefinger. Do not overprocess the dough.

3. Using your fingertips, press the dough firmly and evenly into the bottom and up the sides of the prepared tart pan, being sure that the dough isn't too thick in the corners of the pan. Using a fork, prick the dough all over. Freeze it for 20 minutes. Place the pan on a rimmed baking sheet. Line the dough with aluminum foil and fill it with pie weights or dried beans.

4. Bake the dough until the pastry edges are beginning to brown, about 20 minutes. Lift up and remove the foil and weights. Prick the dough again with the fork and continue baking until the tart shell is lightly browned, about 5 minutes more. Remove it from the oven.

5. Make the filling: Bring the cream to a simmer in a small saucepan over medium heat. (Or heat it in a microwave-safe bowl in a microwave oven on medium power for about 1 minute.) Set it aside.

6. Bring the sugar and ¼ cup (60 ml) water to a boil in a medium, tall saucepan over high heat, stirring constantly to dissolve the sugar. As soon as the sugar comes to a boil, stop stirring. (Don't stir boiling syrup or it will crystallize into a thick glop.) Boil the syrup until it turns deep amber, 3 to 5 minutes. While the syrup is boiling, occasionally swirl the pan by the handle to mix it. Wash down any sugar crystals that form on the sides of the pan by dipping a large pastry brush in cold water and rubbing the wet brush against the crystals. When the syrup is deep amber, reduce the heat to low. Being very careful, slowly stir in the warm cream. The mixture will bubble dramatically, but will eventually subside. Simmer, stirring often, until the caramel is slightly thickened, about 3 minutes. Pour it into a medium heatproof bowl and place it in a larger bowl of water and ice. Let it stand, stirring often, until the caramel is tepid, about 10 minutes.

(continued)

7. Whisk the butter, egg, and vanilla into the caramel. Coarsely chop about half of the nuts and spread them in the tart shell. Top them with the remaining whole nuts. Evenly pour the caramel mixture over the nuts in the pan.

8. Return the tart to the oven and bake it for 10 minutes. Reduce the heat to 350°F (175°C), and continue baking until the filling is bubbling in the center, 15 to 20 minutes more. (If the nuts are browning too fast, tent the tart with aluminum foil.) Transfer the pan to a wire rack and let it stand for 10 minutes. Remove the sides of the pan and let the tart cool completely on the rack. (The tart can be covered with plastic wrap and stored at room temperature for 1 day.)

9. Make the whipped cream: Combine the cream, sugar, and vanilla in a chilled medium bowl. Whip them with an electric mixer on high speed until soft peaks form.

10. Sprinkle the salt over the filling. Slice the tart and serve it with the whipped cream.

Any day that starts with sticky buns is going to be sweet in more ways than one. Amy's is justly famous for their version. The buns are baked pull-apart style, in a rectangular pan, so the buttery caramel and nuts stay primarily on the top. A few minutes after the rolls come out of the oven, flip the pan over onto a tray or plate so the caramel drips down over the rolls. Make sure to scrape all the pecans out of the pan and onto the rolls. They are the best part!

1. Make the dough: Combine the ¼ cup (60 ml) very warm water and the yeast in a small bowl and stir to moisten the yeast. Let the mixture stand for 3 minutes; stir to dissolve the yeast. Pour it into the bowl of a standing heavy-duty mixer.

2. Add the warm water, sugar, butter, and salt to the bowl. Attach the bowl to the mixer and fit it with the paddle attachment. On low speed, add the bread flour, and then enough of the all-purpose flour to make a soft, sticky dough that barely cleans the bowl. Turn off the mixer, remove the paddle attachment, and cover the bowl with a kitchen towel. Let the dough stand for 10 minutes.

3. Fit the mixer with the dough hook. Knead the dough on medium-low speed, until the dough is soft and supple, but tacky to the touch, about 7 minutes.

4. Lightly oil a medium bowl. Scrape the dough out of the mixer bowl onto a lightly floured work surface. Shape it into a ball, place it in the oiled bowl, and turn to coat it with the oil. Cover the bowl with plastic wrap and let it stand in a warm place until the dough is almost doubled in volume, about 2 hours.

5. Meanwhile, make the topping: Warm the brown sugar, butter, and syrup in a small saucepan over low heat, whisking often, until the butter has melted and the sugar is completely moistened and starting to melt (it won't be dissolved). Remove it from the heat and whisk well until the butter is fully absorbed.

6. Butter a 13-by-9-by-2-inch (33-by-23-by-5-cm) baking pan. Pour in the warm brown sugar mixture, tilting the pan so the mixture spreads evenly in the bottom of the pan. Sprinkle the pecans over the caramel, being sure to reach the corners. Let it cool. (The topping must not be warmer than tepid when the dough slices are added.)

7. When the dough has doubled, gently transfer it onto a lightly floured work surface. Try to keep this soft, pillowy dough inflated during handling. Gently pat and stretch the dough, being sure that it isn't sticking, and dusting underneath it with flour as needed, into a 13-by-10-inch (33-by-25-cm) rectangle, with the long side facing you. If the dough resists, cover it loosely with a kitchen towel, let it rest for 5 minutes, and resume stretching.

8. Make the filling: Stir the sugar and cinnamon together in a small bowl until it is evenly mixed. Using your fingertips, spread the butter evenly

(continued)

PECAN STICKY BUNS

AMY'S BREAD

MAKES 12 BUNS

FOR THE DOUGH:

¼ cup (60 ml) very warm water (105° to 115°F/40° to 45°C)

2¼ teaspoons active dry yeast

1¾ cups (420 ml) warm water (90°F/30°C)

⅓ cup (65 g) granulated sugar

5 tablespoons (65 g) unsalted butter, melted

1 tablespoon kosher salt

2¾ cups (355 g) unbleached bread flour

2¾ cups (355 g) unbleached all-purpose flour, plus additional as needed

Vegetable oil, for the bowl

FOR THE TOPPING:

1¼ cups (275 g) packed light brown sugar

14 tablespoons (200 g) unsalted butter, cut into tablespoons, plus softened butter for the pan

2 tablespoons light or dark corn syrup

1½ cups (170 g) pecans, toasted (see page 180) and coarsely chopped

FOR THE FILLING:

⅓ cup (65 g) granulated sugar

1 teaspoon ground cinnamon

6 tablespoons (¾ stick/85 g) unsalted butter, well softened

over the dough to the edges. Sprinkle the cinnamon mixture evenly over the butter. Starting with the bottom edge, roll up the dough jelly-roll fashion into a long log. Pinch the long seam closed.

9. Using a large sharp knife, mark the dough into 12 equal pieces, then cut it into 12 slices. Arrange the slices cut-side down on top of the cooled caramel in the baking pan. Cover the top with oiled plastic wrap, oiled-side down, and let the pan stand in a warm place until the slices have risen and almost completely fill the pan, about 1 hour.

10. Position a rack in the center of the oven and preheat it to 375°F (190°C). Line a half-sheet pan with parchment paper. (The parchment paper will catch any topping that bubbles out of the pan during baking.)

11. Put the pan of sticky buns on the prepared half-sheet pan. Bake for 10 minutes. Reduce the oven temperature to 350°F (175°C) and bake the buns for 35 to 40 minutes more, or until the tops are completely golden brown. It's important to bake the buns long enough so the dough is cooked all the way through and the caramel topping develops properly.

12. Transfer the pan to a wire cake rack and let it cool for 3 minutes. Cover the pan with a large, flat heatproof platter (or even another half-sheet pan). Quickly but carefully invert the pan and platter together to release the sticky buns onto the platter. Immediately scrape out any hot caramel and pecans remaining in the bottom of the pan and spread it on the tops of the buns, filling in any bare spots. Let the buns cool for about 10 minutes, then serve them warm. (The leftover buns can be wrapped in aluminum foil or plastic and stored at room temperature for up to 2 days. Reheat them in a toaster oven before serving.)

TIPS FROM THE PROS

TOASTING NUTS
Amy's Bread

Toasting nuts brings out their oils and makes them even tastier. It is a simple job that only takes a few minutes, and can make all of the difference in your baking. This works for walnuts, pecans, pistachios, and sliced and slivered almonds.

Preheat the oven to 350°F (175°C). Spread the nuts on a large rimmed baking sheet. Bake, stirring occasionally, until the nuts are lightly browned and give off their aroma, 10 to 15 minutes. Transfer them to a plate and let them cool completely before using.

For hazelnuts, bake until the skins are cracked and the flesh underneath the skin is lightly browned, 10 to 15 minutes. Transfer the nuts to a clean kitchen towel, wrap them in the towel, and let them stand for 10 minutes. Then, using the towel, rub off the skins from the nuts. Don't worry if every last bit of skin isn't removed.

Pain de mie ("crumb bread" in French) is probably the epitome of sandwich bread. It gets its name from its firm, tight crumb—your sandwich ingredients won't be slipping through any holes in this bread. It also makes the absolute best toast, strong enough to hold up to thick layers of butter and preserves. Sarabeth's bakes a rectangular pain de mie in a special lidded Pullman loaf pan. Here, they share an ingenious method for the perfect warm and moist environment for rising dough—enclose the filled pan in a large plastic bag with a glass of steaming hot water.

1. Sprinkle the yeast over the warm milk in a small bowl. Let it stand for 5 minutes; stir to dissolve. Pour the mixture into the bowl of a standing heavy-duty mixer and fit it with the paddle attachment. Add the cold milk and sugar. On low speed, beat in half of the flour, then the salt. One tablespoon at a time, add the softened butter and mix until it is absorbed into the dough. Continue adding enough of the flour to make a soft dough that cleans the sides of the bowl. Replace the paddle attachment with the dough hook. Knead the dough on medium-low speed until it is smooth and elastic, about 6 minutes.

2. Butter a medium bowl. Shape the dough into a taut ball. Place it in the bowl and turn it to coat with butter. Cover it tightly with plastic wrap. Let it stand in a warm place until the dough doubles in volume, about 1½ hours.

3. Lightly butter a 9-by-5-inch (23-by-12-cm) loaf pan. Turn out the dough onto a lightly floured work surface. Gently stretch and press the dough into a 10-by-8-inch (25-by-20-cm) rectangle with the long side facing you. To roll it into a loaf, start at the bottom of the dough. Fold up about one third of the dough, and press the seam closed with the heel of your hand. Repeat, then finish rolling it into a loaf, and pinch the long seam closed with your fingertips. Transfer the loaf, seam-side down, to the pan, gently pressing down on the dough to fit it flat in the pan.

4. Slip the pan into a tall plastic bag on a work surface in a warm place. Place a tall glass of very hot water in the bag, and close it tightly. Let it stand until the dough looks inflated but not doubled, about 1 hour.

5. Position a rack in the center of the oven and preheat it to 350°F (175°C).

6. Remove the pan from the bag. Bake until the underside is lightly browned (remove the loaf from the pan to check), about 40 minutes. Do not underbake the loaf or it may collapse. Let cool in the pan for 5 minutes.

7. Remove the loaf from the pan. Transfer it to a wire cake rack and let it cool completely. (The bread can be wrapped in aluminum foil and stored at room temperature for up to 2 days. Or wrap the loaf in plastic wrap, followed by aluminum foil, and freeze for up to 2 months; defrost at room temperature before using.)

PAIN DE MIE

SARABETH'S BAKERY

MAKES 1 (9-BY-5-INCH/23-BY-12-CM) LOAF

1¾ teaspoons active dry yeast

⅓ cup (75 ml) warm (105° to 110°F/ 40° to 45°C) whole milk

1 cup (240 ml) cold whole milk

2 tablespoons plus 2 teaspoons sugar

3¾ cups (465 g) unbleached all-purpose flour, as needed

1 teaspoon fine sea salt

3 tablespoons unsalted butter, well softened, plus more for the bowl and pan

LAMINGTONS

TUCK SHOP

MAKES 16

FOR THE CAKE:

2½ cups (325 g) unbleached all-purpose flour, plus more for the pan

2 teaspoons baking powder

¼ teaspoon fine sea salt

10 tablespoons (1¼ sticks/145 g) unsalted butter, at room temperature, plus more for the pan

⅔ cup (130 g) sugar

2 large eggs, beaten, at room temperature

1 teaspoon pure vanilla extract

½ cup (120 ml) whole milk

½ cup (170 g) raspberry preserves

FOR THE ICING:

4 cups (455 g) confectioners' sugar

½ cup (40 g) natural cocoa powder

3 tablespoons unsalted butter, melted

½ cup (120 ml) boiling water, as needed

2 cups (180 g) unsweetened desiccated coconut, available at natural foods stores and some supermarkets

---

The Lamington is a petit-four gone Down Under. Big, bold, and chocolatey, this Australian specialty is a jam-filled cake cube dipped in chocolate icing and coated with desiccated coconut. Very few Americans have ever seen one before, and if you serve it as a dinner party dessert (serve two per person, perhaps with a scoop of ice cream to fill up the plate), expect it to be the subject of conversation. Or treat yourself to a single Lamington to go with your afternoon cuppa tea.

1. Make the cake: One day before serving, position a rack in the center of the oven and preheat it to 350°F (175°C). Lightly butter an 8-inch (20-cm) square baking dish. Line the bottom with parchment or waxed paper. Dust the inside of the pan with flour and tap out the excess.

2. Sift the flour, baking powder, and salt together into a bowl. Beat the butter in a medium bowl with an electric mixer on high speed until it is creamy, about 1 minute. Gradually beat in the sugar and continue beating until it is light in color and texture, about 3 minutes. Gradually beat in the eggs, followed by the vanilla. Reduce the mixer speed to low. In thirds, add the flour mixture, alternating with two equal additions of the milk, and mix, scraping down the bowl as needed, until the batter is smooth. Spread it evenly in the prepared pan.

3. Bake until a wooden toothpick inserted in the center of the cake comes out clean, 25 to 30 minutes. Let the cake cool in the pan for 10 minutes. Run a knife around the inside of the pan. Invert the cake onto a wire cake rack and remove the paper. Turn the cake right-side up and let it cool.

4. Bring the preserves to a simmer in a small saucepan over medium heat. Strain them through a wire sieve set over a bowl and discard the seeds. Using a large serrated knife, cut the cake in half horizontally. Spread the bottom half with the warm strained preserves. Top it with the other half and press firmly. Wrap the cake in plastic wrap and refrigerate it for at least 8 hours or overnight.

5. Make the icing: Sift the confectioners' sugar and cocoa together into a medium bowl. Add the butter. Whisk in enough of the boiling water to make an icing with the consistency of thick heavy cream, and whisk it until smooth.

6. To assemble the Lamingtons: Line a large rimmed baking sheet with parchment or waxed paper. Place a large wire cooling rack over the sheet. Spread the coconut in a shallow bowl.

7. Unwrap the chilled cake. Using a serrated knife, cut the cake into 16 squares. Place the squares, well apart, top-sides up, on the rack over the baking sheet. Using about half of the icing, slowly pour it over the tops of the cakes. Using a small offset spatula or the back of a spoon, smooth the icing, letting it run down the sides of the cake squares. Let it stand until the icing is barely set, about 5 minutes. One at a time, pick up a square by its bottom and cover any bare areas with more icing. (Don't worry about marring the icing, as it will be covered in coconut.) Return the square, top-side down, to the rack. (If you need more icing, scrape the drips from the parchment paper into the bowl and whisk well.) Let the squares stand until tacky, about 5 minutes.

8. Roll each square in the coconut bowl to coat, return it to the wire rack, and let the icing dry completely, about 2 hours. (The Lamingtons can be stored in an airtight container for up to 2 days.)

Ruthy's and rugelach are synonymous to countless cookie fans, with a recipe originating with Ruthy's grandmother over a hundred years ago. A properly made ruggie is not quickly produced, and be sure to leave room in your refrigerator for chilling the baking sheets containing the rolled nuggets of dough so they hold their shape during baking. You will be well rewarded.

1. Make the dough: Beat the cream cheese and butter together in a large bowl with an electric mixer on high speed until the mixture is light in color and texture, about 3 minutes. Beat in the sugar, followed by the salt and vanilla. Reduce the mixer speed to low. Gradually beat in the flour, mixing just until the ingredients are combined. Turn the dough out onto a lightly floured work surface. Divide it into four equal pieces, then shape each into a thick disk and wrap it in plastic wrap. Refrigerate the dough until it is chilled, at least 1 hour or up to 1 day. (The dough is easiest to handle after 1 to 2 hours of refrigeration, when it is cold but not hard. If it is chilled until hard, let it stand at room temperature for 10 to 20 minutes to soften slightly before rolling.)

2. Make the filling: Combine the walnuts, raisins, sugar, brown sugar, and cinnamon in a small bowl.

3. Working with one chilled dough disk at a time, unwrap a disk and place it on a lightly floured work surface. Dust the top of the dough with flour and roll it out into a 9-inch (23-cm) round. Using a small offset metal spatula, spread the dough with 2 tablespoons of the preserves, leaving a ½-inch (12-mm) border around the circumference of the dough. Sprinkle one fourth of the filling evenly over the preserves, and press it lightly into the preserves to adhere. Using a pizza wheel or sharp knife, cut the dough into 12 equal wedges. (The easiest way to do this is by cutting the dough into quarters, and then cutting each quarter into thirds.) Starting at a wide end, roll up each wedge, and bend each roll slightly into a crescent. Arrange the cookies, pointed ends underneath, on a large rimmed baking sheet or platter. Cover them loosely with plastic wrap and refrigerate until the cookies are chilled, at least 30 minutes and up to 2 hours. Repeat with the remaining dough, preserves, and filling.

4. Position racks in the top third and center of the oven and preheat it to 350°F (175°C). Line two large rimmed baking sheets with parchment paper. Whisk the egg and milk together in a small bowl to make an egg wash. Mix the sugar and cinnamon together in another small bowl for the topping.

5. Arrange the chilled cookies about 1 inch (2.5 cm) apart on the lined baking sheets. Brush them lightly with the egg wash and sprinkle them with the sugar mixture. Bake, switching the positions of the racks from top to bottom and front to back halfway through baking, until they are golden brown, 20 to 25 minutes. Let the rugelach cool on the baking sheets for 5 minutes, then transfer them to wire racks to cool completely. Repeat with the remaining cookies on cooled baking sheets. (The rugelach can be stored in an airtight container at room temperature for up to 5 days.)

RUGELACH

RUTHY'S

MAKES 4 DOZEN

FOR THE DOUGH:

8 ounces (225 g) cream cheese, at room temperature

1 cup (2 sticks/225 g) unsalted butter, at room temperature

¼ cup (50 g) granulated sugar

¼ teaspoon kosher salt

1 teaspoon pure vanilla extract

2⅓ cups (300 g) unbleached all-purpose flour, plus more for rolling

FOR THE FILLING:

1 cup (120 g) finely chopped walnuts

¾ cup (110 g) dark raisins

¼ cup plus 2 tablespoons (75 g) granulated sugar

¼ cup (55 g) packed light brown sugar

1½ teaspoons ground cinnamon

½ cup (160 g) apricot or raspberry preserves, processed until smooth in a food processor

1 large egg

1 tablespoon milk

3 tablespoons granulated sugar

1 teaspoon ground cinnamon

TURTLE WITCH BROWNIES

FAT WITCH

MAKES 16

Softened butter and flour for the pan

¾ cup (1½ sticks/170 g) unsalted butter

4 ounces (115 g) bittersweet (60% cacao) chocolate, finely chopped

1 cup (200 g) sugar

3 large eggs, at room temperature

1 teaspoon pure vanilla extract

½ cup plus 1 tablespoon (75 g) unbleached all-purpose flour

Pinch fine sea salt

½ cup (55 g) coarsely chopped pecans

31 soft caramel candy squares, unwrapped

2 tablespoons lukewarm water

Folks fly into Fat Witch craving this over-the-top goodie, loaded with pecans and with a gooey caramel accent. It's a spellbinding treat that's easy to make at home. Turtles may move slowly, but this treat will disappear quickly. The brownies are very rich, and actually just a step away from being candy, so cut them into small squares when serving.

1. Lightly butter a 9-inch (23-cm) square baking pan. Dust the inside of the pan with flour and tap out the excess.

2. Melt the butter in a medium saucepan over low heat. Remove it from the heat. Add the chocolate and let it stand until softened, about 3 minutes. Whisk it until smooth. Let it stand until it has cooled to room temperature.

3. Beat the sugar, eggs, and vanilla together in a medium bowl with an electric mixer on high speed until they are pale yellow, about 2 minutes. With the mixer on low speed, beat in the chocolate mixture. Sift the flour and salt into the bowl and mix on low speed just until they are combined. Using a rubber spatula, stir in the pecans. Spread only half of the batter evenly in the baking pan. Freeze it while preparing the caramels.

4. Put the caramels and water in a medium microwave-safe bowl. Microwave them on 50% (medium) power for 1 minute. Stir. Continue microwaving and stirring at 20-second intervals until the caramels have melted into a thick liquid. Mix them with a fork to be sure that the caramels are completely melted. Remove the pan from the freezer. Pour the caramel as evenly as possible over the chilled batter, leaving a ½-inch (12-mm) border around the edges. Return the pan to the freezer for 30 minutes.

5. Position a rack in the center of the oven and preheat it to 350°F (175°C).

6. Remove the pan from the freezer. Drop dollops of the remaining batter over the caramel and then spread the batter into an even layer. Bake until a wooden toothpick inserted in the center of the brownie comes out with only a few clinging crumbs, about 30 minutes.

7. Let the brownie cool in the pan on a wire cake rack. Cut it into 16 squares and remove them from the pan. (The brownies can be stored at room temperature in an airtight container for up to 2 days, or individually wrapped in plastic wrap and frozen for up to 2 months.)

Visitors crowd around the boxed cookies at Eleni's, awestruck at the intricately decorated sugar cookies and their bright colors, covering themes from New York City to Hollywood, baseball to football, and every holiday on the calendar. Here, Eleni gives a home-baker version of her sturdy sugar dough and shiny royal icing for cookies that will be the star of your holiday cookie tray. We give instructions for Christmas tree cookies, but the directions can be translated to any simply shaped cookie. Purchase the special equipment and ingredients at craft stores, cake supply shops, and in the baking section of some supermarkets.

1. Make the dough: Beat the butter and sugar in a large bowl with an electric mixer on high speed, scraping down the sides of the bowl as needed, until they are light in color, about 2 minutes. Beat in the vanilla and salt. With the mixer on low speed, gradually beat in the flour, just until the dough is combined. (Do not overbeat the dough.) Gather up the dough into a ball. Divide it in half. Shape each portion into a thick disk and wrap it in plastic wrap. Refrigerate it until chilled, about 1½ hours. (The dough is easiest to roll out if chilled, but not firm. The dough can be refrigerated for up to 2 days, but if it is chilled hard, let it stand at room temperature for 10 to 20 minutes to soften slightly before rolling it out.)

2. Line two large rimmed baking sheets with parchment paper or silicone baking mats. Working with one disk at a time, pound the wrapped dough with a rolling pin to soften it slightly. Unwrap the dough, place it on a lightly floured work surface, and dust the top of the dough with flour. Roll out the dough to ⅛ inch (3 mm) thick, slipping a metal icing spatula under the dough if it sticks. Using a Christmas tree cookie cutter, cut out cookies and transfer them to the baking sheets. If you have the time, refrigerate the cookies on the sheets for at least 10 minutes and up to 1 hour. (This helps them keep their shape.) Gather up the scraps. Roll and cut more cookies until the dough is used up.

3. Position racks in the top third and center of the oven and preheat it to 350°F (175°C).

4. Bake the cookies, switching the position of the pans from top to bottom and front to back halfway through baking, until they are lightly browned, about 12 minutes. Let them cool on the baking sheets for 5 minutes. Transfer the cookies to wire racks and let them cool completely.

5. Make the icing: Combine the confectioners' sugar, ⅓ cup plus 1 tablespoon (90 ml) water, the powdered egg, and lemon juice in the bowl of a standing heavy-duty mixer fitted with the whisk attachment. Mix them on low speed until combined. Increase the speed to medium and beat until the icing is very thick, stiff, and glossy, about 6 minutes. The consistency will be reminiscent of spackling paste. Transfer the icing to a medium bowl and cover it tightly with plastic wrap. (The icing should be covered when not in use, or it will dry out. It can be refrigerated in an airtight container for up to 5 days. Remove from the refrigerator 1 hour prior to use and adjust the consistency with water as needed before using.) Makes about 3½ cups (520 g); enough for 4 dozen 3-inch (7.5-cm) cookies.

(continued)

ELENI'S CHRISTMAS TREE SUGAR COOKIES

ELENI'S

MAKES ABOUT 2½ DOZEN COOKIES

FOR THE DOUGH:

1 cup (2 sticks/220 g) unsalted butter, at room temperature

½ cup (100 g) granulated sugar

1 teaspoon pure vanilla extract

½ teaspoon fine sea salt

2⅓ cups (300 g) all-purpose flour

FOR THE ICING:

4 cups (455 g) confectioners' sugar

2 tablespoons powdered egg whites or meringue powder

1 teaspoon fresh lemon juice

Leaf green and chocolate brown food coloring paste

Special equipment: Christmas tree cookie cutter (about 3 inches/7.5 cm long); 2 disposable plastic pastry bags; ⅛-in (3-mm) plain writing tip; plastic squeeze bottle; small offset metal icing spatula

6. Transfer about ¾ cup (115 g) of the icing to a small bowl, cover it tightly with plastic wrap, and set aside. Add about ½ teaspoon green food coloring paste to the remaining icing and stir well, adding more coloring paste as needed to reach the desired shade for the tree branches. Transfer about 1 cup (150 g) of the icing to a disposable plastic bag fitted with the pastry tip. Look at the cookie to determine the details that you want to highlight: Pipe the outline of the tree, connecting the two sides of the tree with curves to demark the boughs. Return the remaining green icing from the piping bag to its bowl and cover it tightly. Wash and dry the pastry tip.

7. Add about ¼ teaspoon brown food coloring paste into the reserved plain icing and stir well, adding more coloring paste as needed to reach the desired shade for the trunk. Transfer the icing to another disposable plastic pastry bag fitted with the pastry tip. Pipe the outline of the trunk. Return the remaining brown icing from the piping bag to its bowl and cover it tightly. Let the piped outlines on the cookies dry and set for at least 2 hours.

8. Add enough water (2 to 3 tablespoons) to the green icing to give it the consistency of melted ice cream. Fill the plastic squeeze bottle with the green icing. Squeeze the thinned icing into the green-outlined spaces, almost flooding the outlined area. Use a small icing spatula to coax the icing into place. Discard the leftover icing or cover it tightly and refrigerate for up to 3 days for another use. Clean and dry the squeeze bottle.

9. Thin the brown icing with about 2 teaspoons water to give it the consistency of melted ice cream. Fill the plastic squeeze bottle with the brown icing. Fill in the brown-outlined trunk areas with the brown icing, coaxing the icing into place with the spatula, if needed. Let the icing dry and set overnight. Discard the remaining icing or cover it tightly and refrigerate for up to 3 days for another use.

10. The cookies can be stored at room temperature in an airtight covered container, separated by layers of waxed paper, for up to 1 week.

DECORATING COOKIES
Eleni's

It really isn't difficult to achieve the lovely detailed look of my cookies. These guidelines will help you reach cookie perfection.

• *Glossy royal icing, which we use exclusively for our designs, was originally made with fresh egg whites. To keep the icing within food safety standards, we recommend dried egg whites. The icing is used in two consistencies for different results on the same cookie. The basic shapes are piped onto the cookie with thick icing, then the same icing is thinned to fill in (or "flood") the space in each outlined area.*

• *Food coloring paste or gels have richer colors than liquid food coloring. Add them slowly, drop by drop, to the plain icing, to get the desired color.*

• *Patience is a virtue, but especially when decorating cookies. Be sure to allow at least 2 hours for the initial piping to set, then an overnight period to dry the flooded icing.*

• *It is best to flood sections of the cookies in assembly-line fashion, filling one area of a cookie, and progressing to the same area on the next cookie, and so on, rather than flooding the entire cookie at once. By the time you get to the last cookie, the icing in the first cookie will have set slightly, so you can fill in the second area. This keeps the iced sections separate for the tailored look that Eleni's is famous for.*

• *Disposable pastry bags are best for decorating with tinted icing because the coloring can stain plastic-lined canvas bags. Disposable bags can actually be washed and reused a few times. Snip off the pointed end of the bag to make a hole large enough to hold the pastry tip.*

• *A plastic squeeze bottle, which you can find at beauty supply shops as well as craft stores, is the best tool for flooding the thin icing. You may be tempted to skip the purchase and try using a spoon, but you won't get nearly as quick or as neat results.*

STRAWBERRY SHORTCAKES

WITH GINGER BISCUITS

THE GREEN TABLE

SERVES 8

FOR THE SHORTCAKES:

2¼ cups (290 g) unbleached all-purpose flour, plus more for rolling

¼ cup (50 g) sugar

2 tablespoons ground ginger

1 tablespoon baking powder

½ teaspoon fine sea salt

½ cup (70 g) finely chopped crystallized ginger

1 cup (240 ml) heavy cream

1 large egg

FOR THE FILLING:

1 cup (240 ml) heavy cream

2 pounds (910 g) fresh strawberries, hulled and sliced

Strawberry shortcake is one of the most beloved of American desserts. The Green Table has taken a good thing and made it even better by adding ginger—in both ground and crystallized forms—to the dough. The zesty flavor complements the strawberries beautifully. Mary Cleaver, owner of the restaurant, says the dessert is best when made with pasteurized (not ultra-pasteurized) heavy cream from a local dairy and just-picked berries from a nearby farm.

1. Make the shortcakes: Position a rack in the center of the oven and preheat it to 350°F (175°C). Line a large rimmed baking sheet with parchment paper or a silicone baking mat.

2. Sift the flour, sugar, ground ginger, baking powder, and salt together into a medium bowl. Stir in the crystallized ginger, then the cream to make a soft dough; do not overwork the dough. Turn it out onto a lightly floured work surface. Dust the top of the dough with flour and roll it out ¾ inch (2 cm) thick. Using a 2¼-inch- (6-cm-) diameter biscuit cutter, cut out rounds of dough and transfer them to the baking sheet, placing them 2 inches (5 cm) apart. Gather up the scraps, gently press them together, and repeat rolling and cutting until the dough is used up. Beat the egg and 1 tablespoon water together in a small bowl. Lightly brush the tops of the dough rounds with some of the egg wash.

3. Bake until the shortcakes are golden brown, about 20 minutes. Let them cool on the baking sheet for 5 minutes. Transfer them to a wire rack and let the shortcakes cool completely. (The shortcakes are best eaten the day they are made.)

4. Make the filling: Whip the cream in a chilled medium bowl with an electric mixer just until soft peaks form.

5. For each serving, using a serrated knife, cut a shortcake in half horizontally. Place the bottom half on a plate and top it with generous portions of the strawberries and whipped cream. Add the top shortcake half and serve it immediately.

BLACKBERRY BUCKLE

CHELSEA MARKET FAMILY RECIPE

SERVES 8

FOR THE BUCKLE:

1⅔ cups (210 g) unbleached all-purpose flour

1¾ teaspoons baking powder

½ teaspoon fine sea salt

6 tablespoons (¾ stick/85 g) unsalted butter, at room temperature, plus more for the pan

1 cup (200 g) granulated sugar, plus 2 tablespoons for sprinkling

1 large egg, at room temperature

1 teaspoon pure vanilla extract

¾ cup (180 ml) whole milk

12 ounces (340 g) fresh blackberries

Confectioners' sugar, for sifting (optional)

FOR THE WHIPPED CREAM:

¾ cup (80 ml) heavy cream

1 tablespoon confectioners' sugar

½ teaspoon pure vanilla extract

This simple cake is likely to become a favorite at your house, as it has at author Michael Phillips's. You can use blueberries or hulled and halved strawberries instead of the blackberries, or even sliced peaches, plums, or nectarines. It also makes a fine coffee cake to serve hot from the oven for brunch.

1. Position a rack in the center of the oven and preheat it to 350°F (175°C). Lightly butter a 10-inch (25-cm) springform pan.

2. Make the buckle: Sift the flour, baking powder, and salt together. Beat the butter and 1 cup (200 g) of the granulated sugar together in a large bowl with an electric mixer at high speed until it is light in color and texture, about 2 minutes. Beat in the egg and vanilla. Reduce the mixer speed to low. In thirds, add the flour mixture, alternating with two equal additions of the milk, scraping down the sides of the bowl as needed, and mixing until the batter is smooth. Spread it evenly in the pan. Arrange the blackberries on the batter and sprinkle them with the remaining 2 tablespoons granulated sugar.

3. Bake until the buckle is golden and a wooden toothpick inserted in the center of the cake comes out clean, 50 to 60 minutes. Let it cool in the pan on a wire rack for 10 minutes. Run a knife around the inside of the pan to release the cake. Remove the sides of the pan. Sift the confectioners' sugar over the cake, if desired.

4. Make the whipped cream: Combine the cream, confectioners' sugar, and vanilla in a chilled medium bowl. Whip them with an electric mixer on high speed until soft peaks form.

5. Cut the buckle into slices and serve it warm, or cooled to room temperature, with the whipped cream.

Every cook needs a recipe like this one on file for making fruit crisps in season. The topping has just a few easy-to-remember ingredients, and is all the better for its simplicity. Betsy Marger, who occasionally works as a private chef for author Michael Phillips, thinks that juicy pears make the very best crisps, but you can also use an equivalent amount of apples, peaches, or nectarines. If you prefer, instead of baking individual portions, spread the fruit in a 13-by-9-inch (33-by-22-cm) baking dish, add the topping, and bake it for 30 to 40 minutes.

1. Position a rack in the center of the oven and preheat it to 425°F (220°C).

2. Divide the pears evenly among six 1¼-cup (300-ml) large custard cups or individual baking dishes. Place the cups on a large rimmed baking sheet.

3. Stir the flour, sugar, cinnamon, and salt together in a medium bowl to combine. Add the butter and work it into the flour mixture with your fingers until the topping is homogenous and crumbly. Cover the pear wedges in each custard cup with the topping.

4. Bake until the pear juices are bubbling and the topping is crisp and browned, about 25 minutes. Let it cool for 10 minutes. Serve the crisps warm, with the ice cream.

OLD-FASHIONED PEAR CRISPS

CHELSEA MARKET FAMILY RECIPE

SERVES 6

6 firm-ripe Comice or d'Anjou pears, peeled, cored, and cut into sixths

1 cup plus 2 tablespoons (145 g) unbleached all-purpose flour

1 cup (220 g) packed light brown sugar

1 tablespoon ground cinnamon

1 teaspoon fine sea salt

½ cup (1 stick/115 g) unsalted butter, cut into chunks, at room temperature

Vanilla ice cream, for serving

SETTING YOUR TABLE, YOUR WAY

ANTHROPOLOGIE

Inviting friends and family into your home to share a meal is no small task, but many hosts and hostesses, both experienced and green, seemingly do it with ease. These people manage to nail the three corner-stones of a great dinner party: food, folks, and flair.

By food, we mean the entire menu—from salted nibbles to savory roasts to (lots and lots of) Sauvignon Blanc (or any wine!). Folks, of course, refers to your guests, and much like a nut bowl, the right mix of characters can make or break an evening. (Our secret: For every intellectual, invite an eccentric.) And then there is flair, the factor closest to our hearts. One part ambiance, another part personal style, flair includes the right lighting and a pitch-perfect playlist. (Try mixing genres to mimic the desired pace of the evening: Start with indie alt-rock, shift to big-band jazz during dinner, and end the night with effervescent French pop.) Most importantly, be sure not to overlook the space where everyone congregates and inevitably lingers: the table.

Here are six tips to styling yours "just so."

LOSE THE RULES. Ironed linens—says who? Knife's edge inward—if you wish! And never mind bread plates being used for just bread. In other words, make the traditional host/ess protocol work for you, rather than vice versa. Obeying or breaking rules of decorum comes down to the vibe you want to convey. Hosting a casual potluck? Group forks, knives, spoons, and napkins in mini galvanized pails or flowerpots that can easily shuffle from guest to guest. Have a beautifully grained wood table? Skip the tablecloth and opt for a DIY runner of herbs and wildflowers that will show off its rich patina. (Bonus: The natural ingredients will emit the faintest of scents. The flavors of a dinner can be overwhelmed by overly aromatic flower arrangements.)

EMBRACE COLOR. There's a time and place for white porcelain and clear glass, but trust you must: A wash of color leaves a lasting impression. Turn to saturated hues and playful patterns that showcase your personality and evoke the season. We wholeheartedly endorse hand-painted serving platters and bowls, as your guests will get a fun glimpse of original art with each spoonful of food. A spectrum of mix-and-match wine and water glasses—some secondhand, others new—adds unexpected playfulness and texture. Placemats and napkins are wonderful quick-switch conduits of color, too. And let's not forget the meal itself: The freshest ingredients always produce the most spectacular hues.

EXPERIMENT WITH HEIGHT. A cake stand needn't always be occupied by cake, what with so-and-so avoiding carbs and desserts trending scooped versus sliced. Use a cake stand's elevation to your advantage: There is no better stage for a grouping of candles (no fewer than three, please), or a mound of grilled vegetables or buttery croissants. Consider height, too, when adding flowers to the tablescape; just be sure to keep sightlines clear for conversation. Try tall, spindly greens in pitchers and float single buds in teacups. And rather than placing flowers at the center of your table, anchor vessels in a single corner or at the table head.

MAKE ROOM FOR QUIRK. Collectors, take note: There's no better time to dust off your quirky paper-weights, porcelain figurines, and animal-shaped soup tureens than a dinner party. We regularly turn to our personal collections when in need of an attention-grabbing centerpiece or makeshift place card holders. The offbeat charm of these precious finds is guaranteed to spark conversation. Note, too, that food itself makes a charming place card of sorts. At your next brunch, try monogramming the shells of hard-boiled eggs with a fancy colored marker. Once they're in an eggcup, set one atop each place setting. (Bonus points if you doodle a sketch of each guest on the shell!)

ENJOY THE PREP. While many hostesses prefer to set the table the evening prior or the morning of a dinner party, we particularly relish that lovely (but all-too-short) window right before guests arrive, when the greens have been chopped, the oven is warm, and you're dressed just so. Turn up the music, pour yourself a glass of wine, and we assure you: Magic will ensue. (It's a fact: Only you will know if that napkin ring is askew!)

BE LOUD (AND MESSY). You heard us—make a merry noise. Mix, mingle, laugh, dance, splash, spill, and certainly toast with abandon. The most memorable dinner parties are often the most dreadful to clean up. And remember: Plates can always soak—now's the time to soak up your company.

THE SWEET SPOT

HOT & COLD DESSERTS

BLUEBERRY ICE CREAM

RONNYBROOK FARM DAIRY

MAKES 1 QUART (1 L)

18 ounces (510 g) fresh blueberries

1 cup (240 ml) whole milk

1 cup (240 ml) heavy cream, preferably not ultra-pasteurized

1⅓ cups (260 g) sugar

8 large egg yolks, preferably from free-range eggs

This is an Osofsky family favorite (the family behind Ronnybrook Farm), going back to the days when the collective cousins and Nana Osofsky would go blueberry picking in the late summer. Cooking the blueberries concentrates their flavor to make an especially rich version of this treat. If you wish, top each serving with extra blueberries and a drizzle of wildflower honey. (See photo on previous page.)

1. Purée the blueberries in a food processor or blender. You should have 3 cups (720 ml) of purée. Transfer it to a medium heavy-bottomed saucepan and bring it to a boil over medium heat. Reduce the heat to medium-low and simmer, stirring often, until the purée is reduced by half, about 15 minutes. Set it aside.

2. Combine the milk, cream, and ⅔ cup (130 g) of the sugar in a medium heavy-bottomed saucepan. Bring them to a simmer over medium heat, stirring often to dissolve the sugar. Remove the pan from the heat.

3. Set a wire sieve over a medium heatproof bowl near the stove. In a medium bowl, whisk together the egg yolks and remaining ⅔ cup (130 g) sugar until it is thick and pale yellow, about 1 minute. Gradually whisk the hot milk mixture into the egg mixture. Return this mixture to the saucepan and cook it over medium-low heat, stirring constantly with a wooden spoon, until the custard is thick enough to coat the spoon (your finger will cut a swath through the custard on the back of a spoon) and an instant-read thermometer inserted in the custard reads 180°F (82°C), about 3 minutes. Immediately whisk in the blueberry purée. Strain the mixture through the sieve into the bowl. Discard any solids in the sieve. Put the bowl of custard into a larger bowl of iced water and let it stand, stirring occasionally, until it is cold, changing the ice as needed, about 30 minutes. (The mixture can be covered and refrigerated for up to 1 day.)

4. Pour the mixture into an ice-cream maker and process according to the manufacturer's directions. Transfer the soft ice cream to a freezer-safe covered container and freeze until it is firm, at least 4 hours. Scoop the ice cream into serving bowls and serve it immediately.

Nutella, the chocolate and hazelnut spread, has been a European favorite since the 1940s, and it is now easily found at American supermarkets, too. It makes an excellent filling for crêpes, especially with the addition of sliced bananas. Be sure that the bananas are thinly sliced so they will be flexible when the crêpe is folded; otherwise, the bananas can poke through the crêpe. Serve this for dessert, or as an indulgent brunch entrée, with fruit salad and Champagne. Bar Suzette uses local, organic ingredients whenever possible, and recommends them for their recipes. Read the Tips on page 138 for more information before embarking on your crêpe journey. To make this with large crêpes, use 2 tablespoons Nutella per crêpe and 6 banana slices, and fold them into thirds.

1. To make the batter: Process the flour, milk, eggs, oil, and salt together in a blender, stopping the blender to scrape down the batter as needed, until it is smooth. Transfer it to a bowl, cover, and refrigerate it for at least 2 hours.

2. Lightly oil a 7-inch (17-cm) nonstick skillet (measured across the skillet bottom) with a folded paper towel dipped in the oil. (Never spray a nonstick skillet with aerosol cooking spray, as the propellant ingredients in the spray will stick to the surface and will break the pan's warranty.) Heat the skillet over medium heat until it is hot.

3. Pour ¼ cup (60 ml) of the batter into the skillet. Immediately and quickly tilt the pan so the batter swirls into a thin layer that coats the bottom. Fill any empty spots in the crêpe with drips of the batter. Cook until the crêpe looks set and the edges are dry, about 1 minute. Using a heatproof silicone spatula, lift up an edge of the crêpe and flip it over. Cook until the other side is set and lightly browned, about 45 seconds. Transfer it to a plate. Repeat with the remaining batter, separating the crêpes with sheets of parchment or waxed paper. You should have 12 to 14 crepes. The crêpes can be stored at room temperature for up to 2 hours. (For longer storage, let the crêpes cool completely, wrap the stack in plastic wrap, and refrigerate it for up to 2 days or freeze for up to 1 month. Thaw the frozen crêpes before using.)

4. Preheat the oven to 350°F (170°C). Lightly butter a large baking sheet with some of the melted butter.

5. Make the filling: For each crêpe, place a crêpe in front of you, spotted side up. On the bottom right quadrant of the crêpe, smear 1 tablespoon of the Nutella and place 3 banana rounds. Fold the crêpe in quarters to enclose the ingredients. Place it on the baking sheet. Repeat with the remaining crêpes and filling. Brush all of the folded crêpes with the remaining butter.

6. Bake until the crêpes are heated and the Nutella is barely beginning to melt, about 10 minutes. To serve, transfer 2 filled crêpes to a plate. Serve at once.

NUTELLA & BANANA CRÊPES

BAR SUZETTE

SERVES 6; MAKES 6 LARGE OR 12 SMALL CRÊPES

FOR THE CRÊPE BATTER:

1⅔ cups (210 g) unbleached all-purpose flour

1½ cups (360 ml) whole milk

3 large eggs

1 teaspoon extra-virgin olive oil

Pinch fine sea salt

Vegetable oil, for the skillet

3 tablespoons (45 g) unsalted butter, melted

FOR THE FILLING:

12 tablespoons (250 g) chocolate-hazelnut spread, such as Nutella

3 large bananas, very thinly sliced into 36 rounds

Tangy and smooth, this creamy dessert is a cool finish to an elegant meal. Serve it with your favorite berries and tropical fruits (such as raspberries with peeled mango and papaya cubes), perhaps mixed with some minced crystallized ginger.

1. Sprinkle the gelatin over the milk in a small custard cup or ramekin. Let it stand until the mixture swells and softens, about 5 minutes. Heat ¾ cup (180 ml) of the cream in a medium saucepan over low heat until it is hot but not simmering. Add the softened gelatin mixture and stir constantly, without simmering, until the gelatin is completely dissolved, about 2 minutes. Remove it from the heat.

2. Whisk the remaining ¾ cup (180 ml) cream with the sugar, yogurt, sour cream, and lemon juice in a medium bowl until the sugar dissolves. Whisk about ½ cup (120 ml) of the yogurt mixture into the gelatin mixture in the saucepan. Pour the gelatin mixture into the yogurt mixture and whisk until combined.

3. Lightly oil the ramekins. Divide the yogurt mixture among the ramekins and cover each with plastic wrap. Refrigerate them until they are chilled and set, at least 4 hours or up to 2 days.

4. To serve, unwrap the ramekins. Run a dinner knife around the inside of each ramekin, being sure to reach to the bottom to break the air seal. One at a time, place a dessert plate over a ramekin, then invert the ramekin onto the plate. Holding the ramekin and plate together, give them a firm shake to unmold the panna cotta onto the plate. If it is stubborn, dip the ramekin (right-side up) in a bowl of hot water and hold it for 10 seconds, dry the ramekin, and try unmolding it again. Surround each panna cotta with fresh fruit and serve it chilled.

YOGURT PANNA COTTA

WITH TROPICAL FRUITS

BUDDAKAN

SERVES 6

2¼ teaspoons (1 envelope/7g) unflavored gelatin powder

¼ cup (60 ml) whole milk

1½ cups (360 ml) heavy cream

1 cup (200 g) sugar

¾ cup (190 g) plain low-fat yogurt

¾ cup (170 g) sour cream

2 tablespoons fresh lemon juice

Vegetable oil, for the ramekins

2 cups assorted fresh berries and tropical fruits, for serving

Special equipment: 6 (¾-cup/180-ml) ramekins

TRIPLE-CHOCOLATE PUDDING

SARABETH'S BAKERY

SERVES 6

3 tablespoons unsalted butter

4½ ounces (130 g) semisweet chocolate (no more than 62% cacao content), finely chopped

1 ounce (30 g) unsweetened chocolate, finely chopped

3 cups (720 ml) whole milk

1 cup (200 g) sugar

¼ cup (20 g) Dutch-processed cocoa powder

3 tablespoons cornstarch

⅛ teaspoon fine sea salt

3 large eggs plus 1 large egg yolk

¼ cup (60 ml) heavy cream

1 tablespoon dark rum

1 teaspoon pure vanilla extract

Chocolate curls (see Tips), for garnish

Whipped cream (page 176, optional)

Special equipment: 6 (1-cup/240-ml) glass jars or bowls

Who says that chocolate pudding is for kids? Sarabeth's thick-as-mud rendition has two kinds of chocolate bolstered with cocoa to make it a triple threat for chocolate lovers. At the bakery, the pudding is served in small canning jars, and many a buttoned-down type has been seen scraping the jar with their fingers to be sure to get every last bit.

1. Melt the butter in a heatproof bowl over a medium saucepan of hot (not simmering) water. Add the two chocolates and stir often, until they are melted and smooth. Remove the bowl from the saucepan.

2. Heat the milk and ⅓ cup (65 g) of the sugar in a medium saucepan over medium heat until it is steaming.

3. Whisk the remaining ⅔ cup (135 g) sugar with the cocoa, cornstarch, and salt in a heatproof medium bowl. Add the eggs, yolk, and cream and whisk until they are well combined. Gradually whisk in about half of the hot milk mixture. Then, while whisking, pour the egg mixture into the saucepan. Bring it to a full boil over medium heat, whisking often, being sure to reach into the corners of the saucepan. Reduce the heat to low and let it bubble for 30 seconds.

4. Remove the pan from the heat. Strain the pudding into a medium heatproof bowl. Add the melted chocolate mixture, rum, and vanilla and whisk until they are combined. Spoon the pudding into six jars or bowls. Cover each one with a piece of plastic wrap, pressing the wrap directly on the surface of the pudding, and pierce it a few times with the tip of a small sharp knife. (If you like a skin on your pudding, do not cover the jars.) Let the puddings cool at room temperature until they are tepid, about 1 hour. Refrigerate them until chilled, at least 2 hours. (The puddings can be refrigerated for up to 3 days.)

5. To serve, remove the plastic wrap, and top each serving with chocolate curls and whipped cream, if desired. Serve it chilled.

TIPS FROM THE PROS

CHOCOLATE CURLS
Sarabeth's Bakery

Chocolate curls add a professional-looking finish to many desserts. Start with a 4-ounce (115-g) or larger chunk of semisweet or bittersweet chocolate at warm room temperature (about 75°F/25°C); if it is too cold, it will break into shards. Place the chocolate in a warm spot in the kitchen (near the turned-on stove or directly under a counter light) to bring it to the right temperature. Or, barely heat the chocolate in a microwave oven on low power for about 15 seconds. Pressing hard on the chocolate chunk with a swivel-style vegetable peeler, shave curls of chocolate onto a plate. Refrigerate them until ready to serve. Use a fork to move the curls—if you touch them with your fingers, they will melt.

CHOCOLATE GELATO

L'ARTE DEL GELATO

MAKES ABOUT 1 QUART (960 ML)

9 ounces (255 g) bittersweet (66 to 70% cacao) chocolate, finely chopped

½ cup (100 g) granulated sugar

¼ cup (20 g) Dutch-processed cocoa powder

3 tablespoons potato starch (see Note) or cornstarch

2¼ cups (540 ml) whole milk

¼ cup (60 ml) heavy cream

Pinch kosher salt

NOTE: *Potato starch is a fine powder used as a thickener for cooked sauces. You'll find it at stores that carry kosher products and in the baking or gluten-free product section of many supermarkets. For these gelato recipes, cornstarch is a good substitute.*

The owner of L'Arte del Gelato, Francesco Realmuto, says that working with chocolate is like raising a challenging but gifted child. A lot of love and hard work went into this recipe to create a balance of ingredients for both flavor and texture. The end result is a velvety gelato with the perfect proportions—dark but never bitter. Of all L'Arte del Gelato's flavors, this is their personal favorite—high praise, indeed.

1. Put the chocolate in a medium heatproof bowl and set it aside. Whisk the sugar, cocoa, and potato starch together in a medium saucepan. Gradually whisk in enough of the milk to make a smooth paste. Whisk in the remaining milk, the cream, and salt. Cook the mixture over medium heat, whisking often, just until it comes to a full boil and thickens. Pour it over the chocolate and let it stand until the chocolate softens, about 3 minutes. Whisk until it is smooth.

2. Nestle the bowl into a larger bowl of iced water and let them stand, stirring occasionally, until the base is thoroughly chilled, at least 30 minutes. (The chocolate mixture can be covered and refrigerated for up to 1 day.)

3. Pour the mixture into an ice-cream maker and process according to the manufacturer's directions. Transfer the gelato to a freezer-safe covered container and freeze until it is firm, at least 4 hours. Scoop the gelato into serving bowls and serve it at once.

Here is the classic dessert, tiramisú ("pick-me-up" in Italian), in gelato form. The original recipe varies from cook to cook, although espresso, mascarpone, and crisp ladyfingers are the constants. L'Arte del Gelato's version has a bit of brandy and the cookies are served on the side. The gelateria's owner, Francesco Realmuto, explains that the difference between gelato and ice cream is the fat content, as gelato has more milk than cream. In this recipe, the cream factor is provided by the mascarpone.

1. Whisk the sugar and egg yolks together in a medium bowl until the mixture is thick and pale yellow, about 1 minute. Add the mascarpone, espresso, potato starch, and brandy and whisk until they are smooth. Gradually whisk in the milk.

2. Place a wire sieve over a heatproof medium bowl near the stove. Transfer the mascarpone mixture to a medium heavy-bottomed saucepan. Cook it over medium heat, whisking constantly, just until the mixture comes to a simmer and thickens. Do not bring it to a full boil or the egg yolks will curdle. Strain the mixture through the sieve into the bowl; discard any solids. Nestle the bowl of the mascarpone mixture into a larger bowl of iced water and let them stand, stirring occasionally, until the base is thoroughly chilled, changing the ice as needed, at least 30 minutes. (The mixture can be covered and refrigerated for up to 1 day.)

3. Pour the mixture into an ice-cream maker and process according to the manufacturer's directions. Transfer the gelato to a freezer-safe covered container and freeze until it is firm, at least 4 hours. Scoop the gelato into serving bowls and sift a little cocoa on top. Serve it immediately, with the *savoiardi*.

TIRAMISÚ GELATO

L'ARTE DEL GELATO

MAKES ABOUT 1 QUART (960 ML)

¾ cup (150 g) granulated sugar

5 large egg yolks

⅔ cup (150 g) mascarpone cheese

⅓ cup (75 ml) brewed espresso or Italian or French roast coffee

2 tablespoons potato starch (see Note, page 204) or cornstarch

1 tablespoon brandy

2¼ cups (540 ml) whole milk

Dutch-processed cocoa powder, for serving

Savoiardi (crisp Italian ladyfingers), for serving

YELLOW WATERMELON & MINT POPS

PEOPLE'S POPS

MAKES 8

¾ cup (150 g) sugar

5 to 6 large sprigs fresh mint plus
2 teaspoons very thinly sliced fresh mint

1 quart (960 ml) peeled, seeded, and
chopped yellow watermelon

2 tablespoons fresh lemon juice

*Special equipment: 8 (½-cup/120-ml)
ice pop molds (and wooden sticks, if
required for your molds)*

**At first lick, these pops will bring back memories of summer afternoons—but
with the distinction that these sophisticated frozen treats are made with fresh
fruit and herbs. You can use any watermelon, although yellow is an unexpected
change from red. Basil and tarragon are good alternatives to the mint.**

1. Combine the sugar and ¾ cup (180 ml) water in a medium saucepan.
Bring them to a boil, stirring often to dissolve the sugar. Reduce the heat
to medium-low and cover. Simmer until the syrup is lightly thickened,
about 5 minutes. Remove the saucepan from the heat. Stir in the mint
sprigs, and let the pan stand, uncovered, until the syrup is completely
cooled. Drain the syrup in a wire sieve over a bowl, squeezing the mint
between your fingertips to extract the very last drops; discard the mint.

2. Purée the watermelon in a food processor or blender. (If you wish,
leave some of the watermelon in tiny chunks that are small enough to
fit into the mold.) Pour the purée into a bowl. Stir in enough of the mint
syrup to make a very sweet mixture (see Tips). Stir in the sliced mint.
Divide the purée evenly among the eight ice pop molds, leaving a little
clearance at the top of each mold to allow for expansion. Cover the molds
with the lids (adding wooden sticks, if needed).

3. Freeze the pops until they are solid, at least 4 hours. (The pops can
be frozen for up to 1 week.) To serve, run the bottom of the molds briefly
under lukewarm water and unmold.

TIPS FROM THE PROS

PERFECT POPS
People's Pops

Here are some tips to making the most of your frozen pops:

• *There are many different options for ice pop molds, in various shapes and
with or without handles. If your molds require wooden sticks for handles,
be sure to buy a sufficient quantity so you don't run short. You'll find them
at craft shops.*

• *The amount of syrup added to the fruit purée will change according to the
fruit's natural sweetness, so adjust it as necessary. The fruit mixture should
taste quite sugary because freezing dulls the flavors, and the frozen pop will
seem less sweet when eaten.*

• *The pops will expand slightly when frozen, so leave some headroom at the
top of each mold.*

COFFEE BREWING 101

NINTH STREET ESPRESSO

You may not realize it, but creating good espresso is a craft that requires thousands of dollars in equipment and countless hours of training. However, brewing great, consistently flavorful coffee at home is a far simpler and more attainable goal. Keep in mind that everything, from the beans to the filters, affects the flavor. Here is some insider advice and helpful tips to brew coffee at home.

1. Always start with fresh, whole bean coffee. It might seem obvious, but many coffee drinkers brew coffee from stale beans. Roasted coffee has a life span of two weeks, so only buy coffees that display a roast date. Coffee derives its flavors and aromas from the oils contained within the bean, so preserving those oils is crucial. Also, be sure to protect your beans from direct sunlight. When ground beans come into contact with oxygen and light, the oils begin to oxidize within minutes, and the flavor will immediately begin to degrade. Storing coffee in the fridge or freezer won't help. To the contrary, it will do more harm than good, as the coffee will absorb surrounding odors and be impacted by the changed moisture content. Store your beans whole, at room temperature, preferably in the bag supplied by the roaster. A good rule of thumb is to only buy as many coffee beans as you are going to use in a week and always grind them to order.

2. Controlling the brew process, including temperature and brew time, is crucial. Most electric drip brewers aren't capable of achieving the 200°F (90°C) necessary to optimally brew coffee, so consider a couple of manual alternatives:

• A press pot (also known as a French press) uses an infusion method to brew—steep the grounds with heated water in the container, then press the plunger to separate the grounds from the brewed coffee. This allows all of the water and coffee to be in contact throughout the brew cycle. You control the strength of the brew through the grind, dose, and steep time. Since there is no paper filter, none of the essential oils are withheld from the brew.

• Another good option (and personal favorite) is the pour-over method, where you pour heated water over coffee grounds in a filter-lined cone. A great example of this is the iconic Chemex Brewer. The brewed coffee drips through via gravity, but the water temperature and the rate of pouring control the process. It takes a bit of practice to perfect the technique, but it's well worth the effort. This method requires good filters. Poor-quality filters can impart off-flavors and fibers into your brew, as well as disrupt the rate of dripping, making for over- or under-extracted coffee. Buy filters made by and for specialty coffee brewers. Paper filters produce a clean-tasting cup with well-defined flavors, but metal filters work too, especially if you are concerned about the sustainability of disposable filters. Just keep in mind that metal filters tend to allow more particles and solids to pass through, which can change the texture, flavor, and clarity of your cup of coffee (not a bad thing, only a matter of preference).

3. The single most important piece of equipment for making great coffee at home is a good burr grinder. These grinders crush the beans between a pair of flat or conical moving wheels, allowing you to adjust the grind size for the brewing method, and produce a uniform grind without producing too much heat, which will damage the coffee. Because each brewing method exposes ground coffee to hot water in various ways and periods of time, it's important to grind your coffee accordingly. We can't emphasize it enough: Good coffee requires a good grinder!

Infusion methods, such as French press, use a metal screen for filtration, so you want to grind your coffee on the coarser side. For drip and pour-over methods that utilize a paper filter, aim for a medium grind size. Finding the right grind takes a little experimentation, but will drastically affect the quality of the cup.

4. Many folks just eyeball the ratio of coffee to water, but getting more specific here will produce a better cup. For the most consistent results, weigh your coffee and water with a digital scale. Volume can be imprecise—different coffees have different densities, and not every spoon is the same. Begin with 21 grams of coffee for every 12 ounces of water when using a press, and 24 grams of coffee for every 12 ounces of water with a pour-over pot. This is a good starting point; feel free to adjust the measures along with the grind size.

5. The optimal water temperature for brewing coffee is between 198 and 204°F (92 and 95°C). One of the real advantages to brewing manually is that it's easy to get within the ideal temperature range. Just bring the water to a boil, and then let it cool for just under a minute so that it reaches the proper temperature range, and you're ready to pour. A simple kitchen thermometer can help with this.

6. When pouring water over coffee, the "bloom" is the key to a great extraction. Freshly roasted coffee emits small amounts of carbon dioxide that, while harmless, impart flavors that interfere with your palate's ability to taste the coffee's flavors. Think of opening a bottle of seltzer and taking a sip right away—the taste of CO_2 can be very strong and not too pleasant. Blooming the coffee just means starting the brewing process by saturating the grounds with a few ounces of water, letting the mixture stand (or drip) for about 30 seconds to help dissipate the excess CO_2, and then adding the remaining water.

7. Another key to good coffee is cleanliness. Even the smallest amounts of old coffee in your equipment can ruin a good cup of coffee. Clean your brewing gear and grinder daily, and never leave old coffee in the grinder. Stay away from harsh cleaners that tend to leave behind unwanted flavors and residues. A coffee-specific detergent is best, but otherwise use mild soap and water.

In short, if you have a good grinder, your brewer of choice, a kettle (preferably with a nice spout to control the pour), a digital scale, and of course some fresh coffee and good water (use filtered water if you have any doubts), you will make great coffee. The money you spend on this investment will pay off every time you make a cup!

CONTRIBUTORS

& ACKNOWLEDGMENTS

CONTRIBUTORS

Hugh Acheson, Guest Chef
Born in Ottawa, Canada, Hugh Acheson has established his culinary base in Georgia, as chef/partner of Five & Ten, The National, and Empire State South. Hugh's fresh approach to Southern food won him *Food & Wine*'s Best New Chef (2002) and the James Beard Foundation Award for Best Chef: Southeast (2012). His TV appearances as both chef and judge on the *Top Chef* series gained him national recognition, and his first book, *A New Turn in the South* (2011), won a James Beard Foundation Award for best cookbook. www.hughacheson.com

Amy's Bread
Amy's Bread is a well-loved bakery/café that specializes in handmade, traditional breads made from natural, high-quality ingredients. Amy Scherber opened her original location in 1992 in a small storefront in the Hell's Kitchen neighborhood. The bakery expanded in 1996 with a large bread kitchen, followed by the retail café in the Chelsea Market in 1997, and a Greenwich Village café in 2005. Besides the crusty, rustic breads the bakery is known for, Amy's Bread makes morning pastries, sandwiches, and a rotating selection of unique pizzas. www.amysbread.com

Anthropologie
Anthropologie, a store with 175 locations nationwide as well as online, was founded in 1992 and joined the Chelsea Market family in 2010. A lifestyle brand offering clothing, accessories, shoes, beauty, home furnishings, found objects, gifts, and décor, Anthropologie imparts a sense of beauty, optimism, and discovery—an escape from the everyday and a source of inspiration and delight. Buyers and designers travel the world to discover special products and to collaborate with talented artisans. www.anthropologie.com

Bar Suzette
Bar Suzette is an innovative crêpe bar that puts a twist on the French classic with flavors from all over the world. Chefs, co-owners, and childhood friends Peter Tondreau and Troi Lughod discovered that the crêpe is a universal dish, familiar in different forms in almost every culture—in other words, the perfect food for New York City's melting pot of culture and cuisine. Often cited for having the best crêpes in New York, Bar Suzette's creations use the finest ingredients available, many from local sources, including fellow vendors at Chelsea Market. www.barsuzette.com

Michelle Bernstein, Guest Chef
A Miami native, Michelle Bernstein is the executive chef and owner (with her husband) of Michy's restaurant in that city. Her cuisine combines her Jewish and Latin heritage in a thoroughly modern way. She was a winner of the James Beard Foundation Award for Best Chef: South in 2008 and published *Cuisine à Latina* in the same year. Among her multiple TV appearances have been *Iron Chef* and *Top Chef*, where she was a guest judge. Chelsea Market's Sunday Supper has welcomed her cooking expertise since 2009. www.chefmichellebernstein.com

Bowery Kitchen Supply
Bowery Kitchen Supply originally sold refurbished kitchen equipment in the heart of the restaurant furbishing district on the Bowery in 1975 and became one of the inaugural tenants of the Market in 1997. Transforming from a Lower East Side catch-all shop to a chic kitchen supply store, Bowery Kitchen expanded its small-wares department, developed a specialty in cutlery with the largest selection in New York, and added a sandwich shop. Now operated by Howard Nourieli and Robyn Coval, Bowery Kitchen supplies chefs from restaurants around the city and from the Food Network, bars, delicatessens, bakeries, and dozens of other types of food establishments, as well as the serious home cook, with over one hundred brands of equipment. www.bowerykitchens.com

Buon'Italia
When Mimmo and Tonia Magliulo first came to New York from Naples in 1978, finding true Italian ingredients was difficult. They solved the problem by starting Buon'Italia to supply restaurants, hotels, and gourmet stores. In 1997, the family opened their Chelsea Market retail store as a source for all things Italian, selling imported oils, vinegars, cheeses, charcuterie, pastas (fresh, frozen, and dried), grains, truffles, and spices. In the back of the store is an Italian-style salumeria, and at the front, an espresso bar. In a bit of a departure from the Italian theme, but in keeping with its tradition of fine imports, Buon'Italia also has a selection of caviars from Iran and Russia. www.buonitalia.com

Buddakan
With its stunning accoutrements, cathedral-high ceilings, and Buddha paintings on golden walls, Buddakan is a glamorous temple to fine Chinese cuisine. Stephen Starr, a restaurateur who first made his mark in Philadelphia, has brought his sense of style and hospitality smarts to the Big Apple, and made Buddakan one of the hippest and tastiest eateries in town. The restaurant was used for key scenes in the television series *Sex and the City*, and the film based on the show. www.buddakannyc.com

Marco Canora, Guest Chef
Marco Canora, chef, restaurateur, and cookbook writer, runs Terroir on The Porch, the seasonal wine bar on the High Line directly above the Market. There are other four Terroir wine bars in lower Manhattan, and his East Village restaurant, Hearth, is a destination for lovers of Canora's delicious, simple, and healthful food. His first cookbook, *Salt to Taste* (Rodale), was nominated for a James Beard Foundation Cookbook Award and was singled out by both *Food & Wine* and *Gourmet* magazines.

Chelsea Market Baskets
A wholesaler of specialty foods and gift baskets, David Porat met Irwin Cohen just as Cohen was developing plans for Chelsea Market, and, in 1997, Chelsea Market Baskets became one of the Market's original stores. Combining every conceivable food from European as well as local suppliers, Chelsea Market Baskets creates custom-made edible gifts for customers who visit the Market in person as well as online customers. The food gifts now extend to hand-cut artisanal cheeses and cheese platters, prepared and delivered to New York City food lovers. www.chelseamarketbasket.com

Chelsea Thai
Saruj Nimkarn and his family pride themselves on creating an authentic Thai experience tucked into Chelsea Market, offering both freshly prepared Thai food and a grocery section to buy ingredients for Asian cooking at home. One of the early Chelsea Market vendors, Chelsea Thai has maintained its original goals and standards. www.chelseathai.com

Chelsea Wine Vault
Chelsea Wine Vault, along with its sister business Chelsea Wine Storage, has been an anchor of Chelsea Market since the Market first opened in 1997. Founders Dan Barteluce and Don Kurt pride themselves on operating one of New York's friendliest and best-stocked fine wine stores, offering customers a pleasant and

professional wine-buying experience in a beautiful and unique environment. Chelsea Wine Vault maintains its friendly approach and high standards with the motto "We only buy wine we love," catering to a range of different tastes and budgets. Every wine is tasted before it enters the store, most stock consists of small-producer wines, and the staff enjoys teaching customers as much as they like tasting wine. www.chelseawinevault.com

Giada De Laurentiis, Guest Chef
Well known for her popular TV series on the Food Network and her regular appearances on the *TODAY* show, Giada De Laurentiis is a classically trained chef who studied at the Cordon Bleu in Paris before returning to Los Angeles to work at the Ritz-Carlton Fine Dining Room and Wolfgang Puck's Spago. Her first TV show, *Everyday Italian*, debuted in 2003, and several more followed, including *The Next Food Network Star*, on which she was a mentor and judge. Her six cookbooks, of which the most recent is *Weekends with Giada*, have all been *New York Times* bestsellers. www.giadadelaurentiis.com

Dickson's Farmstand Meats
Dickson's Farmstand Meats is a purveyor of a unique selection of artisanal meat and meat products. Its beef, lamb, pork, goat, and poultry are sourced from local farms, chosen for each grower's commitment to producing natural, humanely raised, high-quality, and distinctive meat products. Originally in marketing, Jake Dickson opened his Chelsea Market store in 2009. Dickson's products are selected to satisfy the food needs, discerning tastes, and conscientiousness of the New York City community—grass-fed/grass-finished, organic, heritage breed, and more traditional meat and poultry. www.dicksonsfarmstand.com

Eleni's New York
Raised in Piedmont, a neighborhood of Oakland, California, Eleni Gianopulos has called New York home for nearly twenty-five years. After beginning her corporate career at Time, Inc., she began a side business featuring a family recipe, which quickly became a full-fledged baking business. Since 1997, Eleni's has been a must-stop at the Market, and it was later joined by an Upper East Side location and an expansive Web site, selling "Conversation Cookies™" and other treats. Nationally known for their uniquely designed cookies, Eleni's creations are a favorite of celebrities, luxury brands, Fortune 500 companies, and cookie lovers alike. www.elenis.com

Fat Witch
As a trader on Wall Street, Patricia Helding found herself unwinding from a stressful day by baking in the evenings. After perfecting her brownie recipe, she began taking batches to work, where they were eagerly devoured by her co-workers. She opened her own bakery, specializing in brownies, in 1998. Today, the Fat Witch bakery produces more than 2,500 brownies a day. Helding is also the author of the cookbook *Fat Witch Brownies*. www.fatwitch.com

The Filling Station
The Filling Station became a part of the Chelsea Market in 2010, when Laura Nuter and Megan Cariola teamed up to bring a unique and environmentally friendly concept to the Market. The Filling Station offers a wide selection of exceptional specialty oils, balsamic vinegars, salts, and craft beers, all sold in reusable glass bottles and jars. They provide their customers with an opportunity to taste before purchasing and encourage recycling by offering a discount for customers who bring back their containers for refilling. Stocking only natural ingredients (and often organic or

organically grown), the Filling Station works only with the best importers, distributors, and brewers. www.thefillingstationnyc.com

Bobby Flay, Guest Chef
TV star and eminent chef Bobby Flay is owner and executive chef of twelve restaurants: Mesa Grill in Las Vegas, New York City, and the Bahamas; Bar Americain in New York City and Uncasville, Connecticut; Bobby Flay Steak in Atlantic City; and Bobby's Burger Palace in Long Island, New Jersey, Connecticut, Maryland, and Washington, D.C. In addition to his eleven best-selling cookbooks, Bobby has also been the star of numerous TV programs, including *Throwdown with Bobby Flay*, *Iron Chef*, and *The Next Food Network Star*. Since he is based near the Food Network's headquarters in New York City, Bobby is a frequent visitor to Chelsea Market. www.bobbyflay.com

Marc Forgione, Guest Chef
Marc Forgione is chef-owner of Restaurant Marc Forgione in New York City. He has been the recipient of numerous awards, including Key Newcomer from the Zagat Guide in 2009. Marc is one of the Iron Chefs currently competing on *Iron Chef America*, having won season three of *Next Iron Chef* in 2003. Forgione was long associated with Laurent Tourondel, for whom he served as chef of several of the restaurants and ultimately corporate chef of the BLT Restaurant Group. Marc is the son of legendary New York restaurateur Larry Forgione. www.marcforgione.com

Friedman's Lunch
Under the direction of chef Justin Brunwasser, this contemporary take on the neighborhood delicatessen has made Friedman's a favorite among the Chelsea Market tourists and local diners alike. As one of the original owners has celiac disease, nearly all of the dishes on the menu are gluten free, making Friedman's a destination for those with wheat allergies. Their menu ranges from deli classics like pastrami and roast turkey to fresh salads made with the very freshest ingredients. www.friedmanslunch.com

Giovanni Rana Pastificio & Cucina
Italy's renowned purveyor of fresh stuffed pasta for over fifty years, the Rana family has chosen Chelsea Market for their first American venue. The store embodies two iconic Italian culinary concepts: The *pastificio* (pasta-making area), where the pasta is made from scratch with select quality ingredients, and the *cucina* (kitchen), where the house-made pasta and other creative dishes are prepared to allow guests to enjoy the Italian dining experience.

The Green Table/Cleaver Co.
For nearly thirty-five years—long before "locavore" made it into the *Oxford American Dictionary*—Mary Cleaver has served fresh, flavorful food to city diners. Mary brought The Cleaver Co., her eponymous event planning and catering company, from TriBeCa to the Chelsea Market as an original tenant in 1997. Wanting a wider audience to experience seasonal, local food, Mary opened The Green Table in 2003. Widely recognized for sourcing her high-quality products from regional farms and purveyors, and for supporting small to midsize farms and family farmers, Mary is renowned for her work helping to create a sustainable and humane food system. Whether at a gala for five hundred or a cozy dinner for two at The Green Table, Mary's long-standing conviction—that the best foods are grown, tended, and harvested within a day's drive of your table—is always clear. www.cleaverco.com

Alexandra Guarnaschelli, Guest Chef

Daughter of cookbook editor Maria Guarnaschelli, former culinary student of the acclaimed American chef Larry Forgione, and former sous-chef of the restaurant Daniel (Boulud), Alex Guarnaschelli has an unparalleled cooking pedigree. Currently, Alex is both executive chef of Butter (New York City) and a TV personality, with appearances that include Food Network's *Iron Chef America* as both a challenger and a judge, *Chopped* as a judge, and her own shows, *The Cooking Loft*, as well as *Alex's Day Off*. She has cooked for the Chelsea Market's Sunday Supper since 2009.

Kurt Gutenbrunner, Guest Chef

Kurt Gutenbrunner is owner of an impressive portfolio of top-rated New York City restaurants, including Wallsé, Blaue Gans, Café Kristall, and Café Sabarsky in the Neue Galerie museum. He is also a consultant for such ventures as the Standard Hotel Group's Biergartens in New York and Los Angeles. His first book, *Neue Cuisine*, a celebration of the chef's favorite Austrian recipes, appeared in 2011. Also in 2011, he was awarded the Decoration of Merit in Gold of the Republic of Austria. He has been a regular participant at the Chelsea Market Sunday Supper since 2009. www.kg-ny.com

Jacques Torres Chocolates

Master Pastry Chef Jacques Torres's chain of chocolate factories and retail boutiques are his American Dream come true. In 1986, he became the youngest pastry chef in history to earn the prestigious Meilleur Ouvrier de France (Best Craftsman of France) medal in pastry. In 2000, he launched his first stores and factories featuring his handmade artisanal chocolates and in 2009, he opened his Chelsea Market store. Fondly known as Mr. Chocolate (and the author of three cookbooks, including *A Year in Chocolate* with Judith Choate), Jacques Torres combines traditional French techniques with his vast knowledge and passion for the culinary arts to produce luxe, creative, and edgy chocolate treats inspired by the innovative spirit and energy of the city. Jacques Torres Chocolates is proud to produce real food bursting with real flavor, made without taking any shortcuts or adding any preservatives or artificial flavorings. www.mrchocolate.com

L'Arte del Gelato

Working as a cutter in the Diamond District in the early 2000s, Francesco Realmuto, missed the gelati and sorbetti of his homeland. What began as a hunger pang grew into a quest. He quit his job, found and trained with masters from Sicily to Venice, and learned the classic recipes of the Italian tradition of *dolcefreddo*. In June 2005, he proudly opened his first store in Chelsea Market—selling classic, artisanal gelati and sorbetti made *fresco ogni giorno* (fresh every day), a phrase that is now the company motto. Although L'Arte del Gelato has a branch in the West Village and outdoor stands around New York City, the flagship Chelsea Market Gelateria and Laboratorio will always be best loved for its part in the New York food movement. www.lartedelgelato.com

Anita Lo, Guest Chef

Since *Food & Wine* magazine named Anita Lo one of the ten "Best New Chefs in America in 2001," she has continued to thrive as a renowned New York City chef. Annisa, her signature restaurant, and Rickshaw, her dumpling bar with several locations, showcase her Chinese-American origins, her extensive foreign travel, and her Parisian culinary training. Lo has appeared on *Iron Chef America* and *Top Chef Masters*. Her cuisine has graced the Chelsea Market Sunday Suppers event since 2009. Her book, *Cooking Without Borders*, was published in 2011. www.annisarestaurant.com

The Lobster Place

The Lobster Place was one of the first tenants to move into Chelsea Market, and just as the Market has evolved and grown, so has the store. Rod and Joan MacGregor founded The Lobster Place in the 1970s based on a simple idea: to bring a taste of the Maine coast, with all of its rugged, earnest sensibilities, to New York City. They were among the first entrepreneurs in New York to transport and hold live lobsters, and they built a business selling the crustaceans to the food service trade. When they moved the company to Chelsea Market in the late 1990s, they extended their business to a retail clientele and a full range of seafood products. Under the management of the founders' son, Ian, The Lobster Place is now the largest and most diverse retail seafood market on the East Coast, selling everything from a variety of fresh oysters to sea urchins and beautiful ultra-fresh fish. www.lobsterplace.com

Los Tacos No. 1

Los Tacos No. 1 was created after three close friends from Tijuana, Mexico, and Brawley, California, decided to bring the authentic Mexican taco to the East Coast of the United States. The authentic taste comes from family recipes and from fresh, simple, and tasteful ingredients straight from home. In every taco from Los Tacos No. 1, you'll savor true Mexican culture and flavor. www.lostacos1.com

Lucy's Whey

Lucy Kazickas opened her original store in East Hampton, New York, in 2008, and her Chelsea Market outpost in 2009, both dedicated to a passion for all forms of cheese. Lucy's Whey offers a comprehensive, carefully chosen selection of artisan and farmstead cheeses, all made in the United States. Declaring a mission that showcases quality American cheeses, supports the craftspeople and farms that make and grow good food, and educates the public about artisan cheeses, Lucy's Whey curates its selection carefully. Each cheese is unique and presents distinctive flavors that reflect the region and ingenuity of the cheesemaker. The staff at Lucy's Whey are dedicated cheesemongers, with extensive experience selling, making, and teaching about cheese. www.lucyswhey.com

Manhattan Fruit Exchange

As it became one of the first businesses to join the Chelsea Market, Manhattan Fruit Exchange transformed from a wholesale to a retail business, extending their market from restaurants and retailers directly to everyday customers. Offering a wide array of seasonal produce, the Manhattan Fruit Exchange also prides itself on reasonable prices on unusual fruits and vegetables, such as dragon fruit, passion fruit, and a variety of baby vegetables. Little by little, over the years, the business grew into a multipurpose grocery, offering freshly made juices, imported cheese selections, coffee, fresh herbs, microgreens, and dried goods, as well as the impeccably fresh produce for which they are best known. www.manhattanfruitex.com

Morimoto

Chef Masaharu Morimoto—known to millions as the star of *Iron Chef* and *Iron Chef America*—has garnered critical and popular acclaim for his seamless integration of Western and Japanese ingredients. He currently has nine celebrated restaurants around the world, from Mumbai to Napa. His eponymous restaurant at Chelsea Market opened in 2006, and won a James Beard Foundation Award for Outstanding Restaurant Design. *Morimoto: The New Art of Japanese Cooking*, his first cookbook, was awarded by the International Association of Culinary Professionals in both the "Chef and Restaurant" and "First Book" categories. www.moriomotorestaurant.com

Ninth Street Espresso

Ken Nye, owner of Ninth Street Espresso, is one of New York City's most prominent coffee experts. Since he opened his first specialty coffee store in the East Village in 2001, it has expanded to three separate locations and become a mainstay for coffee purists. In other words, Ninth Street Espresso is where coffee lovers can find the perfect cappuccino, but not flavored syrups or other additives. Launched in 2007, the Chelsea Market location—strategically situated near the Market's central fountain—is one of the busiest specialty coffee bars in America. Ken believes in elevating the standards of coffee while shedding its often snobby reputation. www.ninthstreetespresso.com

Nut Box

A paean to all manner of nuts, at The Nut Box you will find stacks of neatly packaged top-quality nuts and seeds, as well fine snacks like luscious dried fruits and chocolate- or yogurt-covered goodies. Owner James Locke opened his first shop in Brooklyn's Cobble Hill, and now has outposts at the Market and in the East Village.

One Lucky Duck

A native of Newton, Massachusetts, Sarma Melngailis moved to New York City in 1994 to work in the financial industry. Five years and several jobs later, she left that business to attend the French Culinary Institute. In 2003, with a partner, she opened a raw food restaurant, Pure Food and Wine, and in 2005, started oneluckyduck.com, which has a retail store at Chelsea Market. The business is known for and strives to be the definitive source for the very best of everything for raw and organic, eco-happy daily living, which includes freshly made juices, shakes, salads, and other takeaway, as well as a selection of raw sweets and packaged snacks. She is the co-author of *Raw Food Real Food* and *Living Raw Food*. www.oneluckyduck.com

People's Pops

People's Pops began as a one-day experiment based on a hunch by friends Joel Horowitz, David Carrell, and Nathalie Jordi that "the world deserves a better ice pop." As the business grew, the mission remained the same—to showcase the best local, sustainably grown fruit and herbs in creative handmade ice pops and shaved ice. People's Pops are found all over New York City and its environs at specialty shops and pop-up locations, as well as their pop stand at the Market. Their cookbook, *People's Pops*, was released in 2012. www.peoplespops.com

Posman Books

The climate for bookstores changed greatly in the decade from 1999 (when the first Posman Books opened in Grand Central Terminal) to 2009, the debut of the Chelsea Market store. Throughout the years, the family owners and bookstore staff at Posman have seen opportunities to evolve, expand, and grow stronger as New York City independent booksellers. Like the very best independent bookstores, proprietors Eugene and Maxene Posman have an experienced and well-read staff, an unbiased yet discriminating selection, and a commitment to the communities they serve. A third Posman Books recently opened at Rockefeller Center. www.posmanbooks.com

Ronnybrook Farm Dairy

In 1941, long before anyone had heard of megafarms or agricorporations, Nana and Papa Osofsky started a small dairy farm,

naming it for their eldest son, Ronny. In 1991, Ronnybrook Farm became Ronnybrook Farm Dairy when the family decided to eliminate the middleman by producing their own line of premium dairy products with milk from their cows and selling it directly to consumers at greenmarkets, stores, and restaurants. The Chelsea Market store now combines a dairy store with a counter restaurant. Today, Rick Osofsky and the extended Osofsky family continue to work its Hudson Valley pastures, making milk products as they have for three generations, in small batches, delivered at peak freshness, pasteurized and without the use of rBST. www.ronnybrook.com

Ruthy's Bakery

Starting out with a century-old recipe from her great-grandmother Ruth, Patrizia Alessi has maintained the same original flavors and goodness of homemade food in her bakery and take-out offerings. There are old-fashioned cheesecakes and classic rugelach for sale, as well as scrumptious baked goods and a large selection of savory salads, sandwiches, and more. A part of Chelsea Market since it first opened, Ruthy's is an institution with its repeat visitors and steadfast fans. www.ruthys.com

Marcus Samuelsson, Guest Chef

Born in Ethiopia and raised in Sweden, Marcus Samuelsson has brought an eclectic mix of influences to his New York culinary career. Named Best Chef: New York City by the James Beard Foundation while he was executive chef at Aquavit at the age of twenty-four, he went on to open several restaurants, including his latest, Red Rooster, located in Harlem and named Best Neighborhood Joint by the *New York Times*. In 2009, Samuelsson hosted President Barack Obama's first state dinner. Among his many TV appearances was *Top Chef Masters* in 2010, which he won, and then donated the $100,000 prize to UNICEF's "tap project." He also won *Chopped All Stars: Judges Remix* in 2012. Author of four cookbooks, he debuted his latest work, *Yes, Chef*, an autobiography and *New York Times* bestseller, in 2012. www.marcussamuelsson.com

Samurai Sharpening Service

On Wednesdays and Saturdays, Margery Cohen is a familiar figure at her stand in the hall, sharpening knives on her grinding wheel and whetstones for restaurant chefs, Food Network stars, and neighborhood home cooks. She has been sharpening knives since the 1970s, starting in the fish business on the New Jersey shore, moving to Berkeley Bowl in California and honing her skills, and then returning to the East Coast to establish Samurai Sharpening Service at the Market and on location at her clients' establishments. www.samaurisharpening.com

Sarabeth's Bakery

In 1981, Sarabeth began making orange-apricot marmalade in her home kitchen from a family recipe and selling it to local food shops. From that home kitchen beginning, Sarabeth—with her husband and business partner, Bill Levine—grew a prominent business, including a jam factory, a wholesale-retail bakery café in Chelsea Market, and nine restaurants. Although the business continues to expand, Sarabeth enjoys experimenting with new recipes in her Chelsea Market baking kitchen, enjoying the baking traditions of the building as part of the National Biscuit Company. Her book, *Sarabeth's Bakery: From My Hands to Yours*, was nominated for a James Beard Foundation Award in the Baking category. www.sarabeth.com

Jesse Schenker, Guest Chef

A native of Florida, Jesse Schenker became a New York Rising Star Chef in 2011. Previously he had cooked at some of New York's most illustrious restaurants, including Thomas Keller's East Coast outpost, Per Se, and Gordon Ramsay at the London. He opened Recette, his own contemporary urban restaurant, in New York City in 2010, when he was just twenty-seven years old. www.jesseschenker.com

Spices and Tease

Four generations ago, the ancestors of François Athea and Bruno Benzacken, the cousins who own Spices and Tease, started a small spice business in the environs of Naples, Italy. In the early 1960s, one branch of the family expanded the business to the South of France and then to Paris, where they are still today in Galeries Lafayette, providing exceptional-quality spices to French connoisseurs and chefs. In 2003, the two cousins decided to come to America to share their approach to culinary excellence and their family legacy of nearly a century of trading spices and teas with the best farms and small producers all over the world. Spices and Tease, which joined Chelsea Market in 2013, boasts thirty varieties of proprietary spice blends, countless pure whole and ground spices, eighteen kinds of pepper, thirteen types of gourmet salt, 180 exotic imported teas, plus a wealth of natural teas, herbs, seeds, and botanicals. www.spicesandtease.com

Bill Telepan, Guest Chef

A graduate of the Culinary Institute of America, Bill Telepan has worked with some of the world's top chefs, including Alain Chapel, Daniel Boulud, and Alfred Portale. His cookbook, *Inspired by Ingredients*, was published in 2004, and in 2005 he opened his own restaurant, Telepan. Since 2008, he has been the executive chef of Wellness in the Schools, the nonprofit organization where he works with the New York City Department of Education to make New York City school food healthier and more delicious. He has been a long-time supporter of Chelsea Market's Sunday Suppers. www.telepan-ny.com

The Tippler

Tucked beneath New York's celebrated Chelsea Market, the Tippler inhabits a historic space that had not been revealed to the public in over one hundred years. Classic architectural elements like brick archways and locally salvaged artifacts like reclaimed train rails from the nearby High Line enhance the interior. Artfully prepared cocktails, craft beers, and esoteric wines by the glass are offered, along with simply prepared food. Tad Carducci and Paul Tanguay, known together as "The Tippling Bros.," have spent their lives in the restaurant and bar industry and are the creative forces behind the bar program at the Tippler, where their credo is "Let a bar be a bar." www.thetippler.com

Tuck Shop

Niall Grant and Melbourne chef Lincoln Davies opened their first Tuck Shop (a tuck shop is a sandwich or snack shop), celebrating specialties of Australia, in the East Village, which was augmented by a branch at the Market in 2010. They are especially known for their selection of meat pies, which are handmade with carefully selected ingredients. www.thetuckshopnyc.com

ACKNOWLEDGMENTS

This book wouldn't have been possible without the inspiration and endless support of the following people and organizations:

First and foremost, I'd like to thank my coauthor, Rick Rodgers, whose wisdom and insight made sense of my ramblings. Irwin Cohen, who with great foresight, through tireless work and long hours, created the Market and inspired countless New Yorkers to embrace New York's food heritage, continues to inspire me. I am grateful to everyone at Jamestown, especially my partners Christoph Kahl, Matt Bronfman, and Lee Wright. Also to Alane Berkowitz and Ben Gainey, who, as stewards of the Market, have inspired its dynamism, and Charlie, Mario, and Daryl Curmi and the entire engineering department for bringing their own brand of creative display and details to the Market every day.

To the cookbook team: Multitasking project manager Lauren Shakely, my partner Dominick Coyne, literary agent David McCormick, and his associate Bridget McCarthy all helped keep the project moving forward under tight deadlines. Michael Ginsberg and Shannon Hansen in the Jamestown office made many contributions to the success of the book. Our photographer, Jennifer May, captured the lively imagery of the Market and its food. Her team included the talented Jessica Band, food stylist, and Raina Kattleson, prop stylist. A special thanks to Sarabeth Levine for introducing us to Rick Rodgers, Susan Ungaro of the James Beard Foundation for her early support, and to culinary expert extraordinaire, Karen Karp of Karp Resources, for her insights on the history of the Chelsea neighborhood. I am also grateful to Betsy Marger, Glen Siegel, and Orianne Cosentino for their recipe contributions.

Thank you to all of the innovative vendors and tenants of Chelsea Market, especially The Food Network, which continues to put food on the main stage in America.

And last but not least, thank you to my publisher, Leslie Stoker, and everyone at Stewart, Tabori & Chang for believing in this project. Leslie brought an incredible team to the project, including our editor, Elinor Hutton, book designer Rachel Willey, and publicist Claire Bamundo.

—*Michael Phillips*

Our project manager, Lauren Shakely, was a fantastic team player, and I learned many invaluable lessons in traffic control and good publishing practices from her. My kitchen assistant, Diane Kniss, and my spouse, Patrick Fisher, were, as always, stalwart associates in helping me get the book out of the kitchen and into the computer. Peggy Fallon then helped me get it out of the computer and onto the page. Sarabeth Levine played matchmaker with Jamestown and me. Michael Ginsberg and Shannon Hansen were always there to answer my many questions about operations at the market. A special thank-you goes to Jennifer May, Jessica Band, and Raina Katheson for so effectively capturing the essence of the Market in the photographs. I am also thrilled to be working with Stewart, Tabori & Chang's Leslie Stoker, the book's fine editor Elinor Hutton, copy editor Ann Martin Rolke, and managing editor Ivy McFadden. Above all, my hat is off to the vendors at the Market and the contributing chefs who shared such mouthwatering recipes and make New York such a delicious place to live.

—*Rick Rodgers*

RECIPE CREDITS

"Champagne-Orange Cocktail" and "White Sangría with Strawberries and Lime" courtesy of Chelsea Wine Vault.

"Derek Smalls," "Top Cat," "Snowgroni," "Spicy Mixed Nuts," "Spice and Herb-Marinated Olives," "Oysters with Cucumber Mignonette," and "Tapenade" courtesy of The Tippler.

"Tranquility," "Char Siu Pork Belly Buns," "Mongolian Rack of Lamb with Crystallized Ginger Crust," "Stir-Fried Cauliflower with Chile-Garlic Sauce," and "Yogurt Panna Cotta with Tropical Fruits" courtesy of Buddakan.

"Berry Blue Shake" and "Spicy Sesame Salad" courtesy of One Lucky Duck.

"Moroccan Mint Iced Tea," "Grilled Kale, Tomato, and Flageolet Bruschetta," "Turkish Lentil and Bulgur Salad," "Pork Chops with Mojo Marinade," and "Cuban Black Beans with Bacon and Sofrito" courtesy of Spices and Tease.

"Lots of Hot Chocolates" courtesy of Jacques Torres. "Lots of Hot Chocolates" adapted from *A Year In Chocolate*, by Jacques Torres, Stewart, Tabori & Chang, 2008.

"Deviled Eggs with Bacon and Relish," "Seafood and Andouille Gumbo," "Striped Bass en Papillote with Preserved Lemon Butter," "Butternut Squash and Potato Gratin," and "Strawberry Shortcakes with Ginger Biscuits" courtesy of The Green Table.

"Tuna Pizza with Anchovy Aïoli" and "Braised Black Cod with Vegetable Ragout" courtesy of Morimoto NY Venture. "Tuna Pizza with Anchovy Aïoli" and "Braised Black Cod with Vegetable Ragout" reprinted from *Morimoto: The New Art of Japanese Cooking* by permission of DK Publishing, a division of the Penguin Group (USA) Inc. Text copyright © 2007 Masaharu Morimoto; Copyright © 2007 Dorling Kindersley Limited.

"The Velvety Cream of Tomato Soup," "Pain de Mie," and "Triple-Chocolate Pudding" courtesy of Sarabeth's Bakery. "Pain de Mie" and "Triple-Chocolate Pudding" adapted from *Sarabeth's Bakery: From My Hands to Yours*, by Sarabeth Levine, Rizzoli, 2010.

"Cold Cucumber Soup with Yogurt and Mint," "Blue Cheese Risotto with Wild Mushrooms," "Pasta with Creamy Roasted Tomato Sauce," and "Blueberry Ice Cream" courtesy of Ronnybrook Farm Dairy.

"Chicken, Mushroom, and Coconut Milk Soup (Tom Ka Gai)" and "Thai Chicken with Holy Basil (Pad Gra Prow)" courtesy of Chelsea Thai.

"Upstate Chili," "Old-Fashioned Beef Stew with Wild Mushrooms," and "Brined and Rubbed Chicken" courtesy of Dickson's Farmstand Meats.

"Metalbelly's Market Chili" courtesy of Michael Ginsberg.

"Watermelon, Arugula, and Pecan Salad" courtesy of Manhattan Fruit Exchange.

"Tomatoes and Mozzarella with Smoked Basil Vinaigrette" and "Salted Caramel-Nut Tart" courtesy of The Filling Station.

"Beet Salad with Pickled Green Garlic and Tarragon-Yogurt Dressing" courtesy of Jesse Schenker.

"Summer Farro Salad" courtesy of Marco Canora. "Summer Farro Salad" adapted from *Salt to Taste: The Key to Confident, Delicious Cooking*, by Marco Canora and Catherine Young, Rodale Books, 2009.

"Old School Potato Salad," "Grilled Vegetable and Pesto Lasagna," and "Rugelach" courtesy of Ruthy's.

"Grilled Salmon Salad with White Beans and Dill Dressing," "Fish Tacos with Citrus-Fennel Slaw and Tomatillo Salsa," and "Brown Rice Bowl with Asian Vegetables and Sesame-Lime Dressing" courtesy of Friedman's Lunch.

"Cured Salmon with Mâche Salad" courtesy of Alexandra Guarnaschelli.

"Carne Asada Tacos" courtesy of Los Tacos No. 1.

"Flatiron Steaks with a Berry, Port, and Wine Reduction" and "Potato Mille-Feuille with Blue Cheese and Herbs" courtesy of Marc Forgione.

"Guinness Steak and Mushroom Pies," "Roasted Brussels Sprouts," and "Lamingtons" courtesy of Tuck Shop.

"Meatballs in Red Sauce" and "Pasta with Tuna, Broccoli, and Cherry Tomatoes" courtesy of Buon'Italia.

"Bobotie" courtesy of Marcus Samuelsson. "Bobotie" from *Soul of a New Cuisine: A Discovery of the Foods and Flavors of Africa*, by Marcus Samuelsson. Copyright © 2006 by Marcus Samuelsson. Reprinted by permission of Houghton Mifflin Harcourt Publishing Company. All rights reserved.

"Pasta al Forno," "Chocolate Gelato," and "Tiramisú Gelato" courtesy of L'Arte del Gelato.

"Glen's Bourguignon Burgers" courtesy of Glen Siegel.

"Buttermilk Fried Chicken with Honeyed Hot Sauce and Kohlrabi Slaw" courtesy of Hugh Acheson.

"Chicken Cacciatore Pasta" courtesy of Bill Telepan.

"Roast Chicken with Balsamic Glaze" and "Summer Tomato Tart," courtesy of Dominick Coyne.

"Roasted Turkey with Jalapeño-Sage-Orange Butter, and Red Chile–Berry Gravy" and "Wild Rice and Goat Cheese Dressing" courtesy of Bobby Flay.

"Duck Breasts with Five Spices and Grapes" courtesy of Anita Lo.

"Seared Scallops with Brown Butter and Chive Sauce" and "Crispy Crab Cakes with Tartar Sauce" courtesy of The Lobster Place.

"Lobster, Leek, and Brussels Sprouts Gratin" courtesy of Michelle Bernstein.

"Provençal Fish Stew," "Garlic-Butter Mashed Potatoes," and "Dandelion Sauté with Onion and Fennel" courtesy of Orianne Cosentino.

"Shrimp and Sausage Cioppino" courtesy of Giada De Laurentiis.

"Apple and Brie Crêpes with Baby Greens" and "Nutella and Banana Crêpes" courtesy of Bar Suzette.

"Grilled Artisan Cheddar and Fig Jam Sandwich" and "The Ultimate Macaroni and Cheese" courtesy of Lucy's Whey.

"Tomato and Olive Pizza" and "Pecan Sticky Buns" courtesy of Amy's Bread.

"Tonarelli with Artichokes and Pecorino Romano" courtesy of Giovanni Rana Pastificio & Cucina.

"Fresh Herbed Quark Spätzle" courtesy of Kurt Gutenbrunner. "Fresh Herbed Quark Spätzle" adapted from *Neue Cuisine: The Elegant Tastes of Vienna* by Kurt Gutenbrunner with Jane Sigal, Rizzoli, 2011.

"Turtle Witch Brownies" courtesy of Fat Witch Bakery. "Turtle Witch Brownies" adapted from *Fat Witch Brownies: Brownies, Blondies, and Bars from New York's Legendary Fat Witch Bakery*, by Patricia Helding, Rodale Books, 2010.

"Eleni's Christmas Tree Sugar Cookies" courtesy of Eleni's.

"Old-Fashioned Pear Crisps" courtesy of Betsy Marger.

"Yellow Watermelon and Mint Pops" courtesy of People's Pops.

Chelsea Market will donate its proceeds from sales of this book, after expenses, to two charities:

Charity: Water is a nonprofit organization bringing clean, safe drinking water to people in developing countries. One hundred percent of all public donations to Charity: Water directly fund water projects, and the organization proves every dollar using photos and GPS coordinates on a map. Although few Americans have lived in a place where water does not simply come from a tap, there are 800 million people on the planet who don't have clean water. The coins tossed into the fountain at the center of Chelsea Market are also donated to Charity:Water.

Wellness in the Schools (WITS) is a NYC-based nonprofit organization that inspires healthy eating, environmental awareness, and fitness as a way of life for kids in public schools across the country. Through meaningful public/private partnerships with school leadership, teachers, chefs, coaches, parents, and kids, WITS has created innovative wellness programming, including Cook for Kids, Green for Kids, and Coach for Kids. These programs provide healthy foods, healthy environments, and opportunities for regular play to help kids learn and grow.

In 2005, a group of concerned NYC public school parents, led by WITS Executive Director Nancy Easton, united as Wellness in the Schools in the conviction that healthier bodies make healthier minds and that conversely, unhealthy school environments interfere with student health, school attendance, and academic achievement. What started in a single NYC classroom has become a nationally acclaimed school wellness model, currently reaching over thirty thousand students across three states (New York, Kentucky, and Florida). Our goal is simple: We want our children to have the best possible environment in which to learn.

Note: Some of the recipes in this book contain raw or undercooked eggs, which have been known to carry the potentially harmful salmonella bacterium and should not be served to the very young, the infirm, or the elderly.

Published in 2013 by Stewart, Tabori & Chang
An imprint of ABRAMS

Text copyright © 2013 Jamestown Premier Chelsea Market L.P.
Photography copyright © 2013 Jennifer May, with the following exceptions:
    Pages 2, 6, 12, and 83: Sarah Dorio
    Page 8: photographer unknown, courtesy of Chelsea Market
    Page 11: photographer unknown, courtesy of the High Line
    Page 43: Courtesy of Buddakan
    Pages 49, 66, 89, 106, 118, 136, 139, 143, 158, and 177: Michael Turkell
    Page 51: George Manley
    Pages 59, 90, 163, and 204: Katherine Slingluff
    Page 64: Robert Whitman
    Pages 78 and 195: Max Flatow
    Front case: Sarah Dorio (center); George Manley (bottom left); Michael Turkell (bottom second from left)
    Back case: Michael Turkell (top left, bottom left, and bottom right); Katherine Slingluff (top second from right); photographer unknown, courtesy of Chelsea Market (center)
    Case spine: Sarah Dorio

See page 223 for recipe credits.

Library of Congress Control Number: 2013009924
ISBN: 978-1-61769-037-2

Editor: Elinor Hutton
Designer: Rachel Willey
Production Manager: Tina Cameron

The text of this book was composed in Archer, Berthold Akzidenz Grotesk, Trade Gothic, and Stymie.

Printed and bound in the U.S.A.

10 9 8 7 6 5 4 3 2 1

Stewart, Tabori & Chang books are available at special discounts when purchased in quantity for premiums and promotions as well as fundraising or educational use. Special editions can also be created to specification. For details, contact specialsales@abramsbooks.com or the address below.

THE ART OF BOOKS SINCE 1949
115 West 18th Street
New York, NY 10011
www.abramsbooks.com